# ONE YEAR®
# ALONE
## *with* GOD

 *366 Devotions on the Names of God*

## AVA PENNINGTON

**R**
**Revell**
a division of Baker Publishing Group
Grand Rapids, Michigan

© 2010 by Ava Pennington

Published by Revell
a division of Baker Publishing Group
P.O. Box 6287, Grand Rapids, MI 49516-6287
www.revellbooks.com

Printed in the United States of America

Library of Congress Cataloging-in-Publication Data
Pennington, Ava, 1958–
    One year alone with God : 366 devotions on the names of God / Ava Pennington.
       p.   cm.
    Includes index.
    ISBN 978-0-8007-1951-7 (cloth)
    1. God (Christianity)—Name—Meditations. 2. Devotional calendars. I. Title.
BT180.N2.P46 2010
242′.2—dc22                                          2010014860

Unless otherwise indicated, Scripture is taken from the New American Standard Bible®, Copyright © 1960, 1962, 1963, 1968, 1971, 1972, 1973, 1975, 1977, 1995 by The Lockman Foundation. Used by permission.

Scripture marked GW is taken from GOD'S WORD®, a copyrighted work of God's Word to the Nations. Quotations are used by permission. Copyright 1995 by God's Word to the Nations. All rights reserved.

Scripture marked KJV is taken from the King James Version of the Bible.

Scripture marked Message is taken from *The Message* by Eugene H. Peterson, copyright © 1993, 1994, 1995, 1996, 2000, 2001, 2002. Used by permission of NavPress Publishing Group. All rights reserved.

Scripture marked NIV is taken from the Holy Bible, New International Version®, NIV®. Copyright © 1973, 1978, 1984 by Biblica, Inc.™ Used by permission of Zondervan. All rights reserved worldwide. www.zondervan.com

Scripture marked NLT is taken from the *Holy Bible*, New Living Translation, copyright © 1996. Used by permission of Tyndale House Publishers, Inc., Wheaton, Illinois 60189. All rights reserved.

*One Year* and *The One Year* are registered trademarks of Tyndale House Publishers, Inc. Used by permission of Tyndale House Publishers, Inc. All rights reserved.

10   11   12   13   14   15   16       7   6   5   4   3   2   1

To the glory of God,
whose name is worthy of all praise

# CONTENTS

5

Contents

# ACKNOWLEDGMENTS

I am ever grateful for the team of prayer warriors who faithfully interceded before the throne of God each day as I wrote. Thank you, Frankie, Karon, and Marilyn.

I am also grateful for the blessing of fellow writers who caught the vision of this devotional and encouraged me to write with excellence to glorify our awesome God. Thank you, Joyce, Sharon, Jenness, Faith, and Della.

Most important of all, I am forever grateful for the love and encouragement of my precious husband. He picked up the pieces and kept our home running smoothly while I immersed myself in the names and attributes of God. Thank you, Russ, for your unconditional love.

To God be the glory as His name is lifted up!

# INTRODUCTION

Shakespeare once asked, "What's in a name?"

When it comes to our wonderful God, the answer is, "Everything!"

Many strange ideas are floating around our world today as to who or what God is. Some have been passed down from generation to generation, even within the church.

People often speak of "my God" or "your God." *My God would never allow pain and suffering. Your God is archaic. My God is . . .* and so it goes.

What is your understanding of who God is and how He works? Is it a biblical perspective, or have you been molding your understanding of God to fit your desires and expectations? If your perspective is not biblical, then it's time to look at who *God* says He is and how *God* says He works.

Every name of God revealed in the Bible shows us something about His character and His ways. As the multiple facets of a cut diamond combine to reflect its brilliance, the names and attributes of God combine to reveal the transcendence of His nature and the glory of His ways.

With each new revelation, it's as if God whispers to us, "Come closer, My child. I have something new I want to tell you about Me." The more we learn, the easier it is to trust Him and rely on Him.

In *One Year Alone with God*, we will explore 122 names and attributes of God in three ways. In the first devotional for each name or attribute, we will "look up" to see how and why God describes Himself the way He does.

9

Even then, it is possible to have an intellectual understanding of who God is without changing who *we* are in relation to Him. The apostle Paul exhorts us to "be imitators of God" (Eph. 5:1). In the second devotional, we will "look in," as we focus on how the particular name or characteristic applies to our lives, and how it changes or strengthens our relationship with God.

> Look for the arrow symbols by each name or attribute of God to indicate whether the devotional is focusing on looking ▲ up ▲, ▶ in ◀, or ◀ out ▶.

Finally, in the third devotional focused on the same name or attribute, we will "look out," as we apply what we are learning about God and ourselves to our relationships with others.

Use the next 366 days to learn who God is according to how He revealed Himself in His Word. As you do, it is my prayer that your relationship with Him will deepen more intimately than you ever imagined.

# ARE YOU READY?

## Exodus 33:12–23

Give to the LORD the glory his name deserves.

1 Chronicles 16:29 GW

How intimately do you know God? How intimately do you *want* to know Him?

Moses knew God in a way few other people knew Him. It's possible for us to know God in a similar way, simply by making the same request Moses did. "Let me know Your ways that I may know You" (Exod. 33:13).

After God said He would go with Moses and the people, Moses still was not satisfied. He made a bolder request of the Lord: "Show me Your glory!" (Exod. 33:18). Instead of becoming angry with Moses, God granted his request, causing His glory to pass by him.

What is the glory of the Lord? It is the combination of all His attributes. When He passed Moses in the cleft of the rock, God proclaimed His goodness, graciousness, and compassion. God's glory is who He is. It is impossible to separate His glory from His character and His ways.

As we read God's Word and spend time with Him in prayer, He opens our spiritual eyes to see His glory in ways we had not previously recognized. Are you ready to see His glory?

*Lord God, I want to know Your ways more intimately than I have, that I may know You.*

Have I become complacent in my relationship with the Lord? How will I look for Him to show me His ways today?

# MISSING THE POINT
## John 5:39–47

Whatever you do, do everything to the glory of God.

1 Corinthians 10:31 GW

We like to be praised. Even if we are embarrassed by public praise, something inside of us still responds to the approval and admiration of others.

The religious leaders in Jesus's time praised themselves and each other for having gotten it right. They believed God's Word saved them, and since they followed His Word to the tiniest letter, they presumed they needed nothing else.

However, Jesus rebuked them for being so busy patting themselves on the back that they missed what the Scriptures said. Everything in the Law and the Prophets of the Old Testament pointed to the Messiah, Jesus Christ. Yet even with all their study, they missed the message.

How often today do we miss the Scriptures' message because we are too busy chasing the glory of being thought of as "good" Christians? We praise ourselves for obeying parts of the Bible, while ignoring portions that expose the lie of our careful image. When our motive for good works is to garner the praise of others, we trade the glory of God for the glory of men.

*Glorious Lord, forgive me for the times I have exchanged Your glory for the praise of others. Help me keep my focus on You and You alone, rather than on the admiration of others.*

What can I do today to seek God's glory instead of my own?

12

# IT'S NOT ABOUT ME
## Romans 15:5–12

Accept one another, just as Christ also
accepted us to the glory of God.

Romans 15:7

I t's not about me. You'd think I would get that by now, but I need
to be reminded of it on a daily basis, if not more so. Some early
Christians apparently had the same problem.

The ancient city of Rome was the capital of the empire, and the
believers there formed an assorted group. Jews and Gentiles, yes,
but diversity existed among the Gentiles too. Now, as Christians,
they came together to worship Yahweh's Son, Jesus. Disagreements
regarding how to worship Him flowed naturally from their cultural
differences.

When the apostle Paul wrote to the church in Rome, he encouraged them to "be of the same mind with one another according to
Christ Jesus" (Rom. 15:5), but not so they would have less stress, raise
money more easily, or have a simpler time witnessing to others. Paul
told them to be of the same mind to "glorify the God and Father of
our Lord Jesus Christ" (Rom. 15:6).

We need to remember this in the body of Christ today. It was not
about them, and it is not about us. It is always about the glory of
God.

*Glorious Lord, may everything I say and do today*
*bring glory to only You.*

Whom do I need to contact today to "clear the air" so that our
unity will glorify God?

# WHAT MAKES GOD, GOD?
## Deuteronomy 32:1–4

Your Father in heaven is perfect.

Matthew 5:48 GW

What makes our God, God above all gods? Are there particular characteristics He must have to be God? If He is missing one or two of those attributes, can He still be God?

The gods of ancient Greece and Rome were fickle and unpredictable. The goddess of love was an adulteress, the god of light flayed his enemy alive, and the god of wine hosted an ongoing party resulting in debauchery and death. Their failings mimicked and magnified the flaws of their human worshipers.

Not so with the God of the Bible. The Lord is perfect in all His ways. Although the Bible uses human terms to describe Him, He is not human. Because He is not impulsive or capricious, His worshipers never have to guess at what pleases Him. He is complete and consistent in all His ways, lacking in nothing. Instead of reflecting our failings, He offers the solution for them.

God is perfect. *That* is what makes Him God.

> *Lord, I praise You, for You are complete perfection,*
> *without any flaw to compromise who You are.*

How do the human characteristics used to describe God's perfection affect my view of Him?

# ONLY HUMAN

## James 1:1–4

Let endurance have its perfect result, so that
you may be perfect and complete.

James 1:4

I'm only human!" How regularly we use this plaintive cry to excuse
our failings. Since we're only human, no one—not even God—
should expect us to be perfect.

Yet the Bible tells us God *does* expect us to be perfect, as He is
perfect. This does not mean we can be the same as God. It means
we are to grow until we reach the maturity God intended for us to
have. Not only does the Lord rightly expect this of us, He tells us
how to do it.

James began his letter to Jewish believers in the early church by
encouraging them to view their persecution and suffering as something
that would achieve positive results in their lives. These trials tested
their faith and cultivated endurance or perseverance. As the believers
endured, God used those opportunities to cause them to grow spiritually, producing mature Christians with a faith so dependent on the
Lord that they would be complete, lacking nothing.

Our trials can achieve the same results today. We're only human,
but we *can* grow into maturity!

> Lord God, forgive me for the times I excuse my fail-
> ings instead of growing to maturity and completion
> through faith in You.

When have I used "I'm only human" as an excuse for my failings? How can God use that situation to grow me to spiritual
maturity?

# PRAYING FOR PERFECTION
## Colossians 4:10–13

Epaphras, who is . . . always laboring earnestly for
you in his prayers, that you may stand perfect.

Colossians 4:12

Have you, or someone you know, ever entered into a relationship with the intent of changing the other person? These types of relationships often fail. Although people can and do change, *we* are not the ones responsible for changing them.

However, the Bible does tell us we can have a part not only in changing other people but also in helping them to the maturity and perfection God desires for each one of us.

When the apostle Paul closed his letter to the Colossian Christians, he included greetings from an old friend. Although Epaphras could not be with them to teach, mentor, and encourage, he prayed earnestly that they would stand perfect and fully assured in the will of God.

Today, you and I also have a role to play in the perfection of others. We can pray daily for them to mature as God uses their experiences to bring them to His perfection. It's not about changing others for our convenience; it's about others becoming all God intends for them to be.

*Heavenly Father, help me pray for the perfection*
*of others for their ultimate good rather than for*
*my convenience.*

Who does God want me to pray for today as He works to mature and perfect them?

# THREE IN ONE
## John 10:22–39

From the first I have not spoken in secret,
From the time it took place, I was there.
And now the Lord GOD has sent Me, and His Spirit.

Isaiah 48:16

People have been preoccupied with the number three throughout world history. We divide time into past, present, and future. We categorize matter by animal, mineral, or vegetable. Writers, speakers, and mathematicians are familiar with the "rule of three," which holds that people more easily remember lists of three things.

Perhaps we are drawn to the number three because it helps us understand the wonder of our awesome God. Although the word *trinity* is not found in the Bible, it describes the truth found in the pages of Scripture. God is three in one. Three persons, one in essence. Father, Son, and Holy Spirit in perfect and equal union.

Isaiah prophesied that God would send His Messiah *and* His Spirit, and Jesus confirmed His deity when He said, "I and the Father are one" (John 10:30). His listeners did not understand the nature of the triune God then, and we have difficulty understanding Him today. Yet our lack of understanding does not negate our privilege of belonging to God: Father, Son, and Holy Spirit.

*Father, thank You for revealing Your triune nature*
*by sending Your Son and Your Spirit.*

How will I worship God in His triune nature today: Father, Son, and Holy Spirit?

# IN WHOSE NAME?
## Matthew 28:16–20

Therefore, go and make disciples of all the nations, baptizing
them in the name of the Father and the Son and the Holy Spirit.

Matthew 28:19 NLT

Have friends or acquaintances tried to convert you to their
religion or to their church? Perhaps they sent you flyers about
events, or cornered you while they advocated doctrine you
do not agree with. Of course, *we* would never do that to anyone else,
would we?

Christians can be misguided in their sharing. We may become so
enamored of our pastor, church, or denomination that we forget Jesus
Christ's instructions to us. His Great Commission is threefold: we
are to make disciples, baptize, and teach.

When we make disciples, we must remember that we are disciples
of Christ, not of a particular pastor or teacher. When Christians are
baptized, it is not in the name of a particular church, but in the singular name of the triune God: "the Father and the Son and the Holy
Spirit." When we teach, we are teaching the commands of Christ,
not of a denomination.

Our goal should never be to convert someone to a doctrine, religion,
or tradition. Our goal is to introduce people to our glorious triune
God, and let His Spirit convert them to Him.

*Lord God, help me point people to You: Father,*
*Son, and Holy Spirit.*

How can I introduce someone to God today without trying to
convert him or her to my church?

# UNITY IN DIVERSITY
## 1 Corinthians 12:12–27

By one Spirit we were all baptized into one body.
1 Corinthians 12:13 GW

Experts have identified at least eight thousand different Christian denominations throughout the world. Some groups clash over anything from doctrine to control over Christian sites in Israel. The location believed to be the setting of Jesus Christ's tomb is divided among six different Christian groups, and Israeli police must intervene when disputes become physical.

How these conflicts must grieve the heart of God! Jesus specifically prayed that we would all be "completely united" so the world would know that God sent His Son for us (John 17:23 GW). Our lack of unity interferes with our witness to the world.

Unity does not mean compromising essential biblical truths. We must recognize the difference between biblical truth and personal preferences. The fact that salvation is a gift of God's grace is a biblical truth. The color of the carpet in the sanctuary is a personal preference, yet churches have divided over less.

Christians are the body of Christ on earth, and we need to start behaving like it.

*Lord, help me reflect the unity of the Trinity in my relationships with other Christians.*

How can I differentiate between biblical truth and personal preferences in my relationships with other Christians this week?

# RELATIONSHIP
## Psalm 110:1–7

The LORD says to my Lord:
"Sit at My right hand
Until I make Your enemies a footstool for Your feet."

Psalm 110:1

Would you like to eavesdrop on the persons of our triune God? You can!

God allowed David to record a conversation in Psalm 110 between two persons in the Trinity. If we had any doubts as to the identity of the speakers, Jesus removed them when He confronted the Pharisees. Some religious leaders had interpreted the passage as David speaking to his son, but Jesus corrected them (Matt. 22:41–46).

The psalm is a clear account of a personal conversation between God the Father and God the Son. "The LORD" spoke to "my Lord," and said, "Sit at My right hand."

Several years ago, a series of movies popularized the phrase, "May the Force be with you." Although the movies are fictional accounts, they encouraged the view that there is a powerful but impersonal force operating in the universe. However, God is both personal and relational. His relationships begin within the Trinity, between the Father, Son, and Spirit. Then, when He created us, God gave *us* the capacity for relationships—the most important of which is our relationship with Him.

*Holy Lord, thank You for bringing me into a personal and intimate relationship with You.*

How can I make my relationship with the triune God a priority today?

# PERSONAL RESEMBLANCE
## Genesis 1:26–2:7

So God created humans in his image.

Genesis 1:27 GW

Snow can be captivating—snowflakes swirl about, wet to the touch and melting as they land, until enough fall to form a white blanket that muffles a noisy world. Undetected by the naked eye, no two snowflakes are alike. Each one is a unique creation.

When God created humanity, He created us as unique beings. No two people are the same. However, He said something about people that He did not say about anything else in His creation: "Let Us make man in Our image, according to Our likeness" (Gen. 1:26).

God does not look like me, and He is not bald like my husband, so what does "in Our image" mean? The meaning of this Hebrew word for *image* is associated with resemblance. We resemble God because we are moral and personal beings. We have the ability to discern right from wrong. He has created each of us with a mind, will, and emotions. We have personality: innate qualities that distinguish us, one from another.

God is personal, each Person of the Godhead equal yet distinguished from the other, and He made us in His image. Does our behavior reflect the One we were created to resemble?

*Father, forgive me for when I have failed to resemble*
*You in thought, word, and deed.*

What can I do today to reflect my resemblance to my personal God?

# FELLOWSHIP
### 1 John 1:1–4

> The grace of the Lord Jesus Christ, and the love of God,
> and the fellowship of the Holy Spirit, be with you all.
>
> 2 Corinthians 13:14

Christians seem to have a specialized vocabulary for almost everything. We don't just enjoy good things, we are *blessed*. We don't simply enter into a relationship with God, we *ask Jesus into our hearts*. We don't merely depend on God daily, we *live the Spirit-filled life*.

When it comes to spending time with friends, Christians don't just socialize, we *fellowship*. However, fellowshiping is not the same as socializing. Socializing focuses on interacting with others, mingling on a friendly level. Fellowship is deeper. It entails time spent in relationships with those who share our beliefs, values, and experiences. When we fellowship with others who also desire to grow in intimacy with God, the result is encouragement and unity.

The greatest, purest fellowship is the fellowship among the three persons of the Trinity. God the Father, God the Son, and God the Holy Spirit share an eternal relationship, unbroken and untainted. What a *blessing* that we can share in *fellowship* with God, and with others!

*Dear Lord, thank You for the privilege of fellowship*
*with You through Your Son, Jesus.*

What specific arrangements can I make this week to fellowship with other Christians?

*Elohim*

# MIGHTY CREATOR
## Job 38:1–41

In the beginning God created the heavens and the earth.

Genesis 1:1 NLT

The first name by which God revealed Himself in His Word is the name "God" or *Elohim*. It introduces Him as our mighty Creator God.

We've read it so often, it may have lost its impact: "In the beginning . . ." God took nothing and made *something*. From the vast reservoirs of the oceans to the diminutive plankton swimming in them. From the endless expanse of the heavens to the tiny fireflies lighting up the night sky. From majestic mountain peaks to industrious ants burrowing in hidden valleys.

And the colors! Cornflower blue and lemon yellow, cherry blossom pink and forest green, pictured in God's mind before He painted them on the world's canvas. Our Creator also fashioned shapes and textures, sounds and smells—all extolling the glory of His Triune nature.

For not only was God the Father involved in creation, so were God the Son and God the Holy Spirit. John's Gospel says, "All things came into being through Him [Jesus]" (John 1:3). Genesis 1:2 notes, "the Spirit of God was moving over the surface of the waters." All three Persons of the Trinity played a part in creating a world that would bring glory to its Creator, our Elohim.

> *Elohim, help me see Your glory revealed in the creative beauty of the world around me.*

How will I take time today to see Elohim, my Creator God, in my natural surroundings?

*Elohim*

# NO MISTAKES
## Psalm 139:13–18

You knitted me together inside my mother.

Psalm 139:13 GW

I do not like looking in the mirror. When I do, I often wonder why God made my nose too long, my mouth too wide, and my height too short.

King David marveled at God's skill in creating each of us. David had no doubt that God is intimately involved in the formation of every individual life. The Creator, Elohim, "knits" us together in the hidden recesses of our mothers' wombs, skillfully forming us in wonderful ways.

At conception, our life is so tiny, we cannot be seen with the unassisted human eye. Still, Elohim not only sees us, He determined beforehand who we are. Smaller than a grain of sand, yet genetically complete, we are already distinctive individuals. Inherited genes decide our eye and hair color, height, and everything else that forms our individual characteristics. We do not grow *into* a life after conception; rather, we *are* a life that continues to grow as God determines.

Elohim intended everything in His creation to glorify Him, including you and me. That includes the timing of our birth, our family, ethnicity, abilities, and everything else that makes us who we are. He made each one of us unique, and when God creates, He never makes mistakes!

*Elohim, help me see that You have created me uniquely to accomplish Your purposes.*

How does knowing God as my Elohim change how I view my circumstances and myself?

*Elohim*

# EVERY NATION
## Genesis 9:1–7

> You created everything. . . . You bought people
> with your blood to be God's own. They are from
> every tribe, language, people, and nation.
>
> Revelation 4:11; 5:9 GW

In 1963, Martin Luther King Jr. said, "At 11:00 on Sunday morning . . . we stand at the most segregated hour in this nation." Today, many Christians still worship God with people who look and act like themselves—racially, socially, economically, and politically.

For years, in my "majority" world, I did not understand why being in the minority made people feel uncomfortable. Then at a co-worker's wedding reception, my husband and I were one of only two "minority" couples out of 150 people. The other guests were friendly, yet I still felt out of place. Until that moment, I hadn't made much effort to spend time with people different from me.

How we must hurt God's heart when we interact with others based on their similarity to us. I can almost hear God say, "There's a *reason* I didn't make everyone just like you!"

Someday in eternity, we will all stand before Elohim's throne, praising Him for who He is and thanking Him for who we are: redeemed people from every tribe, language, and nation. Until that day, we still have many friends to make.

*Elohim, You created people from all nations. Help
me see You in all Your children.*

How can I seek friendships this week with people who are different from me?

*Yahweh*

# Two Questions
## Exodus 3:1–14

God spoke to Moses, "I am the LORD."

Exodus 6:2 GW

Using a burning bush that did not burn up, God introduced Himself to Moses and declared He would use Moses to deliver Israel from Egyptian slavery. Moses, of course, had a few questions.

Moses's first question was, "Who am I?" (Exod. 3:11). God did not answer it directly. It didn't matter who Moses was, because God would be with him. In other words, "Moses, it's not about *you*!"

Moses's second question was more daring. What was God's name? For the past four hundred years, the Israelites had lived in a nation that worshiped hundreds of gods. How could he talk to his people of yet another god? However, the One speaking to him was "the LORD"—*Yahweh*. The one, true, living God, self-existent and holy, not dependent on anyone or anything.

The Lord alone is to be worshiped. Yet just as the Israelites struggled with idolatry, so we do today. Our idols may not be statues of gold or silver. They may be good things: a spouse, children, a job, a sport or hobby, or even ministry. Anything that causes us to disobey or neglect God can become an idol for us.

Nothing must ever compete with the Great "I Am" for preeminence. There is room for only one God in our lives. He is the Lord, and His name is Yahweh.

*Yahweh, show me where things or people compete*
*with You for first place in my life.*

Does anything in my life vie with Yahweh for supremacy? If so, what needs to change?

*Yahweh*

# Trust in the Name
## Psalm 20:1–9

We will boast in the name of the LORD our God.

Psalm 20:7 GW

Names can be significant, especially in the Bible. In biblical times, a name often reflected a person's character or background. Even today, one cannot know someone intimately without at the very least knowing his or her name.

When God told Moses His name, He separated Himself from the multitude of gods worshiped in the ancient world. While other nations trusted in their military might, Yahweh would be all Israel needed for her defense. When fear caused others to run in circles, Yahweh would be a refuge of safety. Israel would come to rely on the power of the name of the Lord.

God's name is as mighty today as it was the day He revealed it to Moses. The economy may falter, natural disasters may cut swaths of destruction across the earth, and relationships may crumble, but we know and trust in the name of the Lord our God.

Everything else will disappoint, but He is Yahweh, and He will never fail.

*Yahweh, show me where I have been running to other things and other people instead of first running to You whenever I am afraid.*

What issues are causing me concern? How does knowing God's name help me face my problems today?

*Yahweh*

# WHY BOTHER?
## Leviticus 19:9–18

Love your neighbor as you love yourself. I am the LORD.

Leviticus 19:18 GW

With all the laws the Lord gave the ancient Israelites, it's easy to imagine some of the people wanting to ask, "Why bother?" The Lord required them to follow the tiniest details, even in their relationships, but did it really matter?

When Yahweh provided the people His instructions for relating to each other, He also gave them the reason. Their behavior mattered because of who He is. Fifteen times in this chapter, God repeats, "I am the LORD." God had placed His name in Israel, and He expected them to honor Him in all they did. Compassion for the needy, honesty, justice, forgiveness, and love are a few of the ways they could demonstrate that they belonged to Yahweh.

The Lord still requires us to reflect who we belong to in our relationships. Jesus told His followers, "Everyone will know that you are my disciples because of your love for each other" (John 13:35 GW). If we did not tell others we are Christians, would they know?

If we belong to Yahweh, the world will see it in our relationships.

> *Yahweh, I want my relationships to reflect that I belong to You. Help me treat others as You treat me.*

How can I respond to others today in a way that proclaims I belong to Yahweh?

*Adonai*

# BEST-LAID PLANS
## Genesis 15:1–21

"Lord GOD, what wilt thou give me, seeing I go childless?"

Genesis 15:2 KJV

Conventional wisdom tells us that to be successful, we should become adept at planning. Good planning helps us manage resources and minimize unexpected challenges.

God had promised to bless Abram, and Abram had become wealthy. Even so, the promise of an heir had yet to be fulfilled, and Abram and his wife had become too old to have children.

Abram offered God a plan. He could adopt an heir according to the practices of his day. God was not interested in this or any other suggestion. His promise would be fulfilled in His way. He revealed Himself to Abram by a new name—*Adonai*—the Lord.

Abram called God, "Lord God." He understood that the Lord—Adonai—had the right to command him. Abram's sole assignment was to take God at His word. Like Abram, we need to trust God's plans for our lives. He is our Lord, and He has the right to command us. Ours is the privilege to believe and obey Him. The only appropriate response is to yield to His lordship.

One day, the world will acknowledge God is Adonai and that the title "Lord" also belongs to God's Son, Jesus. For now, we must learn to write our plans in pencil and carry a big eraser.

*Adonai, You are my Lord. Show me where my plans do not agree with Your plans.*

How can I implement my plans today in a way that leaves room for God's changes?

*Adonai*

# HANDS AND HEARTS
## Luke 14:25–33

No servant can serve two masters.

Luke 16:13

A recent survey revealed that 76 percent of Americans identify themselves as Christian. Although this is lower than previous years, it still means more than three-quarters of the United States' population claim the name *Christian*.

While these may be impressive numbers, Jesus told His followers that simply calling Him "Lord" is not enough to please God. Our lives must reflect an immediate and consistent obedience to our Adonai. Anything less belies our claims to be His followers.

Rather than choosing outright disobedience, some of us *delay* our obedience. We obey at our convenience, or according to our own plans or circumstances. Nevertheless, delayed obedience is still not obedience. Our delays essentially tell God we know better than He does.

Another way we defy Adonai's lordship is to obey Him for the wrong reasons. Pursuing good works to fulfill our own agendas results in right actions done for self-serving motives.

Are we truly devoted to the One we call "Lord"? If so, we will do what He says, both with our hands . . . and with our hearts.

*Adonai, I commit myself to complete obedience to*
*You in my actions and my motivation.*

What commands of Adonai have I neglected to obey? How will I obey Him today?

*Adonai*

# WHO'S IN CHARGE?
## Colossians 3:17–25

He . . . gave Him as head over all things to the church.

Ephesians 1:22

Every year, thousands of people nominate their bosses in a contest for the worst boss in the country. The entries describe instances of low pay, unreasonable work, and a lack of respect.

Such horror stories in the working world should not be surprising. After all, many of these people are not Christians. They don't know better if they don't know Christ.

Sadly, relationships in our families or in the Christian community may yield similar experiences. Left unchecked, our old natures have a way of reasserting themselves.

The apostle Paul urged us to be different from the world. Christ, our Adonai, is the head of the church, and we are to imitate Him in all our relationships. In Colossians 3:17, Paul reminds us we are to "do all in the name of the Lord Jesus, giving thanks through Him to God the Father" because we are working for the Lord, not for men.

Our Adonai is to be in charge in our families, in our churches, and in our workplaces. The relationships of husbands and wives, parents and children, and employers and employees are all under His authority. Let's take our eyes off people and look to the One we are really serving.

*Adonai, whatever I do in word or deed, help me do*
*it in obedience to You for Your glory.*

How does knowing that Adonai is my ultimate authority affect my earthly relationships?

*El Olam*

# BEFORE TIME BEGAN
## Psalm 90:1–17

You are God from everlasting to everlasting.

Psalm 90:2 GW

How quickly time passes, and how little control we have over its passage! Sometimes it feels like we are slaves to it. Still, the currents of time do not control God. The Eternal God—*El Olam*—existed before time began and will exist after time ceases to be measured. The Great "I Am" always *is*.

God is outside of time because He created it. We measure our days by the earth's rotation around the sun, but God is the One who hung the sun in its place and set the earth on its rotation. Days, nights, months, and years are all a measure of what He created.

Because God is eternal and outside of time, His plan for our redemption did not begin when Adam and Eve first sinned in the Garden of Eden. God did not need to dream up a contingency plan. Sending His Son, Jesus, to atone for our sin was always His intention. Revelation 13:8 tells us Jesus Christ ("the Lamb") was "slain from the foundation of the world" (KJV).

Centuries have passed since the Garden, but God did not forget our need. In the fullness of time, the Eternal God—El Olam—revealed His plan of salvation to a waiting world.

*El Olam, help me use the passage of time as Your tool to enable me to appreciate life.*

How can I honor God in the way I use my time today?

*El Olam*

# WASTING TIME
## Jeremiah 10:1–10

Be careful how you walk, not as unwise men but
as wise, making the most of your time.

Ephesians 5:15–16

I am always looking for time-saving devices. To El Olam, a day may be as a thousand years, but for me, twenty-four hours is never enough time to complete my to-do list, no matter how organized I try to be. Although I welcome anything that will help me save time, lately I wonder what I'm saving it *for*.

Long ago, God spoke through the prophet Jeremiah to rebuke His people for chasing after idols—worthless objects that drew them away from Him. These wasteful, sinful pursuits drained the people's time and energy, distracting them from serving the Eternal God—the only One worthy of their worship.

Today, our idols may be more sophisticated than ancient idols of gold, silver, and wood, but they are no less destructive. We may sacrifice our time on the altar of financial security but lose our integrity as we grasp for the next dollar. We may sacrifice our time on the altar of ambition but lose our families as we climb the corporate ladder. Either way, we lose.

Time is a gift. Let's use it wisely.

> *El Olam, help me to glorify You in the way I use
> my opportunities.*

How much time will I spend on activities of eternal value today?

*El Olam*

# LIVING FOREVER
## 2 Corinthians 5:1–9

> These will go away into eternal punish-
> ment, but the righteous into eternal life.
>
> Matthew 25:46

Two things in our world will last forever: God's Word and people. Every human being will experience a resurrection into eternity, some to eternal life with God, some to eternal condemnation. Since El Olam values people enough to cause them to live forever, they need to hear the Good News of salvation. God chose us for this mission because we have experienced His redemption. He has lifted us from the filth of sin to stand cleansed in His presence.

This privilege of telling others about the Lord should be a priority for all believers. Too often, though, we are self-conscious or ill-equipped to share our faith. Frequently, we're just too busy to learn how to clearly communicate the gospel and too busy to do it after we've learned.

One reason God does not take us to heaven immediately upon our salvation is so we can share the Good News of redemption with others who need it as much as we do. Martin Luther described this as "one beggar telling another beggar where to find bread."

Who will we see in eternity because we took the time to share?

*El Olam, help me see the eternal value of others*
*because Christ died for them, as He died for me.*

How can I invest in relationships with others today in a way that will yield eternal fruit?

*El Elyon*

# NO LIMITS
## Genesis 14:1–24

Blessed be Abram by God Most High, Creator of heaven and earth.

Genesis 14:19 NLT

In the ancient world, people believed physical boundaries governed deities. They believed that specific territories limited each nation's gods. If one nation conquered another, it meant their god crossed beyond their territory and was stronger than their opponent's god.

Then along came Abram, who belonged to *El Elyon*—God Most High. The repetition in this name of God—*El El*—emphasizes His power and might. El Elyon is the mightiest of the mighty, the strongest of the strong. He is Creator and owner of all things, stronger than anything in the physical or the spiritual world. Neither geographical nor spiritual boundaries could stop the Most High God from giving Abram victory over the kings who had kidnapped Lot.

Abram's understanding of God Most High caused him to trust God beyond the actual battle. He realized the power of El Elyon would care for him in every area of life.

It is tempting for us to put God in a religious box and take Him out only on Sundays. But El Elyon is the Lord of every part of our life: spiritual, physical, mental, and emotional. Like Abram, let's trust Him in every area.

> *El Elyon, thank You that there is no problem in my life too large for You to handle.*

How have I partitioned my life, trusting God in certain areas but not in others?

*El Elyon*

# NO ONE HIGHER
## Daniel 4:4–37

The Most High rules over the kingdoms of the world.

Daniel 4:25 NLT

Sometimes blessings can lure us into a dangerous state of self-sufficiency.

That's what happened to King Nebuchadnezzar. Instead of being grateful for his position, the king believed his throne and prosperity resulted from his own efforts. He failed to recognize that El Elyon, God Most High, established and removed rulers to fulfill His divine purposes.

Daniel warned him that unless he acknowledged the Most High God, he would lose everything. Nebuchadnezzar ignored the warning and suffered El Elyon's judgment.

We may not own a palace or rule a nation, but we can still fall prey to the same danger Nebuchadnezzar did. Material blessings can lead us to believe our prosperity is due to our own efforts. We brag about our homes or our jobs and rest in the security of growing bank accounts.

God Most High does not provide these things for our glory and honor. He blesses us to fulfill His purposes through us. Employment layoffs, foreclosures, accidents, illnesses, and other crises remind us we have less control over our positions and prosperity than we may think.

Let's give El Elyon, God Most High, all the glory and credit for His blessings.

*El Elyon, use all that I am and all that I have for*
*Your glory and Your purposes.*

How can I use my blessings and accomplishments to honor El Elyon today?

*El Elyon*

# WITNESS TO THE POWER
## Mark 5:1–20

What business do we have with each other,
Jesus, Son of the Most High God?

Mark 5:7

I f God Most High appeared on your doorstep, would His presence bring you joy or would you ask Him to leave?

A multitude of evil spirits tormented the Gerasene demon-possessed man. Local residents feared him. Chains could not contain him. When Jesus brought healing, He once again proved He is El Elyon, God Most High. Even the demons recognized His authority.

The townspeople should have been thrilled by the miraculous healing, but they feared Jesus more than before. They dreaded the power of El Elyon. They feared the effect His presence had on their livelihoods. When they lost their herd of pigs, they pleaded with Jesus to leave.

Today, we may wonder at the fear and hostility exhibited toward us, perhaps by our own families, simply because we have chosen to follow Christ. Our initial reaction may be to retreat to Christian friends and isolate ourselves from an unbelieving world. Yet when the man who had been demon possessed begged to leave his home and family to go with Jesus, Jesus sent him back to be a witness to the power of God Most High. El Elyon calls us to do the same.

*El Elyon, use me to share the joy of belonging to
You with an unbelieving world.*

How do I respond when others react with hostility to my faith?
How should I respond?

*El Roi*

# WATCHFUL EYES
## Genesis 16:1–14

The LORD looks down from heaven and sees the whole human race.

Psalm 33:13 NLT

Science has provided us with the remarkable ability to pinpoint and see a particular location on earth from heaven. Yet God has always done this—and without satellites!

Sarai's servant, Hagar, found herself in a difficult situation. Unable to conceive, Sarai suggested that her husband father a child with her servant. This may sound odd today, but it was a common practice, and Hagar probably had little choice. Still, once Hagar conceived, she forgot her position and looked on her mistress with contempt.

Sarai resented Hagar and her pregnancy. Her mistreatment caused Hagar to flee into the desert, where she had an encounter with the living God. Hagar called His name *El Roi*, "The God Who Sees Me." The God of Abraham had taken notice of an Egyptian servant and her situation. El Roi sent her back to her mistress and gave her the grace to endure. He also promised to multiply Hagar's descendants through her son, Ishmael.

How many times have we been stuck in a difficult situation, wondering if anyone knows or sees us? No matter how alone we may feel, El Roi's watchful eye is always on us.

> *El Roi, help me remember that no matter where I am, I am never out of Your sight.*

How does knowing that God always sees me bring me comfort today?

*El Roi*

# LIVING IN SECRET
## Matthew 6:1–8

Man looks at the outward appearance, but
the LORD looks at the heart.

1 Samuel 16:7

Shakespeare once said, "All the world's a stage, and all the men and women merely players." That may be true for some, but when it comes to Christians, God isn't interested in seeing actors going through religious motions.

Doing good things to impress people, or even to impress God, is doing them with wrong motives. The people of Jesus's day had seen enough of that. Religious leaders made a point of attracting attention when they did their good deeds. They hungered for the applause of others.

Jesus denounced this behavior and pointed to a new way of living out our faith: the secret life. He didn't mean for us to hide our faith. He meant that our motive for doing good is to please El Roi, The God Who Sees Me. Jesus illustrated His point with familiar activities. He told His followers to give, pray, and fast in secret, rather than doing these things for the praise of others.

It is not easy to work in secret. We may feel underappreciated or ill-used when others receive credit for our efforts. But El Roi sees both our efforts and the desires of our hearts. He will reward us, and His reward is always better than fleeting applause.

*El Roi, today I commit to serving You wholeheart-
edly rather than seeking the praise of others.*

What motivates my good works? How do I respond to a lack of appreciation by others?

*El Roi*

# DO I SEE WHAT HE SEES?
## James 2:14–18

Whoever has the world's goods, and sees his brother in need and closes his heart against him, how does the love of God abide in him?

1 John 3:17

My neighbor became ill several weeks ago and needed help. I didn't know because I was busy teaching a Bible study, writing a book, and preparing to speak at a retreat. I noticed her absence, but I did not see her need.

Most of us have too much to do and too little time to do it. We're busy accomplishing great things for the Lord. We rush around in ministry, but we may fail to minister to the needs around us.

In his letter to believers, James identified an inconsistency in Christians who claim to have faith in God but who don't accompany their claims with action. James did not speak about this in the context of evangelism. He made a point of saying, "Suppose a *brother or sister* is without" (James 2:15 NIV, emphasis added)." It is not enough to dismiss someone with a few spiritual wishes and prayers. El Roi wants us to see their need and do something about it.

How often do we miss someone's need, not because we don't care, but because we're simply too busy to see what El Roi sees?

*El Roi, open my eyes to the person whose need You want me to meet in Your name.*

How can I look beyond the surface of my relationships to meet the needs El Roi sees?

*El Shaddai*

# HE CAN DO IT
## Genesis 17:1–8

> When Abram was 99 years old, the LORD appeared to him. He said to Abram, "I am God Almighty. Live in my presence with integrity."
>
> Genesis 17:1 GW

I sometimes struggle with how God chooses to work in my difficult circumstances. It's not that I don't think He can resolve the difficult situation. It's usually the timing that gets me. God frequently waits until I am at the end of my resources before He steps in.

Abram understood what it meant to wait on God. God had been promising him a son for twenty-five years. Abram's wife no longer had the ability to bear children, and God had refused his helpful suggestions to adopt a faithful servant or father a child with another woman.

Abram could only trust and wait. When he reached the end of his resources—with no suggestions left—God again promised him descendants. This time, God changed Abram's name to "Abraham" (Gen. 17:5) to confirm His word. Before He did, however, He revealed Himself by a new name: God Almighty—*El Shaddai*—the One who is all-sufficient to carry out His promises.

By El Shaddai's power and sufficiency, Sarai, now "Sarah" (Gen. 17:15), bore a son. Almighty God did not need Abraham's help to fulfill His word then, and He does not need our help to fulfill it today.

> *El Shaddai, I confess my lack of trust in Your sufficiency in difficult circumstances.*

---

In what situation is El Shaddai calling me to wait on Him for the solution to my problem?

*El Shaddai*

# THE FULL STORY
## Ruth 1:1–22

We cannot imagine the power of the Almighty, yet he is
so just and merciful that he does not oppress us.

Job 37:23 NLT

A close friend suffered a series of painful losses in a span of
five months. His father died of cancer in September, and his
brother died in October. His wife was diagnosed with cancer
in December and died in February. During this time, he wrote a letter
that began, "I feel like Job."

Naomi would have understood his feelings. She had left her home-
town with a husband and two sons, returning with only a foreign
daughter-in-law. She described herself as bitter and empty and viewed
El Shaddai, the Almighty God, as One who brought affliction and
hardship.

Naomi didn't know the full story. She had yet to learn that Ruth
would marry a distant relation and that they would care for her in her
old age. She also did not know the child born to them would be in the
line of David and the Messiah. El Shaddai did not share the details
of His plans with Naomi, but His power and sufficiency worked to
fulfill His purposes through her.

Today, my friend has not allowed his circumstances to embitter
him. He knows who he belongs to. El Shaddai is fulfilling His plans
and purposes, even through the darkest days.

> *El Shaddai, help me trust Your sufficiency in all that
> I am facing today.*

What situation is provoking me to bitterness instead of trust in
El Shaddai's sufficiency?

*El Shaddai*

# APPEARANCES ARE DECEIVING
## Numbers 24:1–25

> We give thanks to you, Lord God Almighty.
> Revelation 11:17 NLT

We live in a world where evil frequently triumphs, and those who follow Jesus Christ are the objects of attack and mockery. It appears El Shaddai can no longer care for His people.

That's what the world wants us to think. They are wrong.

Actually, things haven't changed much in several thousand years. After Israel's deliverance from Egyptian slavery, the nation prepared to claim the land God had promised them. The Moabite people living in the area, however, had different plans.

Their king hired Balaam to curse the Israelites so he could defeat them in battle. Despite the king's schemes, God would not allow His people to be cursed. After two failed attempts, Balaam spoke the words El Shaddai gave him, prophesying Israel's victory and prosperity. All the while, Israel camped in the valley, unaware of God Almighty's protection and care.

El Shaddai overrode the evil intentions of Israel's enemies and used those same enemies to bless His people. Today, no matter how much the world seeks to attack the followers of Christ, we need not fear. El Shaddai uses even our enemies to fulfill His purposes.

> *El Shaddai, help me rest in Your power and suffi-ciency as You care for me.*

When I am attacked, how can I react in a way that shows my confidence in El Shaddai?

*El Qanna*

# THE BEST FOR US
## Deuteronomy 6:10–19

You shall not worship any other god, for the LORD,
whose name is Jealous, is a jealous God.

Exodus 34:14

A celebrity talk show host recently told her television audience that she didn't feel right believing in a God who says He is jealous. On the face of it, the statement that God is a jealous God does sound strange.

Jealousy is a powerful emotion. It can devastate relationships and destroy lives. So why would the eternal, sovereign, almighty God name Himself "Jealous"?

When God says He is a jealous God, He is *not* saying He is jealous *of* us or of something we have. He is also *not* saying He is fearful of losing His position in our lives, the way a person might be possessive in a human relationship. What He *is* saying is that He is jealous *for* us. We are so precious to Him that He wants the highest and best for us, which can only be found when He is first in our lives. He knows that when we love anyone or anything else more than Him, we harm ourselves and damage our relationship with Him.

The God of the Bible is jealous for our sake. He deserves no less than all our worship.

*El Qanna, thank You for being a jealous God who wants the highest and best for me.*

What affection do I have for people or things that would arouse God's jealousy?

*El Qanna*

# PROTECT THE RELATIONSHIP
## 2 Corinthians 11:1–4

I am jealous for you with the jealousy of God himself. For
I promised you as a pure bride to one husband, Christ.

2 Corinthians 11:2 NLT

We naturally protect what is precious to us, whether it is a person or a possession.

*El Qanna*, our jealous God, is protective of us and always wants what is best for us. How diligent are we, however, in protecting our relationship with Him?

The apostle Paul had a warning for the early church in Corinth. He was concerned that false teaching would lead them astray and affect their devotion to Christ. He cautioned them to be on guard against any teachings that put forth a "different" Jesus.

Today, it is popular to be spiritual, but *spiritual* is not always the same as *Christian*. Bestselling authors tout spiritual beliefs they claim are consistent with belief in Jesus Christ. Then they go on to define a Jesus who is very different from the Jesus described in the Bible. Like the early church in Corinth, we are in danger of being led astray to follow a god who is not God at all. Vigilance is needed to ensure that we are not merely devoted to *a* god, but to *the* God.

El Qanna is jealous for us. Are we as jealous to protect our devotion to Him?

> *El Qanna, I confess I have not always protected my
> relationship with You as I should.*

What specific thing can I do today to help protect my devotion
to the Lord?

*El Qanna*

# ENVY NOT
## Psalm 37:1–22

Don't worry about the wicked. Don't envy those who do wrong.

Psalm 37:1 NLT

With each passing day, it seems evil is becoming more and more rampant in our world. Those who do wrong get rewarded. At the very least, they seem to avoid punishment of any kind. Yet here *we* are, obeying God and abiding by His "rules." Sometimes it is just plain hard not to envy those who do not live according to God and His Word.

The psalmist, King David, understood the frustration of watching evildoers prosper. Although it appeared they were getting away with evil, he knew the time of judgment would come. David encouraged God's people to keep an eternal perspective. God delights to bless those who put Him first, and He will judge those who make gods of their own desires.

Our jealous God is protective of us. We are also called to jealously protect our devotion to Him. Those who belong to El Qanna do not need to envy others because their prosperity is short-lived. God will always provide the best for His children.

*El Qanna, help me not to envy others. Thank You*
*for the assurance that nothing anyone else has will*
*ever exceed Your best for me.*

Whom do I envy, and why do I envy this person? What does El Qanna's Word say about my envy?

*Yahweh Jireh*

# HE'LL SEE TO IT!
## Genesis 22:1–18

Abraham called the name of that place The LORD Will Provide.

Genesis 22:14

Some people like to think of God as a cosmic Santa with an inexhaustible sack of gifts. However, when the Lord revealed His name as Provider, it had nothing to do with the provision of material things. Instead, He chose circumstances involving something much more significant.

God called Abraham to offer a sacrifice that would clearly show his obedience. God asked him to sacrifice Isaac, the son Abraham waited twenty-five years to receive. It must have been agonizing for Abraham as each step brought him closer to losing his precious son. Still, he obediently trusted God, and God responded to his obedience by providing a substitute sacrifice.

Abraham memorialized God's provision by naming the place *Yahweh Jireh*, "The LORD Will Provide" (Gen. 22:14). While several Hebrew words can be translated as *provide*, this particular word is related to seeing or recognizing something. In this case, the Lord saw, in advance, Abraham's need for a substitute sacrifice for Isaac and provided a ram in a nearby thicket.

Our greatest need today is the need for a substitute to pay the penalty for our sin and die in our place. Yahweh Jireh saw our need before time began and provided His Son.

> *Yahweh Jireh, thank You for seeing my need and sacrificing Your Son as my substitute.*

Is it easier for me to trust the Lord for eternal life than to trust Him for today's needs?

*Yahweh Jireh*

# ABUNDANT PROVISION
## 1 Kings 17:1–16

My God will supply all your needs according to His riches in glory in Christ Jesus.

Philippians 4:19

When we only have a little, we tend to hold tightly to the little we have. By doing so, we miss God's best for us.

Like others in Israel, the widow at Zarephath suffered from the drought God had sent as a judgment on the nation. By the time the prophet Elijah came to her, she had only enough ingredients for a final meal before she and her son faced death by starvation.

Yahweh Jireh had determined she would feed His prophet during the drought. Elijah instructed her to provide him a meal and then make something for herself and her son.

The widow could have held tightly to the little she had, suspicious of unsubstantiated promises. Still, she did as he asked, and her supply of flour and oil lasted until the rains arrived.

The Lord could have supernaturally provided for Elijah without the widow, but she would have missed the blessing of abundant provision. Still, her blessing depended on her obedience and trust that Yahweh Jireh would provide for her situation.

Do we miss God's abundant provision because we hold tightly to the little we have?

> *Yahweh Jireh, help me use what I have as You direct,
> and to trust that You will provide.*

What is Yahweh Jireh calling me to hold loosely as I anticipate His abundant provision?

*Yahweh Jireh*

# AM I THE ANSWER?
## Genesis 45:4–11; 50:15–21

Don't be afraid! I will provide for you and your children.

Genesis 50:21 GW

Have you ever been the answer to your own prayer?

After Joseph's brothers sold him into slavery, he must have missed his father and his younger brother. In his intimate relationship with God, he would have prayed for Yahweh Jireh's provision for them, and maybe even for his other brothers too!

God raised Joseph to a high position in Egypt to prepare the nation for a coming famine. Joseph's success attracted foreigners, including his brothers, to Egypt in search of food. Joseph's family eventually settled there under his provision, and he became the answer to his own prayer.

I have prayed for God to provide food for a family, encouragement for a sick person, or someone to share the gospel with an acquaintance. I wonder how many of those prayers Yahweh Jireh intended for me to answer. Surely *I* could have purchased groceries for an out-of-work friend, visited a hospitalized patient to pray with them, or invited a neighbor to Bible study.

Of course, Yahweh Jireh can provide for His children through supernatural means. Sometimes, though, He wants us to be the answer to our own prayers.

> *Yahweh Jireh, help me obey You when You want*
> *me to be the answer to my prayers.*

How might Yahweh Jireh want me to provide for someone I am praying for today?

*Yahweh Rapha*

# THE PHYSICIAN
## Exodus 15:22–27

For I am the LORD who heals you.

Exodus 15:26 NLT

The human body is an intricate creation, one we usually take for granted until we suffer illness or injury. Then our priority shifts to seeking healing. When God first revealed Himself in His Word as our Healer, though, He showed us that *His* priorities regarding healing are different.

During their Egyptian slavery, the Israelites had absorbed the pagan perspectives of their oppressors. When God freed them, the new nation had to learn what it meant to belong to Yahweh. After God parted the Red Sea, He tested Israel with undrinkable water. They responded by complaining instead of remembering Yahweh's mighty deliverance a mere three days earlier.

God purified the water but also taught the Israelites His priorities. He wanted them to put aside the things they had learned in Egypt and obey Him. Their first priority needed to be a healed relationship with Yahweh. If they put the Lord first, He would bless them spiritually *and* physically. He would be to them *Yahweh Rapha*, The Lord Who Heals.

God is concerned about our physical health. However, He is more concerned about our spiritual health found only in a right relationship with Him through Jesus Christ.

> *Yahweh Rapha, help me see my life through Your perspective and with Your priorities.*

How can I make a healthy relationship with Yahweh Rapha my priority today?

*Yahweh Rapha*

# THE PATIENT
## Psalm 38:1–22

Heal me, O LORD, and I will be healed;
Save me and I will be saved.

Jeremiah 17:14

Guilt is more than a bad feeling. It can cause physical complications such as hypertension, insomnia, or ulcers. More importantly, guilt can destroy relationships with others and with the Lord.

David understood the physical and emotional burden of his sin. We feel his pain and guilt in Psalm 38. Anxiousness weighed on his spirit, his wounds festered, and his strength failed. Yet he wisely did not seek help from family or friends. His only hope for relief was in the Lord.

Today, the Lord is frequently the last place we go for healing. We cover our wounds with a bandage and hope the pain fades as we seek the world's solutions. Counselors say guilt is old-fashioned baggage that should be discarded. Friends affirm our right to enjoy life without constraint. Alcohol and drugs temporarily deaden the pain. Yet the guilt and pain remain.

All the while, Yahweh Rapha waits for us to turn to Him. When we surrender to the Lord, He will treat the guilt that causes our pain. He sent His Son for that very purpose.

Only Yahweh Rapha could heal David, and He is the only one who can heal us today.

> *Yahweh Rapha, I am Your patient. Search me for the secret sin that wounds my soul.*

---

What guilt have I tried to cover? How can I submit it to Yahweh Rapha for healing?

*Yahweh Rapha*

# VITAL NUTRIENTS

## Colossians 3:5–14

So, as those who have been chosen of God, holy and beloved, put on
a heart of compassion, kindness, humility, gentleness and patience.

Colossians 3:12

Malnutrition is associated with a variety of diseases. A lack
of vitamin D causes rickets, vitamin C deficiency causes
scurvy, and beriberi results from a lack of thiamine. In
each case, healing is introduced through proper diet and nutritional
supplements.

Just as our bodies have nutritional requirements to remain healthy,
our relationships also have nutritional needs. Relationships are living
things. Feed them properly, they thrive. The Bible tells us to cultivate
our relationships with the vital nutrients of speaking truth, kindness,
compassion, and relating to others with humility, gentleness, patience,
and forgiveness.

Yahweh Rapha healed our relationship with Him through His
Son, Jesus Christ. Now He beckons us to share this message with a
hurting world. To do that, we must become vessels of healing as we
convey to others the same grace God shows us. There is truth in the
adage, "You may be the only Bible some people will ever read." If
others don't feel safe with us in our relationships, they won't consider
trusting our Savior.

> *Yahweh Rapha, help me be sensitive to the people*
> *You have brought into my life.*

Which of my relationships needs a healing touch? How can I
initiate healing today?

*Yahweh Nissi*

# A BANNER DEFENSE
## Exodus 17:8–16

> Moses built an altar and named it The LORD is My Banner.
>
> Exodus 17:15

In ancient times, military leaders proudly marched under a flag or a shiny metal ornament held on a tall pole for all to see. This banner, or standard, accompanied armies into battle and rallied the soldiers to fight for their cause. If the banner fell, so did hope for victory.

Yahweh had upheld Israel through the plagues, brought them out of Egyptian slavery, and protected them through the Red Sea. Then the Amalekites posed a new danger.

While Joshua valiantly led the Israelites into battle, Moses stood on a hill, holding the staff God had used to work miracles on their behalf. As long as Moses held the staff high, the Israelites prevailed. When he dropped his arms, the battle turned against them. The raised staff proclaimed their dependence on *Yahweh Nissi*, The Lord My Banner. They did not win their victory on the battlefield. Victory was achieved by the One under whose banner they marched.

Yahweh Nissi still leads the way for His people today. He is our defense, the One who protects us under the banner of His holy name. Though our spiritual adversary seeks our defeat, our victory is assured because we belong to Yahweh Nissi.

*Yahweh Nissi, thank You for being my shield and protector in all circumstances.*

How has God revealed Himself to me as Yahweh Nissi, The Lord My Banner, this week?

*Yahweh Nissi*

# LIFT UP THE CROSS
## Numbers 21:4–9

As Moses lifted up the snake on a pole in the
desert, so the Son of Man must be lifted up. Then
everyone who believes in him will have eternal life.

John 3:14–15 GW

Crucifixion is a brutal method of execution. Yet today, millions of Christians wear a cross to signify who they are and what they believe. To an unbelieving world, it makes no more sense than wearing a miniature electric chair around our necks.

The Israelites probably had similar thoughts when they first heard God's cure for the plague of poisonous snakes. God told Moses to construct a bronze snake, the image of the cause of their suffering, and put it on a standard for the people to see. When they looked at it in faith, they would be healed. They had a choice: look and live, or look for a different cure and die.

Through His crucifixion, Jesus Christ took the sin of the world on Himself. Looking at the cross, we see His payment for our sin. He is our only hope of salvation. We have a choice: look to the cross and live, or look for a different cure and die.

The Lord My Banner raised His standard: the cross lifted high. It signifies that we belong to Jesus Christ, our Yahweh Nissi.

*Yahweh Nissi, thank You for lifting Christ on the
cross to be the cure for my sin.*

Have I looked to the cross as the only cure for my sin? If not, why not?

*Yahweh Nissi*

# UNDER HIS BANNER
## 1 Corinthians 9:19–23

I am not ashamed of the gospel, because it is the
power of God for the salvation of everyone who
believes: first for the Jew, then for the Gentile.

Romans 1:16 NIV

It's natural to want to be like everyone else. People who are different tend to attract negative attention. However, in our haste to fit in, we may push Christ out.

The apostle Paul made a practice of relating to others on their terms, but he never forgot his intention to win people to Christ. Paul was not ashamed to live under Yahweh's banner.

Today, our desire for acceptance may override our desire to witness for Christ. Instead of living under Yahweh's banner, we hide the cross of Christ under a blanket.

Do our co-workers know to whom we belong? As we strive for advancement, do we compromise our witness for Christ? Do our neighbors know we belong to Yahweh Nissi? Do we join in neighborhood gossipfests, or do we share God's love to encourage those who are hurting?

Living under the banner of Yahweh Nissi means resting in the One we belong to, trusting that He is our sure defense, and living a life that points people to Him.

*Yahweh Nissi, I confess I do not always live in a way
that points people to You. Help me to be unashamed
of the cross as I live under Your banner.*

How have I hidden my allegiance to Yahweh Nissi instead of living under His banner?

*Yahweh Sabaoth*

# THE CHAMPION
## 1 Samuel 17:1–9, 32–51

I come to you in the name of the LORD of hosts, the God
of the armies of Israel, whom you have taunted.

1 Samuel 17:45

Most of us remember the school bully. If we weren't singled out for his or her unwanted attention, then we knew the unfortunate person who was. Victims of a bully all wish for a champion to take up their cause and take down their tormentor.

Imagine how Israel's army felt in the face of Goliath's taunts. Israel belonged to Yahweh, yet none had the courage to face the Philistine giant. They needed a champion to fight for them.

A young shepherd understood what others missed. Goliath's taunts were not only against Israel, they were against the "armies of the living God" (1 Sam. 17:36). To taunt Israel was to taunt Israel's God.

With courage fueled by experience, David prepared to fight. *Yahweh Sabaoth*, the Lord of Hosts, had fought for him before. David trusted the Lord to give him victory once again.

Although Israel's army marched under Yahweh's banner, they doubted the power of the Lord of Hosts. But the Lord waited for someone to step forward in faith. He used David to show Himself mighty in battle on behalf of His people and for the sake of His own Name.

*Yahweh Sabaoth, show Yourself mighty for Your*
*glory as I step out in faith today.*

How does knowing I belong to Yahweh Sabaoth change the way I view those I fear?

*Yahweh Sabaoth*

# SPIRITUAL REALITY
## 2 Kings 6:8–17

Bless the LORD, all you His hosts,
You who serve Him, doing His will.

Psalm 103:21

Watching a 3-D film without 3-D glasses keeps us from enjoying the movie's full effects. Likewise in life, when we believe that what we see is all there is, we miss opportunities to enjoy the full measure of the grace and power of God. The result is often a sense of defeat and of being overwhelmed by people and circumstances.

Elisha's servant could see only the enemy's army surrounding the city with horses and chariots. His reaction was predictably fearful. Elisha did not attempt to convince his servant to give up his fear. Instead, he prayed the Lord would open his servant's eyes to the unseen reality. The enemy might have surrounded the city, but the armies of Yahweh had surrounded the enemy—and the whole mountain!

In Ephesians 6:12, the apostle Paul warns that "our struggle is not against flesh and blood, but against the . . . spiritual forces of wickedness in the heavenly places." Just because we cannot see this spiritual world does not make it any less real. Even so, though our enemy may scheme and attack, we have no need to fear if we belong to Yahweh Sabaoth. The Lord of Hosts fights our battles and gives us the victory.

> *Yahweh Sabaoth, open my eyes to the spiritual realities around me.*

How can I change my perspective so that nothing blocks my view of Yahweh Sabaoth?

*Yahweh Sabaoth*

# VINDICATED
## Isaiah 54:11–17

The LORD is fighting for you! So be still!
Exodus 14:14 GW

Few things cause us to react more strongly than when we are wrongly accused or attacked. We're eager to assert our innocence and demand our rights as we protest the injustice.

Yahweh Sabaoth instructs us to respond differently. If we belong to Him, we are to trust Him to fight for us and to vindicate us. Although we know God will keep His word, we still may struggle with the *when* and the *how* of His promises. *When* will God vindicate us? *How* will He do it? Will we have the satisfaction of seeing our tormentors suffer as we have suffered?

After Isaiah prophesied judgment to Israel, he confirmed the Lord's defense of them. However, waiting for Yahweh Sabaoth to act in His time and in His way meant many would die before they saw His vindication against their oppressors. It did not seem fair, but God would accomplish His perfect will for their ultimate good and for His glory.

Jesus also had something to say about what to do when we are wrongly accused or persecuted for Him. Luke 21:14–15 tells us not to worry about our defense. When we need it, He will give us the right words at the right time, because Yahweh Sabaoth is our sure defender.

> *Lord of Hosts, help me to be still and trust You as*
> *You fight on my behalf.*

How do I respond when I am wrongfully accused? Is this response usually helpful?

*Yahweh Shalom*

# THE SOURCE OF PEACE
## Judges 6:1–24

We have peace with God through our Lord Jesus Christ.

Romans 5:1

If anyone needed peace, Gideon did. He so feared the Midianite raiders oppressing Israel that he hid in a winepress to thresh wheat. Afraid God had abandoned His people, Gideon wondered if the Lord could still be trusted to be their protector. Then, when he realized he had spoken directly with God, Gideon feared he would die because he had actually seen Yahweh.

God revealed Himself to this fearful man. He quieted Gideon's fears and appointed him to deliver Israel from the Midianites. Reassured, Gideon built an altar and called it *Yahweh Shalom*, "The LORD is Peace" (Judg. 6:24). The knowledge that he was at peace with God gave Gideon the freedom to accomplish what God had called him to do.

A thousand years later, God again spoke peace to fearful men. Jesus said, "My peace I give to you; not as the world gives. . . . Do not let your heart be troubled" (John 14:27).

Others promise peace, but Jesus is the only One who brings real peace because He *is* peace. True peace is more than the absence of hostility or fear. True peace is the gift God gives when He reconciles us to Him through Jesus Christ, the Prince of Peace.

*Yahweh Shalom, help me remember that peace apart from You is not real peace at all.*

Whom can I share the true peace of God with today?

*Yahweh Shalom*

# THE PRACTICE OF PEACE
## Philippians 4:6–9

You will keep in perfect peace all who trust in
you, whose thoughts are fixed on you!

Isaiah 26:3 NLT

If Christians should not be anxious for anything, why do so many of us spend our nights lying in bed, staring at the ceiling, body exhausted but mind racing?

The prophet Isaiah noted that God's peace results from keeping our minds focused on the Lord. Additionally, when God tells us to do something in His Word, He always tells us *how* to do it. In the fight to keep our mind focused on Him, the battle plan is found in Philippians 4:6–9.

First, we are to ask for God's help in releasing anxious thoughts as we thankfully acknowledge His grace and mercy. When we do, Yahweh Shalom gives us a peace beyond our understanding that stands guard over our hearts and minds.

Then, to prevent anxious thoughts from returning, God tells us to fill our thoughts with things that are honorable, pure, lovely, and worthy of praise.

Finally, it's not enough to do this once. We need to practice it repeatedly until it becomes a habit. When we do, Yahweh Shalom blesses us with His perfect peace.

> *Yahweh Shalom, help me release my anxious thoughts to You as I rest in Your care.*

How am I allowing fear and worry to control my thoughts and steal my peace?

*Yahweh Shalom*

# MAKING PEACE

## Luke 12:49–53

"Do you think I came to bring peace to earth? No!"

Luke 12:51 GW

Are you a peacekeeper or a peacemaker?

Peacekeepers avoid conflict at all costs. Their motto is, "Don't rock the boat." Peacemakers focus on reconciliation, and they recognize that healthy conflict may be necessary for reconciliation to occur.

Jesus was a peacemaker. He was more concerned with *making* peace than He was with *keeping* peace. His earthly life—and His death—centered on making peace between God and humans. Yet some of the things He said did not sound peaceable at all.

Jesus understood that real peace does not ignore conflict. True peace addresses the cause of the problem to remove it permanently. For us to have peace with God, Jesus dealt with the problem of our sin with finality and in the most violent way possible.

Being a disciple of Jesus Christ means we are to say what people *need* to hear rather than what they *want* to hear. Of course, we are to do so gently and lovingly. Avoiding conflict may be easier, but Yahweh Shalom doesn't call us to take the easy way. He calls us to be peacemakers.

> *Yahweh Shalom, help me speak Your words of*
> *peace to a world at enmity with You.*

In which of my relationships have I avoided speaking God's words of peace?

*Yahweh Tsidkenu*

# STAIN REMOVER
## Jeremiah 23:1–8

This is His name by which He will be called,
"The LORD our righteousness."

Jeremiah 23:6

Television crime dramas regularly use forensic science to solve crimes. Although the offender may scrub away telltale blood, crime solvers discover the stain and catch the criminal.

For thousands of years, the ancient Israelites depended on a system of sacrifices to remove sin's stain, and adhered to God's commandments to provide a righteous covering.

But they discovered that no one can keep the Law in its entirety. A gulf exists between sinful men and holy God. While sacrifices temporarily covered sin, they could not bridge the divide. The rituals revealed their need for God's righteousness and the futility of trying to earn it.

The sacrifices also pointed to the coming Messiah, the One who would permanently pay for, and remove, sin. *Yahweh Tsidkenu*, The Lord Our Righteousness, provided the gift of His Son to cleanse sin's stain and declare us righteous by giving us His righteousness.

We can do nothing to cover our sin. Our only solution is the righteousness God gives us in Jesus Christ. No sin is too large for the Lord to cover for us. Then He goes a step further: He not only gives us a righteousness that covers our sin, He removes it forever.

*Yahweh Tsidkenu, thank You for permanently removing the stain of my sin.*

What sin have I tried to hide instead of confessing it and receiving God's righteousness?

*Yahweh Tsidkenu*

# New Clothes
## Matthew 23:25–33

Unless your righteousness surpasses that of the scribes and
Pharisees, you will not enter the kingdom of heaven.

Matthew 5:20

In Hans Christian Andersen's tale, "The Emperor's New Clothes,"
a gullible ruler believes he is wearing valuable clothing, only to
discover he is not wearing anything.

Jesus warned His followers to guard against a similar delusion.
The Pharisees clothed themselves in ritual, convinced that their high,
righteous standards earned them God's approval.

However, the prophet Isaiah wrote, "All our righteous deeds are like
a filthy garment" (Isa. 64:6). Jesus called the Pharisees "hypocrites"
(Matt. 23:25). He said our righteousness must surpass theirs to enter
heaven. These words must have shocked His listeners. If the Pharisees,
with all their religious knowledge, could not get into heaven, what
chance did the average person have?

Religious rituals mean nothing without a change of heart. To exceed
the righteousness of the Pharisees is to begin with the righteousness
Yahweh Tsidkenu gives us through Jesus Christ. Only then will we
truly be clean on the inside. Anything else is nothing more than filthy
rags. When Jesus gives us His righteousness, we exchange our rags
for the riches of His new clothes.

*Yahweh Tsidkenu, give me a hunger and thirst for
Your righteousness alone.*

How have I tried to impress God with the rags of my own righteousness this week?

*Yahweh Tsidkenu*

# THERMOSTAT OR THERMOMETER?
## Proverbs 1:10–19

Do not walk in the way with them.
Keep your feet from their path.

Proverbs 1:15

Are you a thermostat or a thermometer?

Thermostats set the temperature, while thermometers reflect the existing environment. When we go along with the crowd, we function like human thermometers, reflecting the moral standards of others. Our desire for their approval is stronger than our desire to please Yahweh Tsidkenu. But when we speak up, gently and respectfully, we can influence other people and raise the moral standard, functioning more like a thermostat than a thermometer.

Throughout His earthly ministry, Jesus challenged the people not to go along with the status quo if it violated God's standards. John the Baptist is another example of one who took an unpopular stand when he rebuked Herod for an adulterous relationship (Mark 6:17–18).

If we belong to Yahweh Tsidkenu, we will reflect His righteousness no matter where we are or who we are with.

> *Yahweh Tsidkenu, I want to stand for Your righteousness. Help me be a thermostat instead of a thermometer.*

When have I gone along with the crowd even though I knew it was wrong? How can I begin to prepare myself today to stand alone for righteousness?

*Yahweh Mekoddishkem*

# SET APART
## Exodus 31:12–18

You shall not profane My holy name. . . .
I am the LORD who sanctifies you.

Leviticus 22:32

When God delivered Israel from Egypt, He also delivered them from the influences of a pagan religion. At Mount Sinai, Yahweh gave Israel His law and entered into a covenant with them. He set them apart as His people and told them how to please Him.

Israel had to learn that they could not set themselves apart as God's own people, no matter how many commandments they observed. Being sanctified, or set apart, was something God did *for* them. Obedience was to be their response.

To confirm this as His work, God revealed Himself as *Yahweh Mekoddishkem*, The Lord Who Sanctifies You. He did this as He affirmed the Sabbath, a weekly day of rest for His people. God intended it to be a sign for them, and for a watching world, that Israel was different. Yahweh Mekoddishkem had declared them righteous, and He would keep them righteous.

The revelation of this new name together with the Sabbath reminds us to rest in the Lord. Yahweh Mekoddishkem will work in our lives to make us all He intends for us to be.

> *Yahweh Mekoddishkem, thank You for Your sanctifying work in me and for me, because I belong to You.*

Do I live in a way that shows a watching world I belong to Yahweh Mekoddishkem?

*Yahweh Mekoddishkem*

# YIELDING CONTROL
### Galatians 5:16–25

Now may the God of peace Himself sanctify you entirely.

1 Thessalonians 5:23

God has declared us righteous through Christ's finished work on the cross. However, our thoughts, words, and deeds don't always match what God has declared us to be.

Inconsistencies between who we are and who we should be often trigger our resolve to improve. We make resolutions to be more loving, patient, kind, or self-controlled. We determine to try harder, work smarter, do better. Still, we fail again and again.

Just as we cannot *declare* ourselves righteous by our own efforts, we also cannot *make* ourselves righteous. "Love, joy, peace, patience, kindness, goodness, faithfulness, gentleness, self-control" are called "fruit of the Spirit" (Gal. 5:22–23) because it is the Holy Spirit who develops them in us.

This is not about trying harder; this is about yielding control. Only then can God love others through us, give us His joy, or develop patience in us far beyond our natural inclination.

As we surrender to Yahweh Mekoddishkem, He works to sanctify us and make us more like His Son. Our behavior will begin to match what He has already declared us to be: new creations in Christ.

*Yahweh Mekoddishkem, help me surrender to the work of Your Spirit in my life today.*

In what area do I need to yield to the Holy Spirit to produce the fruit I am lacking?

*Yahweh Mekoddishkem*

# PERFECT CHURCH
## Hebrews 2:11–18

For both He who sanctifies and those who are
sanctified are all from one Father.

Hebrews 2:11

A couple I know has been searching for the perfect church, but none meets their standards. Churches are too big, too small, too quiet, too loud, too traditional, or too contemporary.
These differences would not bother Jesus, as long as the people trust Him for salvation and honor Yahweh Mekoddishkem. He is "not ashamed" (Heb. 2:11) to refer to Christians as His brothers and sisters because He has declared us righteous and set apart for our heavenly Father's praise.

We can easily develop a critical sense as we compare ourselves to other believers or our church to other churches. We focus on the unimportant and forget that Yahweh Mekoddishkem sanctifies *all* believers through Jesus Christ. We each may be in different places on our spiritual journey, but if we have trusted Christ as Lord and Savior, then we are on the same spiritual road.

When we become dissatisfied with our own church or critical of another, let's remember one small point: even if we found the perfect church, it would cease to be perfect the moment we entered the front door.

*Yahweh Mekoddishkem, forgive me for the things
I've said that tear down other believers.*

How can I encourage Christians who are struggling, without seeming to criticize the church they attend?

*Yahweh Rohi*

# THE GREAT SHEPHERD
## Ezekiel 34:11–16, 22–31

I am the good shepherd; I know my own sheep, and they know me.

John 10:14 NLT

A picture of Jesus wearing a flowing robe and carrying a fluffy lamb in His arms is a familiar image in many church nurseries. It invokes thoughts of a tender and compassionate shepherd as children are introduced to the Savior.

As we get older, though, this picture of a gentle and tender God may fail to be enough for us. Life becomes demanding, and only the tough succeed. How can a tender shepherd who cares for little lambs help adults courageously fighting difficult battles with hardened enemies?

This kind of thinking proves that we don't understand what a shepherd really does. Yes, he is gentle and caring, and he knows each of his sheep by name. But a good shepherd is also strong and fierce when necessary. He is the first and only line of defense for his sheep, protecting them from a variety of predators who see the sheep as easy pickings. David, in his shepherd days, killed lions and bears to protect his flock (1 Sam. 17:37), proving that shepherding is not for the fainthearted!

*Yahweh Rohi*, The Lord My Shepherd, is our tender provider and our strong defender. He knows our enemy better than we do. He protects us and rescues us when we fall. He is exactly who we need, no matter how old we are.

*Yahweh Rohi, thank You that I can never outgrow*
*my need of You, my Shepherd.*

When have I insisted on my own way instead of staying close to my Shepherd?

68

*Yahweh Rohi*

# THE SHEEP
## Psalm 100

All of us like sheep have gone astray,
Each of us has turned to his own way.

Isaiah 53:6

O f all the animals we could be compared to, would we ever pick sheep? Sheep are helpless, fearful, and stubborn. They are dependent on their shepherd for food sources, and they have no defenses against predators.

God compared us to sheep, specifically sheep that have gone astray. We have turned from the rich pastureland Yahweh Rohi provides, and we have sought greener pastures. Wandering from the safety of the sheepfold, we easily become ensnared by the adversary of our souls.

The ability to return to our Shepherd carries a greater cost than we could ever imagine or pay. God paid the price for us—the supreme price of His Son's life—to bring us into His flock.

Even when we are part of His flock, Yahweh Rohi will discipline us, as a shepherd uses his staff to get the attention of a stubborn sheep. He may allow hardship to drive us closer to Him, as a shepherd might break the leg of a wandering sheep. Yet as the shepherd carries the injured lamb and keeps it close, Yahweh Rohi carries us until our Shepherd's voice is more appealing than the attraction of distant pastures.

*Yahweh Rohi, I confess I often follow the world's lure instead of my Shepherd's voice.*

How can I listen more closely to my Shepherd's voice today?

*Yahweh Rohi*

# THE SHEPHERDS
## 1 Corinthians 9:7–14

"Simon, son of John, do you love Me?" . . . He
said to him, "Shepherd My sheep."

John 21:16

Full-time ministry is not the best choice if your goal is fame and fortune. Hundreds of thousands of people serve in relative obscurity on the mission field and in large and small churches around the world. They do so because Yahweh Rohi called them to shepherd His sheep.

Answering Yahweh Rohi's call to shepherd means shouldering unusual responsibilities and pressures. Pastors have the unique charge of guarding and developing the spiritual health of their flock. Even as they do so, they and their families are expected to live up to a standard few others would willingly accept. Despite all this, they obey the voice of their Shepherd.

Shepherds have a responsibility to their flocks, but flocks also have a responsibility to their shepherds. We can pray for our shepherds, encourage them verbally or with a card, and support their ministries financially and with our time and effort. We can also be generous with praise and sparing with criticism. Above all, we can love and appreciate them for their obedience to the Great Shepherd on our behalf.

Our shepherds have a job to do—and so do the sheep.

*Yahweh Rohi, help me be supportive of the shepherds You have placed over Your flock.*

How can I show appreciation to my pastor and my pastor's family today?

*Yahweh Shammah*

# THE PRIVILEGE OF HIS PRESENCE
## Ezekiel 10:1–4, 18–19; 11:22–23; 48:35

> The LORD's glory had filled the LORD's temple.
>
> 2 Chronicles 7:2 GW

How easy is it to take the Lord's presence for granted?

Four hundred years after the glory of the Lord first occupied the temple, the Israelites had become unaffected by Yahweh's presence. The nation had forsaken God, and God judged them through captivity by the conquering nations of Assyria and Babylon. During the Babylonian captivity, the Lord gave Ezekiel a vision of the departure of God's glory from the temple in Jerusalem. God's people had lost the privilege of His presence.

What about us? When we attend church, do we go through the motions of worship, or are we aware of the presence of Yahweh? In our daily quiet time with the Lord, do we say a few routine prayers and read a few obligatory Bible verses, or are we grateful for the opportunity to enter His throne room? He is always present with us, whether we acknowledge Him or not.

Israel is waiting for the day when Jerusalem will be named *Yahweh Shammah*, The Lord Is There. For Christians, the Lord is *here*. Do we appreciate the privilege of His presence?

> *Yahweh Shammah, thank You for the privilege of entering Your holy presence through the saving work of Jesus Christ.*

What have I allowed to interfere with Yahweh's presence in my life this past week?

*Yahweh Shammah*

# RECOGNIZING HIS PRESENCE
## 1 Kings 19:9–14

GOD wasn't in the fire; and after the fire a gentle and quiet whisper.

1 Kings 19:12 Message

God often used miraculous signs and wonders in the Bible to confirm His presence and His work. There is a danger, however, in associating *only* these things with the presence of God.

By the power of Yahweh, Elijah had won a miraculous victory over the prophets of Baal. Afterward, with his life in jeopardy, he ran into the wilderness, feeling very much alone. God ministered to His weary servant in an unusual way. Yahweh did not reveal His presence in the power of hurricane-force winds. He did not reveal His presence in the strength of an earthquake. Nor did He reveal His presence in the burning intensity of fire.

Instead, Yahweh Shammah made His presence known in the "sound of a gentle blowing" (1 Kings 19:12). One translation calls it a "still small voice" (KJV). When Elijah refocused his attention away from miraculous signs and wonders, he was able to recognize Yahweh's presence. Only then was he ready for the next assignment the Lord had for him.

Rather than searching for Yahweh Shammah in out-of-the-ordinary events, let's look for His presence today in the whispers of our daily routines.

*Yahweh Shammah, help me to be aware of Your presence in the dailyness of life.*

How do I need to refocus my attention to recognize the Lord's presence today?

*Yahweh Shammah*

# REJOICING IN HIS PRESENCE
## Revelation 21:1–5

I will come again. Then I will bring you into my
presence so that you will be where I am.

John 14:3 GW

We will spend eternity with the Lord. That's very good.
However, we will also spend eternity with Christians.
Depending on the quality of our existing relationships
with other believers here on earth, we may or may not view *that* as
very good.

When God said in His Word that He will dwell among us, He meant
*all* believers in Christ. Not only the ones who agree with our politics
or the ones who enjoy singing the same hymns or praise choruses we
enjoy. When God says He will dwell among us, He includes every person who has received the gift of salvation offered by Jesus Christ.

We all know Christians who are difficult people. The person who
always says the wrong thing. The one who monopolizes every conversation. We might even be that person to someone else. Do we treat every
Christian as if God dwells in them? We should, because He does.

We will live forever, rejoicing with the Lord and with His people—
*all* of His people. With that in mind, let's learn to rejoice with them
here.

*Yahweh Shammah, help me see Your presence in
all Your children.*

What difficult person is the Lord asking me to love because He
is present in them?

# REVERENCE AND INTIMACY
## Deuteronomy 32:5–14

> When Israel was a youth I loved him,
> And out of Egypt I called My son.
>
> Hosea 11:1

While God is regularly referred to as our "Father" in the New Testament, He also spoke of Himself as the Father of the nation of Israel in the Old Testament. In Deuteronomy, Moses sang of how God purchased Israel from slavery and fathered the nation to be His own people.

Jesus upset the religious leaders of His day by encouraging His followers to consider God not just as the Father of the nation but also as a personal Father. Paul wrote in Galatians 4:6, "Because you are sons, God has sent forth the Spirit of His Son into our hearts, crying, 'Abba! Father!'" *Abba* refers to an intimate relationship, similar to *Papa* in English.

God the Father is the One who chose Israel as His people, and He is the same God who created us for intimate relationship with Him. He is both, and we are to respond to Him intimately, yet with reverence.

Our heavenly Father requires nothing less than reverential awe without fright and intimacy without disrespect. Our relationship and our worship should reflect both.

> *Heavenly Father, I worship You and love You as the*
> *God of the universe and my Abba.*

How can I experience intimacy without sacrificing reverential awe in my quiet time with God today?

# PERFECT FATHER
## Matthew 6:25–34

Your heavenly Father already knows all your needs.

Matthew 6:32 NLT

Have you or someone you know been disappointed by an earthly father? Do memories of an abusive or neglectful father cause you to mistrust your heavenly Father? Perhaps you have regrets about your own role as a parent.

Children naturally base their view of their heavenly Father on what they experience with their earthly father. If they feel loved by an earthly father who cares for them with kindness and compassion, then they will probably view their heavenly Father the same way.

Earthly fathers may or may not choose their roles willingly or fulfill their roles adequately. Although they may fail to meet their children's needs, their failures do not reflect the character of our heavenly Father. God intentionally chose us to be His children through faith in Christ. He is aware of our needs and is always working for our ultimate good and for His glory.

We have imperfect fathers and we are imperfect children, but the Lord will never be anything but a perfect heavenly Father.

*Heavenly Father, thank You for the assurance that You will never fail me.*

Has a poor relationship with an earthly father caused me to mistrust my heavenly Father? If so, how can I change my perspective of my heavenly Father today?

# BIRTHRIGHT
## John 1:6–13

They are reborn! This is not a physical birth resulting from
human passion or plan—this rebirth comes from God.

John 1:13 NLT

The world is quick to say we are *all* God's children. However, that is not what the Bible says. God's Word tells us that the Father-child relationship we have with Him has nothing to do with our natural birth into the human race. If anything, our birth into a humanity tainted with sin is what keeps us from a relationship with Him.

John wrote in his Gospel that the right to refer to the living God of the universe as our Father is given to us when we believe in His Son. "But to all who believed him and accepted him, he gave the right to become children of God" (John 1:12 NLT). Belief that Jesus Christ is the Son of God, the only way of salvation, is the only way to restore the Father-child relationship that sin destroyed.

Everyone must face this decision individually. We may be born to Christian parents, but no one is born a Christian, at least not by their first birth. If we don't speak up, others will never learn how to receive the right to become a child of our heavenly Father.

*Father, thank You for making me Your child through*
*my belief in Jesus Christ.*

With whom can I share the truth of new birth today?

# UNLIMITED ACCESS
## Leviticus 16:1–10

The curtain in the temple was split in two from top to bottom.

Mark 15:38 GW

We are a sinful people separated from a holy God. The Lord emphasized this to the Israelites when He brought them to Mount Sinai and taught them how to worship Him.

Israel learned that God required boundaries in their worship of Him. His presence dwelt in the Holy of Holies, separated from the rest of the tabernacle by a thickly woven curtain. Even the high priest could enter only once a year, and only after appropriate sacrifices.

Jesus Christ's crucifixion paid for our sin and provided access to our holy God in ways the Israelites never imagined. At Christ's death, the massive curtain restricting the Holy of Holies in the temple was split in two from top to bottom—impossible for man to do.

The torn curtain confirmed that God declared Himself accessible to us through the broken body of Christ. Hebrews 10:19–20 tells us, "Because of the blood of Jesus we can now confidently go into the holy place. Jesus has opened a new and living way for us to go through the curtain. (The curtain is his own body.)" (GW).

Christ paid the ultimate price to give us unlimited access. All we have to do is enter.

*Lord, help me never to take my access to You for granted.*

How does knowing I have unlimited access to God change the way I will call to Him?

# ULTIMATE CONFIDENCE
Luke 18:1–5

Therefore let us draw near with confidence to the throne of grace.

Hebrews 4:16

When we pray, we'll never get a busy signal or hear, "Please remain on the line. Your call will be answered in the order it was received." There is never a bad signal, a dropped call, and we never have to ask, "Can You hear me now?"

In Luke 18, Jesus told a parable to illustrate several important lessons about prayer. The widow in His story knew whom she needed to approach, she remained persistent in her request, and she did not doubt she would receive what she required. Our unlimited access to the God of all creation ensures that He will hear us and He will respond. His responses may not always be what we want, but they will always be what we need.

Scripture urges us to pray at all times (Luke 18:1), pray without ceasing (1 Thess. 5:17), and to pray no matter where we are (1 Tim. 2:8). When we do, we have an instantaneous audience with the God of the universe.

No busy signals, no voicemail, and He hears us wherever and whenever we call. That's unlimited access with ultimate confidence.

*Father God, thank You for the assurance that You always hear me when I call to You.*

How does the assurance of God's accessibility give me confidence in prayer today?

# ONE-ANOTHER AVAILABILITY
## Colossians 3:1–16

Use your freedom to serve one another in love.

Galatians 5:13 Message

Christianity is not for Lone Rangers. God intended for us to love and serve each other together as part of a community. The multitude of "one anothers" in the New Testament epistles tells us how to do this.

We are to love one another, pray for one another, and comfort and care for one another. We are commanded to minister to one another, teach one another, and be kind to one another. We are to submit to one another, admonish and exhort one another, forbear and forgive one another . . . and that's not even the complete list!

We cannot do this in isolation. We are blessed to *be* a blessing, not to hoard our blessings. We need the body of Christ, and the body of Christ needs us. If we are too busy doing our own thing, we won't be available to serve. Our availability is linked to God's accessibility. The more we "access" the Lord—by spending time in His presence through prayer, reading His Word, and yielding to His Spirit—the more He equips us to fulfill His purposes among His children.

If there is no accessibility to each other, then there is no "one another."

*Lord, reveal to me where You want me to increase my availability to serve You.*

To whom is God asking me to be accessible today? How can I show them my accessibility?

# DESIGNING HISTORY
## Psalm 22:1–24

Whose architect and builder is God.

Hebrews 11:10

Consider all the events that lined up exactly the way they did to bring you to this moment: the details necessary to bring you and your spouse together, or your parents or grandparents together. How different our lives might have been if the smallest event changed.

God is the Architect of history, arranging it to accomplish His purposes. He designs it all—world events *and* individual life experiences—to work together to display His glory.

Psalm 22 is one example of several hundred prophecies in the Old Testament proclaiming details of the birth, life, and death of the Messiah. Statisticians have proven the virtual impossibility of any one person fulfilling *every* prophecy, yet that is exactly what Jesus Christ did. God designed the details of Jesus's life and described them beforehand so there would be no question as to the validity of Jesus's claims and credentials.

We do not have to be frightened of world events or even the events of our individual lives. The Architect of history designed it and is still in control today.

*Lord God, thank You that I can trust Your design*
*for history and Your design for me.*

How do the fulfilled prophecies of Jesus's first coming help me trust God's design today?

# DESIGNING MY SALVATION
## Acts 8:25–40

*Then the Spirit said to Philip, "Go up and join this chariot."*

Acts 8:29

How did you come to know the Savior?

Perhaps you went forward in church in response to the pastor's invitation. Maybe you realized your need for a Savior while reading the Bible alone in your room. Perhaps a friend shared with you what it meant to be a Christian, and you prayed with him. Maybe you responded to the gospel as a child in Sunday school. Perhaps you have not yet received the gift of salvation.

The book of Acts overflows with descriptions of how people responded—or failed to respond—to the message of the gospel. In today's passage, God directed Philip to meet an Ethiopian and share the meaning of Isaiah's prophecy.

God designs the circumstances of our individual lives to draw us to Him. Only He knows what it will take for each one of us to surrender to Him. For some, hearing the gospel for the first time is enough. Others need to hear the message of salvation multiple times before they respond.

Whatever our experience may be, the Architect of our salvation designed it just for us.

*Heavenly Father, thank You for designing my circumstances to draw me to You.*

How did God design the circumstances of my salvation? If I have not yet responded to His invitation, what is preventing me from responding today?

# DESIGNING MY DAY
## Mark 5:21–43

At that moment Jesus felt power had gone out of him. He turned
around in the crowd and asked, "Who touched my clothes?"

Mark 5:30 GW

I hate interruptions, especially when I have a deadline. Can't people
see I am busy?

Jesus was having a busy day. A synagogue official's daughter
lay dying, and he begged Jesus to heal her. What a prime opportunity
for Jesus to win over one of the religious leaders! Surely He should
have accompanied this important official in haste and with single-
minded determination.

Jesus did not allow the pressure of a dying child to interfere with
another divine appointment arranged by His heavenly Father. Can
you imagine the official counting the minutes when Jesus stopped to
question the crowd? Yet Jesus had time for both needs, and the official's child benefited from a more glorious healing than she would
have earlier.

Just as Jesus trusted His heavenly Father to orchestrate His schedule,
we also must trust the Architect of our days.

> *Dear Lord, forgive me for the times I have ignored*
> *Your divine appointments. Help me keep my sched-*
> *ule flexible to respond to Your promptings.*

How can I prepare to recognize the divine appointments God
has for me today?

# THE STORY
## Acts 2:22–36

You have worked wonders,
Plans formed long ago, with perfect faithfulness.

Isaiah 25:1

I love a good book. When I find authors I enjoy, I wind up reading every book they've written.

God has written His own compelling story. It is a powerful story of creation, unrequited love, betrayal, rebellion, sacrifice, and reconciliation. It includes mystery, romance, deceit, poetry, murder, wisdom, history, miracles, biographies, and battle scenes.

Early in the story, a loving God is betrayed, but He is not surprised by the betrayal. The Divine Author had already written the story's gripping resolution before time began.

Genesis through Revelation, the Bible is the enthralling story of God's relationship with His people. One of the reasons it is so compelling is that the Author has included you and me in His story. He has described our past, present, and future in its pages.

The Bible is the bestselling book of all time. Listen to the Author's heart as you read His book. You'll love how the story ends!

*Lord, You are the Divine Author. Help me to value,
read, and understand Your Word.*

Will I read a less familiar passage of Scripture today, asking the Holy Spirit to give me understanding of His Word?

# THE STORIES
## Jeremiah 31:31–34

You are our letter, written in our hearts, known and read by all men . . . written not with ink but with the Spirit of the living God.

2 Corinthians 3:2–3

The phrase "My life is an open book" takes on special meaning when we become Christians. The Divine Author, God Himself, begins to write on the pages of our hearts.

First, He replaces the old pages of our life. The shameful words on dirty, crumpled pages stained with sin no longer have power to shout accusations. Our Author refuses to remember what was written there. Instead, He gives us pristine paper, waiting to be filled with His story.

Then He proclaims a new title for us: *Christian*, a follower of Christ. He lists a new Table of Contents, revealing the entries to us chapter by chapter. Finally, He writes His full story in and through us: a story of hope, love, redemption, and reconciliation.

While our new story is being written, do we argue with the Author about the plot, the length of the chapters, or the characters He includes? Or do we cooperate with Him, resting in the assurance that, although we haven't read it yet, He knows how the story ends?

*Sovereign Lord, I confess I have argued with You about the details of the new story You are writing in my life. I commit to yielding to Your pen as You complete each new chapter.*

In what area have I argued with God? How can I yield to Him as He writes my story?

# THE LEGACY
## Deuteronomy 6:4–9

We are writing these things so that our joy will be complete.

1 John 1:4 NLT

What legacy are you leaving for those who come after you—your children, grandchildren, students, or friends? When we think of legacies, we might think of monetary or property bequests. The Author of our salvation asks us to leave a different kind of legacy.

As He writes His story on our lives, He wants us to share that story with others, especially the next generation. Through Moses, God explained to His people how to do this.

Before we can share with anyone else, we must know for ourselves who God is and write that knowledge on our own heart. Then we are to teach others, no matter where we are or what we are doing. The four examples Moses gave include when we are at home, when we go out, when we go to sleep, and when we wake up. This covers every aspect of life. We are also to use written reminders of all that God has done for us, so that we and our children will never forget.

The Divine Author is writing the story of our lives. Our assignment is to tell it and keep telling it, that those who come after us may learn of His Son and His love.

*Lord, help me to pass on the story You are writing in my life so others will learn of Your love and faithfulness in Jesus Christ.*

With whom is God asking me to share my story? How can I begin to share it today?

# NO ONE LIKE GOD
## Psalm 19:1–6

Who is like You, majestic in holiness,
Awesome in praises, working wonders?

Exodus 15:11

Technology changes faster than many of us can process. We see the results in everything from routine communication tools to the special effects in Hollywood movies.

That's the problem. We have been wowed by technology to such an extent that we now describe these experiences in terms once reserved for God alone. We ascribe words such as *awesome, amazing,* and *wonderful* to our inventions.

God created a universe out of nothing. Then He made exceptions to the properties and natural laws of His creation with miraculous interventions such as the parting of the Red Sea, Daniel's deliverance in the lions' den, and Jonah's preservation in the stomach of the fish. These miracles were nothing, though, compared to the virgin birth of God's Son, Jesus Christ, to a young Hebrew girl. The most awesome work in all of history occurred when God became man.

Let's reserve words like *awesome* and *amazing* for the One they really belong to, for there is no one and nothing like our awesome God.

> Lord God, I worship You, for there is no one like
> You. You are truly awesome.

What amount of time will I set aside to worship my awesome God today?

# SIGNS AND WONDERS
## Matthew 12:38–42

Only an evil, faithless generation would ask for a miraculous sign.

Matthew 12:39 NLT

Magicians use tricks and illusions to entertain their audience. People are sawed in two. Tigers seem to appear and disappear at a word.

When Jesus used miracles in His earthly ministry, He amazed many with His power and authority. Some, such as the Pharisees and Herod, demanded He perform miracles on command.

However, Jesus was not a magician performing parlor tricks for entertainment. His miracles confirmed His authority over the physical and spiritual world. He healed and fed people to demonstrate how much their loving Father wanted to heal and feed their spirits.

John explained why he included Jesus's miracles in his Gospel. "That you may believe that Jesus is the . . . Son of God, and that by believing in him you will have life" (John 20:31 NLT).

Today, people are hungry for miracles. They follow anyone who performs wonders for them, yet overlook the most significant miracle of all: the miracle of spiritual new birth.

*Awesome Lord, whether or not I see Your miraculous intervention in my circumstances, help me remember You have already given me the greatest miracle of all: new life in You.*

For what miracle have I been praying? Will I trust God today for the outcome, even if He does not intervene as I ask?

# COME AND SEE
## Psalm 66:1–20

Come and see the works of God,
Who is awesome in His deeds.

Psalm 66:5

When we receive good news, our first inclination is usually to tell someone. Did you begin a new job or receive a promotion? Perhaps you learned of a free concert at the local park or discovered a 75-percent-off sale on shoes? Good news, too good to keep to ourselves.

It seems we are eager to speak of almost any good news other than *the* Good News. We may hesitate to speak of the greatness of our God at the office for fear of being branded as a fanatic. Or we may falter in speaking of His awesome works to our neighbors for fear of being labeled "one of *those* people."

Yet the psalmist beckons us to "come and see the works of God . . . and sound His praise abroad" (Psalm 66:5, 8). If we have experienced the awesome deeds of God in our lives, we are to share the news. This does not mean we must carry a ten-pound Bible in our briefcase and pull it out the moment someone says "God bless you" when we sneeze. Sometimes the best way to start is with a simple, "Thank you. He *has* blessed me, and I'm so grateful."

Our awesome God has done great things. Let's not keep it to ourselves!

*Lord, I have hesitated to speak of Your awesome works. Show me how I can start today.*

What fears keep me from speaking to others of my awesome God?

# BUILDING BLOCKS
## Hebrews 3:1–6

For every house is built by someone, but
the builder of all things is God.

Hebrews 3:4

Scientists refer to DNA as the building blocks of life, because it carries the blueprint for each individual living being.

When we think of the building blocks of the church, we might think of wood, stones, or bricks used to build cathedrals. However, God builds His church—His house—with people, not masonry. He builds one person at a time until His household extends across languages, cultures, and nations.

The writer of Hebrews said that *we* are the house of God, a house He built through His Son. He will continue to build His house through Jesus Christ until the last person is in place and Jesus returns to claim His own.

It is up to each of us to take our place in God's house, persevering through faith in our Builder until that day arrives. As we do, we will discover that He is building a glorious house indeed.

> *Lord God, thank You for choosing to build me into Your house. Help me to honor You as I wait for the day Your household is complete.*

What is my position in the household of God? How can I honor my Builder today?

# ARISE AND BUILD
## Nehemiah 2:11–18

Let's rebuild the wall of Jerusalem.

Nehemiah 2:17 GW

When life gets messy and everything falls apart around you, how do you respond?

Nehemiah was the cupbearer to a foreign king when God appointed him to direct the rebuilding of Jerusalem's broken walls. How would he begin such a massive task?

First, he spent three days taking stock of the situation. Then he conducted a discreet inspection with like-minded men, followed by a forthright assessment of the job before him. Finally, he asked the people to join him in the work God had set for him to do. The people's response? "Let us arise and build" (Neh. 2:18).

God is the Master Builder of His church *and* of our lives. Sometimes, however, due to wrong choices or circumstances, our lives fall apart and we need to rebuild. The steps Nehemiah followed can be applied to any situation—personal, business, or spiritual.

Problems are part of life. When they develop, we can wallow in self-pity, or we can follow the leading of our Master Builder and say, "I will arise and build."

*Heavenly Father, I confess I would sometimes rather feel sorry for myself because of past failure than obey Your leading. Strengthen me for the work You have for me to build.*

What area of my life is in disarray? How is God calling me to begin rebuilding today?

# TEAR DOWN OR BUILD UP
## 1 Thessalonians 5:11–18

So encourage each other and build each other up.

1 Thessalonians 5:11 NLT

Whether in physical construction or in relationships, demolition is much easier than building. It is more natural for us to tear down than to build up.

The apostle Paul instructed the Christians at Thessalonica to build up one another. Then he told them how to do it. They could begin by appreciating their spiritual leaders and living in peace with one another. He urged them to correct those who needed correction, encourage the fearful, and help the weak. They were also to be patient and avoid vengefulness. In all these things, he encouraged them to rejoice, pray, and be thankful.

Relationships take work. It is easier to speak ill of people, especially if we do it under the guise of soliciting prayer for them, than it is to build them up. Building up someone costs time and effort. It requires us to overlook their faults and focus on their strengths.

It may be easier to tear down, but when we build people up, the results last for eternity.

*Heavenly Father, forgive me for the times I have tried to build myself up by tearing others down. Help me build up the people You have placed in my life.*

Who do I know who is feeling demolished by life's circumstances? How can I help build them up today?

# MORE THAN PITY
### Nehemiah 9:17–33

You are a merciful and compassionate God.

Nehemiah 9:31 GW

Compassion is more than a feeling of pity. Compassion is what we feel when we see others suffer and are motivated to alleviate their pain.

The Bible repeatedly refers to God as compassionate. Beginning in the Garden of Eden, the Lord could have abandoned Adam and Eve to the consequences of their actions, but He didn't. Instead, He told them of the coming Savior, His solution to the problem of their sin.

After God chose the nation of Israel to be His people, they responded with constant disobedience and rebellion. The Lord warned them of the consequences of their behavior, but they continued to go their own way, crying out to Him when they suffered the penalty for their actions. Again and again, God rescued them from their suffering.

Today, God sees our pain and alleviates our suffering in ways only He can do. He saw the pain of our slavery to sin, and sent us a Savior. He saw our suffering because of separation from Him, and sent His Holy Spirit to indwell us. He does it because He is compassionate.

*Holy Lord, I do not deserve Your compassion, yet*
*You freely give it. Thank You for surrounding me*
*with Your compassion today.*

How has God revealed His compassion to me this past week?

# MORE THAN EMPATHY
## Mark 6:33–44

He saw a large crowd, and He felt compassion for them.

Mark 6:34

God knows when we are hurting. He knows every pain, every disappointment, every tear shed alone in the dark. He knows . . . and He has compassion.

When Jesus first heard about John the Baptist's execution, He withdrew to a quiet place. It must have been difficult news for Him to receive in His humanity. John was his cousin, but more than that, John's death at the hands of Herod foreshadowed His own coming execution.

Still, the crowds followed Jesus, and He did not turn them away. They were sheep without a shepherd. He would not leave them at the mercy of the leaders who had already been responsible for John's cruel death. Jesus ministered to their souls by teaching them, and He ministered to their bodies by feeding them.

When we hurt with a need so intense that no one else could understand, Jesus understands. He doesn't merely tell us everything will be all right. In His compassion, He touches the deepest part of our being with healing and hope.

*Heavenly Father, thank You for not leaving me with platitudes. In Your compassion, You meet my deepest needs with Your healing touch.*

What is my most intense need today? Have I talked to the Lord about it?

# FOR FRIEND AND FOE
## Jonah 4:1–11

Should I not have compassion on Nineveh?

Jonah 4:11

It is easy to have compassion for people I like. What I struggle with is having compassion for people I do *not* like. That's why I can relate to the prophet Jonah.

God told Jonah to proclaim repentance to the Ninevites. Jonah had a problem with this for two reasons. First, Nineveh was the capital of Assyria, a cruel nation that consistently harassed and mistreated Israel. Second, Jonah knew that God is compassionate and that his enemies would receive mercy if they listened to the call for repentance.

Jonah responded by running in the opposite direction. In fact, he had more compassion for a wild plant than he did for a city populated by his enemies.

We will always find it easier to have compassion for the people we like, but we should not stop there. Romans 5:10 tells us God poured out His compassion on us when we were His enemies. He asks us to do the same for our foes.

If we are recipients of God's compassion, we cannot withhold it from others.

> *Lord God, forgive me for the times I have selectively offered compassion. Help me express compassion to those who need it, regardless of my preferences.*

How can I demonstrate compassion today to someone who is antagonistic to me?

# THE COMING FIRE
## 1 Kings 18:20–40

For our God is a consuming fire.

Hebrews 12:29

The battle lines had been drawn: 450 prophets of Baal on one side and the prophet Elijah on the other. Between them stood the people of Israel, whose worship of Yahweh had become corrupted by apathy and pagan practices. The time for a showdown had come.

When the smoke cleared, literally, the Lord had revealed Himself as the one, true, living God. The prophets of Baal were not only defeated; they were executed—not a politically correct ending according to today's culture. Why not "live and let live," allowing them to slink off in defeat instead of killing them? After all, the Lord had already worked through Elijah to prove who the real God was.

God is a consuming fire. He consumed the sacrifice and left no doubt Yahweh is *the* God. Those who proclaimed another god could not be allowed to draw Israel into further sin.

The prophet Joel spoke of a future day when Yahweh will execute judgment on His enemies: "A fire consumes before them and behind them a flame burns" (Joel 2:3). On that day, He will judge evil with finality. Nothing will hold back Yahweh's consuming fire.

*Lord, I confess my discouragement at the apparent unrestrained evil in the world. Thank You for the assurance that evil will last for only a season before You consume it forever.*

How can I take a stand for Yahweh against a rising tide of evil in my community today?

# THE REFINER'S FIRE
## Malachi 3:1–5

I will . . .
Refine them as silver is refined,
And test them as gold is tested.

Zechariah 13:9

The silver is carefully heated until it becomes molten. Slowly, impurities rise to the surface and the dross is skimmed away until the refiner sees his reflection in the pure molten metal. Only then is it removed from the fire to be shaped into a precious and lasting possession.

Yahweh not only judges evil in a consuming fire, He also purifies His children.

The flame may grow hotter than we think we can stand, but only our Refiner knows the temperature needed to loosen the grip of sin and remove it from our lives.

We may argue about the duration—"surely *most* of the sin is gone by now, isn't that good enough?"—but the Refiner will never settle for "good enough." He wants only the best for His children, and that means burning away any impediments in our relationship with Him.

Someday, the refining process will be complete, and the dross of our sin will be fully removed. On that day, the Refiner will see the image of His Son shining in us.

> Lord, thank You that Your consuming fire does not destroy me, but only purifies me to live in Your presence forever.

In what area of my life has Yahweh targeted His refining fire? How can I cooperate with Him as He purifies me?

# BREATHING FIRE
## Deuteronomy 9:1–6

My breath will consume you like a fire.

Isaiah 33:11

A Christian friend recently made several unwise choices. When a severe reaction caught her by surprise, she responded with a verbal backlash, breathing fire on her opponent. However, when Isaiah 33:11 speaks of a consuming fire, it refers to the breath of God, not the breath of people. In defending herself, she usurped God's role as her defender. The outcome is that both she *and* the other person were burned.

This doesn't mean we are never to defend ourselves. In Deuteronomy 9, God did not tell Israel *not* to fight the Canaanites. On the contrary, God commanded them to move into the land and "destroy them quickly" (Deut. 9:3). They would accomplish this, though, by depending on Yahweh's consuming fire to go ahead of them. He would subdue their enemies, and Israel would fight in the knowledge that their victory had already been won.

There will be times when we have to defend ourselves. When those times occur, let's be sure we don't confuse our job description with God's job description. He is the consuming fire; we are not. In spite of our unrighteousness, He goes before us for the sake of His name.

*Lord, I have breathed fire in my own defense and have been burned in the process. Help me trust You to go before me and make all things right.*

To whom have I breathed fire instead of allowing God to go before me in my defense?

# THE BIG PICTURE
### Genesis 9:8–17

> But I will establish My covenant with you.
>
> Genesis 6:18

Rainbows touch the child in each of us. Faint, shimmering colors lift us from our worries as we relish the fleeting delight. However, rainbows also have a more lasting significance.

The first time we see the word *covenant* mentioned in the Bible, God said He would make a covenant with Noah. God then confirmed His agreement, promising He would never again destroy the earth with a flood. It was an unconditional covenant, which meant God's promise did not depend on the actions of Noah or anyone else other than God Himself.

Covenants in the Bible were usually accompanied by a sign. God provided a rainbow as the sign of this covenant. Imagine how Noah felt each time it rained. Did he wonder if it would flood again? The appearance of a rainbow reassured him that God keeps His promises.

A rainbow's arc reminds us that like much of life, we see only in part while God sees the whole. Revelation 4:3 gives us a peek at what God sees. A rainbow surrounds His throne—not a partial arc, but a full circle! God always sees the big picture. His covenants are always for our ultimate good, and He always keeps His word.

*Lord, thank You that I can trust Your faithful Word*
*as You keep covenant with me.*

How does the assurance that God keeps His covenants affect my relationship with Him?

# UNCONDITIONAL RELATIONSHIP
## Hebrews 8:7–13

*This cup which is poured out for you is
the new covenant in My blood.*

Luke 22:20

Have you ever made a conditional promise? "If you do this, then I'll do that." In the Bible, God made several unconditional *and* conditional covenants to draw His people to Him.

Genesis 12:1–3 describes God's *unconditional* covenant with Abraham. God lifted him from obscurity, promising to bless him and to bless the world through him—an early prophecy of the Messiah. Because the covenant was unconditional, its fulfillment depended entirely on God.

Hundreds of years later, God made a *conditional* covenant with the nation of Israel. The old covenant was dependent on the Israelites' behavior. Deuteronomy 30:15–20 tells us obedience to the Law brought blessing, while rebellion resulted in judgment. The demands of the Law illustrated the people's need for their coming Messiah.

When the Messiah came to Israel, God instituted an *unconditional* new covenant with His people. God did all the work through Jesus Christ; we contribute nothing to its fulfillment.

Unconditional covenant, unconditional relationship, unconditional salvation.

*Father God, thank You for accomplishing everything necessary for me to belong to You.*

How have I tried to contribute to my new covenant relationship with God, rather than accepting the completed work of Christ on the cross?

# THE BEST FOR THE BEST
## 1 Samuel 18:1–4; 20:12–17

Then Jonathan made a covenant with David
because he loved him as himself.

1 Samuel 18:3

When we think of biblical covenants, we usually think of covenants between God and humanity, such as the covenants with Noah, Abraham, and the old or new covenants.

The Bible also records covenants made between individual people. One such covenant reflected David's relationship with Jonathan. Jonathan was heir to the throne of Israel, held by his father Saul, the reigning king. David had been anointed to be Saul's successor. David and Jonathan should have been sworn enemies. After all, David was destined to take by appointment what should have belonged to Jonathan by inheritance. Instead of viewing David as a usurper, however, Jonathan's love for David caused him to put David's interests above his own.

Marriage is another example of a covenant between two people. Each person is committed to the other until separated by death. Marriage also represents the unconditional new covenant God has with His people. His love always wants what is best for us.

Covenantal relationship is always the best in me wanting the best for you.

*Lord, help me honor You by being faithful in my*
*covenantal relationships.*

What can I do today in a covenantal relationship to put the other person's interests above my own?

# SIN'S SLAVERY
## Exodus 6:1–8

God is to us a God of deliverances.

Psalm 68:20

Slavery is repulsive. It demeans and denigrates people in ways we cannot imagine. Yet the God of Israel allowed His chosen people to experience slavery for four hundred years.

The Lord permitted the Israelites to suffer harsh oppression until they had nothing and no one left to depend on other than Him. When He finally delivered His people, God did it in a way they would never forget, and in a way for which no one could take the slightest bit of credit.

Today, we congratulate ourselves on being part of a sophisticated society that would never tolerate slavery. Yet we ignore the shackles of sin that bind us more cruelly than any human oppressor. Slavery to sin demeans and degrades us. It causes us to feel ashamed, hopeless, and alone . . . until our Deliverer comes.

God delivered us from slavery to sin in a way we can never forget, and in a way for which no person can take credit. Christ accomplished for us what we could not accomplish for ourselves. The chains of sin and shame fall away when we trust His delivering work on the cross.

*Lord God, thank You for being my Deliverer. May I never underestimate the cruel power of slavery to sin from which You delivered me.*

If I am no longer a slave to sin, why do I still choose to sin? How can I rely on my Deliverer today?

# IGNORE THE LIES
## 2 Kings 18:19–37

Now, O LORD our God, I pray, deliver us . . . that all the kingdoms of the earth may know that You alone, O LORD, are God.

2 Kings 19:19

N o one can help you, not even God." Have you ever heard these words whispered deep in your soul when you are trapped in difficult circumstances?

Not only did King Hezekiah hear this same message from his enemy, the entire city of Jerusalem heard it. What they heard, however, was a lie. Look closely at the enemy's deceptive message. First, he claimed he had the Lord's approval to come against Judah. Then he equated the Lord with the gods of other conquered nations to mock the Jews' apparent helplessness.

Hezekiah knew he had only one defense. He responded by going directly to his Deliverer. No one else had the power to save. The Lord would act on behalf of His people to protect them and once again demonstrate to a watching world that He alone is God.

Our enemy would like nothing better than to cause us to lose faith in the Lord. The enemy's subtle lies are dangerous because they can seem to be supported by our circumstances. No matter how horrendous our situation is, though, it will never be bigger than our Deliverer.

*Lord God, help me look past my circumstances to*
*Your deliverance.*

When have I believed lies about my Deliverer? How will I shut out those lies today?

# NOW I KNOW
## Exodus 18:1–12

Blessed be the LORD who delivered you from the hand of the Egyptians. . . . Now I know that the LORD is greater than all the gods.

Exodus 18:10–11

Actions speak louder than words, especially when someone is trying to convince us of their position. Experience has conditioned us to be skeptical until we see actual results.

Moses's father-in-law, Jethro, must have heard incredible stories from passing caravans about Israel's deliverance from Egypt. Should he trust the stories as reliable or dismiss them as exaggerations? Jethro came to see for himself, bringing Moses's wife and children.

What must it have been like to sit around the fire with Moses and Jethro as Moses recounted Israel's mighty deliverance by the hand of Yahweh? Imagine how Jethro felt as he witnessed the truth of the stories that had passed from caravan to caravan. No other nation's gods had ever shown themselves as mighty as Yahweh in delivering His people.

Today, the verbal testimony of Christians to the might of our Deliverer is only part of the picture. When our lives match our words, then the world will say with Jethro, "Now I know."

> Lord God, I want the world to know You are my
> Deliverer. Show me where my words and my actions
> are not aligned, so that all may see the reality of
> Your power to deliver.

When I speak of my Deliverer, does my life match my testimony?
If not, why not?

# ABOVE ALL
## Isaiah 6:1–8

Exalt the LORD our God,
And worship at His footstool.

Psalm 99:5

The king had died. King Uzziah had been a decent ruler, and the prophet Isaiah might have wondered if the next king would be as good for Israel.

Yahweh made sure that Isaiah's attention did not remain earthbound. God gave Isaiah a vision of the Lord, lofty and exalted—one translation says "high and lifted up" (Isa. 6:1 KJV)—in the temple.

Today, our culture is consumed with celebrity worship. Movie stars, athletes, and politicians capture our attention as the media revels in the most inconsequential details of their professional and private lives. We say the Lord is high and exalted, but do we thirst to see Him as eagerly as we scan television or movie screens for a scene with our favorite actor? Do we hunger for His Word with the same eagerness as the newest issue of an entertainment magazine?

Isaiah had two responses when he saw the Lord. First, he became aware of his own sin. Second, he desired to serve his exalted God. He understood that God is above all other people and all other things.

Let's ensure that nothing competes with the Lord for His rightful place.

*Exalted Lord, forgive me for not always giving You
the worship You deserve.*

What people or activities do I approach with greater eagerness than for my exalted Lord?

# STEPPING DOWN
## Luke 14:7–11

He who humbles himself will be exalted.

Luke 14:11

"You deserve the best." "Look out for Number One." "Get a leg up on the other guy." The world offers much advice, but it's the precise opposite of what Jesus tells us.

It is tempting to want to be first in line, to reach for the best products, to grab for the best seat. After all, we repeatedly hear the message that we deserve the best and the brightest because we *are* the best and the brightest.

However, God is the exalted Lord, high and lifted up. When we begin to understand who we are in relation to who God is, we will gladly wait for Him to exalt us, when and where He chooses. When He does, the result is always better than we could ever accomplish for ourselves.

Jesus taught us "the greatest among you shall be your servant" (Matt. 23:11). Servants never run for the best seat. Instead, they run to *serve* the one in the best seat.

Exalting "Number One" is a good thing . . . as long as Number One is our exalted God.

> *Father, thank You that Your "best" for me is always*
> *better than the "best" I could accomplish for myself.*
> *Help me to exalt You in all that I say and do.*

In what area have I been exalting myself instead of waiting for God to exalt me?

# STEPPING OUT
## Proverbs 11:1–11

Righteousness exalts a nation,
But sin is a disgrace to any people.

Proverbs 14:34

What makes a great nation? Some say it is military power, economic influence, or an educated population. Others suggest it is the ability to cooperate with other world powers or a willingness to assist less developed nations. Throughout history, nations have exalted themselves on the world stage by establishing empires or flexing their military muscles.

However, a nation cannot survive on military power alone. Scholars point to the ancient Roman Empire as an example of the downfall of a nation due, in large part, to moral disintegration and political corruption. Proverbs 11:11 reminds us, "By the blessing of the upright a city is exalted, but by the mouth of the wicked it is torn down."

Too often, we limit our ministry to within the church rather than serving as salt and light (Matt. 5:13–16) in the neighborhoods and cities across our country. When we step out of our comfort zone, God is glorified. When God is glorified, the nation is exalted.

*Lord, help me glorify You in my community. Reveal to me where I can be salt and light in a culture that seeks to be exalted on its own terms rather than according to Your Word.*

Where is God calling me to serve Him outside my church and in my community?

# FORGIVEN, NOT FORGOTTEN
## Hebrews 10:10–18

Their sins and lawless acts
I will remember no more.

Hebrews 10:17 NIV

Is God more like a forgetful grandfather or an elephant that never forgets?

When it comes to our sin, God is more like an elephant that never forgets. In the Bible, *forgetting* is not the same as *not remembering*. God does not say He forgets our sin. He is not like a great-great-grandfather with memory lapses. There is nothing faulty about our awesome God, including His memory! When God forgives our sin, it is not that He suddenly becomes forgetful. The Bible says He *does not remember* our sin.

This difference is significant because whenever the Bible speaks of God remembering someone or something, He has not forgotten them in the way people forget. Rather, references to His remembering always signal that God is about to take action. When He remembers sin, it is to bring judgment. When He says He will *not* remember our sin, it is because He forgives us by not counting it against us. He paid the penalty of our sin with the shed blood of His Son.

What a comfort to know that our sin does not float in and out of God's memory. Instead, God has made an irrevocable decision to never, ever count our sin against us.

*Holy Lord, thank You for the complete and irrevocable forgiveness I have in Christ.*

How does knowing that God does not remember my sin affect how I view His forgiveness?

# FORGIVING MYSELF
## 1 Timothy 1:12–16

Christ Jesus came into the world to save
sinners—and I was the worst of them all.

1 Timothy 1:15 NLT

Of all the people in the world who have done stupid, annoying, nasty things that affect me personally, perhaps the most difficult person to forgive is *me*. I am not alone in this struggle. A friend recently asked how to forgive herself for something she had done years earlier. She had received forgiveness from God and the people involved, but the action still haunted her. No matter how hard she tried, she could not forgive herself.

Once God has forgiven us and we have made any necessary restitution, we may think the next step is to forget the experience ever happened. This can be like someone saying, "Don't think of purple zebras." Of course, we immediately think of purple zebras! The harder we try to forget, the more we end up remembering.

The apostle Paul did not try to forget his past. He used it as a reminder of the magnitude of God's grace and forgiveness. When the forgiven past pushes its way into the present, don't fight to forget it. Instead, claim it as a reminder of God's personal and permanent forgiveness.

*Heavenly Father, thank You that Your forgiveness
is always greater than my sin.*

How can I use the memory of forgiven sin to strengthen my relationship with God today?

# PASS IT ON
## Matthew 6:9–15

Forgive us as we forgive others.

Matthew 6:12 GW

We cannot stop people from hurting us, but we may attempt to punish them by not forgiving. The problem is that *we* are the ones who are punished when we withhold forgiveness.

We know God has forgiven us. We know God tells us to forgive others. Still, we may tell ourselves a different message. *They do not deserve my forgiveness. They have not been punished enough for causing me pain. They will be let off the hook if I forgive them.*

The God of all creation forgave us at the cost of the life of His Son. Now He calls us to forgive others at a much lesser cost to ourselves. When we fail to forgive, we become our own victims, locked in a prison of resentment while holding the key. Failure to forgive destroys individuals, and it destroys relationships. The only one who is happy is Satan.

Don't forget, *we* did not deserve God's forgiveness. *We* have not been punished enough for the pain *we* have brought to the heart of God. His forgiveness does not excuse *our* sin.

We have been freely forgiven, and we are to freely forgive. Pass it on.

*Dear Lord, forgive me for the times I have withheld forgiveness. Help me forgive others as You have forgiven me.*

From whom have I withheld forgiveness? Will I extend forgiveness to this person today?

# BATTLE-WEARY
## 2 Samuel 22:1–33

God is my strong fortress; he has made my way safe.

2 Samuel 22:33 NLT

Some days, life feels like a series of battles. It may be a battle just to wake up in the morning if we went to bed late the night before. We may battle traffic on our commute to work or while taking the children to school. Co-workers or neighbors may clash with us over seemingly inconsequential matters. Then there's the battle for a table and fast service during the lunch rush. Finally, we combat rush-hour traffic back home only to face a new set of family battles.

David understood what it was like to live in a constant state of battle. Although Samuel anointed him as the next king of Israel, he spent at least ten weary years running for his life from King Saul. David had no palace or fortress to retreat to other than God Himself. Yet God was enough for David. No other fortress could have afforded the safety God provided him.

God is still a fortress for His people today. His arms are both gentle and strong as He secures us in an unbreachable hold. The strongest fortress of brick and stone does not measure up to the Lord when His weary children rest in Him.

*Lord God, thank You for being my secure fortress.*
*Help me rest in the shelter of Your strong hold.*

Where do I *first* run when I am fearful? How has God shown Himself to be my fortress?

# RECOVERING GROUND
## 2 Corinthians 10:1–5

For the weapons of our warfare are . . .
for the destruction of fortresses.

2 Corinthians 10:4

God is not the only One who uses fortresses and strongholds. Our enemy, Satan, specializes in building strongholds in our lives whenever we let down our guard.

The apostle Paul reminded us that we are fighting a war, but it is not a physical battle. We are at war with spiritual powers whose goal is to take ground in our lives that we have ceded due to sin. When we practice sin, we give the enemy an opportunity to grab a toehold, then a foothold, and finally, a stronghold in our lives.

We can break the power of the enemy's stronghold by running to the fortress of our mighty God. From the safety of His fortress, we confess wrong thinking and shut out thoughts that contradict God's Word. Are we justifying unforgiveness or fits of wrath or pride? Confess it, and claim the forgiveness that comes from Christ's sacrifice.

Satan may be powerful, but our God is more powerful. We can successfully battle the enemy's strongholds only when we run to God, our mighty fortress.

> *Holy Lord, I confess the times I have allowed sinful strongholds to develop in my life. Help me slam the door on wrong thinking that contradicts Your Word.*

Where has the enemy constructed toeholds, footholds, or strongholds in my life? How will I begin to break them down today?

# POWER OF THE IMAGINATION
## Proverbs 18:10–16

The wealth of the rich is their fortified city;
they imagine it an unscalable wall.

Proverbs 18:11 NIV

Have you ever wished for the financial security associated with a bigger bank account? Have you ever gravitated to people who are better off than you, hoping to benefit from their resources, perhaps even indirectly?

There is nothing wrong with having money. God provides us with financial resources to accomplish His purposes. Problems arise when our desire for financial security causes us to use money as a fortress we run to, rather than a tool we use. The writer of Proverbs reminded us that the safety associated with wealth is not real. This fortress is a product of our imagination. One investment scandal or glitch in the stock market can wipe out financial balances in a moment.

God's Word cautions us to be watchful in our relationships. If we are not careful, we will slip into the subtle trap of seeking those with wealth to replace the Lord as our fortress.

> *Heavenly Father, forgive me for the times I have been dissatisfied with my financial resources. Help me view money as a tool for Your use, rather than a fortress to which I can run.*

Have I sought relationships based on the financial resources of the other person? What is God calling me to do with these relationships?

# RETURN ON INVESTMENT
## Isaiah 5:1–7

What more could have been done for my vineyard
than I have done for it?

Isaiah 5:4 NIV

After I moved from New York to Florida, one of the first things I planted was an orange tree. I weeded, I fertilized, and I sprayed, but the tree remained small and scrawny. No growth, no blossoms, no fruit. Even pruning failed to stimulate growth. Gardening experts could not help me. After several years, the tree finally died. When I pulled it from the ground, I discovered the roots had not spread into the surrounding soil. The tree never reached its potential.

The prophet Isaiah described God as a vineyard owner disappointed by His vineyard. He cultivated the vineyard and prepared for a fruitful crop, but the crop was worthless. After investing His efforts into the vineyard, few would dispute that God had a right to expect a return on His investment.

Think about all God has invested in us—salvation, spiritual gifts, His grace, His mercies. What "yield" is God seeing? Sour grapes, or the fruit of obedience and spiritual growth?

> Lord, thank You for planting me in Your vineyard.
> Help me respond by producing fruit that honors
> You.

How would my Gardener evaluate the fruit I yield? How can I be more fruitful?

# FRUITFUL PRUNING
## John 15:1–6

*Every branch that bears fruit, He prunes it
so that it may bear more fruit.*

John 15:2

A healthy, fruitful plant is usually a well-pruned plant. It may not always make sense to us, but sometimes less is more. Pruning, however, is not the same as trimming.

When we trim a plant, we merely cut it back in size without concern for which branches we are cutting. But pruning requires skill. We must know where and when to prune a plant for it to yield the greatest crop of fruit. Skillful pruning removes dead branches and fast-growing shoots that draw nutrients from the fruit-bearing branches. The result is a more fruitful plant.

When we are fruitful for God, He doesn't just pat us on the back and give us a big thumbs-up. The more fruitful we are, the more He prunes. It is a painful process. God may prune people, things, or habits from our lives. In every situation, His goal for us is an abundantly fruitful life.

When our master Gardener prunes us, we can argue and complain, or we can eagerly anticipate our increased fruitfulness.

*Heavenly Father, forgive me for the times I have
complained about Your pruning. Help me willingly
surrender to You so I might bear more fruit.*

What area has the Lord been pruning in my life? Have I been complaining about the pruning process? How can I cooperate with His pruning today?

# GARDENERS

## 1 Corinthians 3:1–8

I planted, and Apollos watered, but God made it grow.

1 Corinthians 3:6 GW

My neighbors travel to a vacation home for several months during the hottest part of the year. They once asked me to water and fertilize several newly planted trees during their absence. When they returned the next season, their trees had yielded crops of oranges, lemons, and limes.

The apostle Paul likened the spiritual growth of the early Christians to plants that had been planted and watered by a team of gardeners. Paul understood that no matter who planted or watered, God alone was responsible for their growth.

God still uses His people to "plant" and "water" new Christians across the street and around the world. We should be careful, however, as we tenderly nurture new believers through discipleship. Just as cacti and rose bushes require different amounts of water, new believers learn and grow in different ways. The process of discipleship requires an investment of time and effort to know the individual and his or her needs.

When we follow the master Gardener's direction in discipling others, we may plant or we may water, but God is the One who will cause a fruitful yield.

*Lord, help me recognize opportunities You provide
to plant and water for Your kingdom.*

How can I cultivate a relationship with someone God has placed in my life to disciple?

115

# THE GIFT GIVER
## 2 Corinthians 9:6–15

Thanks be to God for His indescribable gift!

2 Corinthians 9:15

Friends gave us an extravagant present when we moved into our new house. The framed scroll was a costly gift we never would have purchased for ourselves. It is a beautiful addition to our home, as well as a daily reminder of a special relationship.

When we think of the attributes of God, words like *loving*, *holy*, and *faithful* easily come to mind. We should also remember to add the word *generous*. God works in our lives in ways "far more abundantly beyond all that we ask or think" (Eph. 3:20).

However, if God never gave us another thing in answer to our requests, would it be enough? This may be difficult to answer until we consider what He has *already* given us. We are the recipients of the extravagant gift of salvation, a gift so costly we could never have purchased it ourselves. Then, in addition to the gift of eternal life, He showers us with gifts in this life.

Salvation is the most generous gift we could be given, and it is a daily reminder of our restored relationship with Him. "Thanks be to God for His indescribable gift!"

> *Lord, thank You for not holding back what was most costly to You to give me a gift that is most precious to me.*

In addition to the costly gift of salvation, what other gifts can I thank God for today?

# GIVING BACK
## Malachi 3:8–12

The generous prosper and are satisfied; those who
refresh others will themselves be refreshed.

Proverbs 11:25 NLT

A variety of financial management programs promise to help
people get out of debt and manage their money. These programs have several common components, including careful
budgeting, saving, and spending.

While these are all good things to do, God's financial management program also includes giving back to Him. Psalm 24:1 says, "The earth is the LORD's, and all it contains." When we give back to God, we are acknowledging His ownership.

Yet it can be a struggle to give God even 10 percent of what we have. Perhaps this is because we prefer to view ourselves as owners, rather than as stewards, of what He has given us. We take credit for earning our resources, and we forget that Deuteronomy 8:18 says, "Remember the LORD your God, for it is He who is giving you power to make wealth."

The first step to financial health is to generously give back to God what is His.

*Lord God, forgive me for holding back what belongs*
*to You. Help me to see myself as a steward of what*
*You have entrusted to me.*

Have I been giving God the portion of my income that belongs to Him? If not, why not?

# PAY IT FORWARD
## 2 Samuel 9:1–13

> When you give a reception, invite the poor
> . . . and you will be blessed, since they do
> not have the means to repay you.
>
> Luke 14:13–14

How do you choose the right gift for someone? Do you base it on your budget, the recipient's needs and interests, or how much time you have to shop? Perhaps you make your selection based on the value of what that person last gave you.

King David finally had the throne God promised him years earlier. In the process, his friend Jonathan had died. David could have easily forgotten about Jonathan's family, focusing instead on the business of ruling the nation. Besides, Jonathan's crippled son was destitute and could offer the new king nothing except the potential trouble of a rival claim to the throne.

None of this mattered to David. God had given him much, and David wanted to pass that generosity forward. He honored Jonathan's memory by giving to someone who would never be able to repay the kindness.

David gave generously because he understood the truth that no matter how much we give, we will never be able to out-give God.

*Lord, help me to be as generous with others as You have been with me.*

What will I do for someone less fortunate today to reflect God's generosity to me?

# No Strings Attached
## Ephesians 2:1–10

> "For I am gracious," declares the LORD.
>
> Jeremiah 3:12

Is it possible to earn God's love? Millions of people around the world think so. Ask why they think they're going to heaven, and they'll answer, "I've tried to be a good person" or "I've done good things." But how many good works are enough to meet God's holy standards?

The Bible tells us salvation is not earned through being good or doing good. We can never be good enough to bridge the gap between a holy God and sinful humanity. Christians understand this and trust in God's gracious gift of Christ's finished work on the cross for salvation. It is only by His grace—His undeserved favor—that we are restored to Him.

Some believers, however, begin their relationship with God by grace through faith, only to continue their Christian life based on their own works. Their faulty reasoning concludes: "God saved me by His grace, which I could never earn or deserve. To be a good Christian, though, I must say and do all the right things so God will continue to love me."

Our gracious God saves us and keeps us. We do good works, not to *earn* His love, but to *thank* Him for the love He has freely given, no strings attached. That's why it's called *grace*.

> *Gracious Lord, thank You for giving me what I*
> *could never be good enough to earn.*

How have I been trying to prove my worthiness to God after receiving His salvation?

# DON'T ABUSE IT
## Romans 6:1–23

Shall we sin because we are not under law
but under grace? May it never be!

Romans 6:15

Grace almost sounds too good to be true. If I can't do anything to cause God to love me more or to make Him love me less, does that mean I can live in whatever way I want and confess it later? To paraphrase the apostle Paul, "Absolutely not!"

Paul reminded us that since we have received the undeserved gift of God's salvation, we are granted new life. Along with this new life comes freedom from sin's slavery and a new heart's desire to please the Lord who so graciously saved us. We now have the power to say *no* to sin and say *yes* to obedience to God—not in our own strength, but in the grace God imparts.

Growing in grace means becoming more and more like Christ. It means sinning less and obeying God more. Our heart's desire is to please God, and our gratitude for His salvation is reflected in our thoughts, words, and deeds. As we grow in grace, we should see a continuing trend away from sin, replaced by a progression in righteousness.

Abusing His grace is the last thing we should want to do.

*Gracious Lord, may I never abuse the grace You so
lovingly and freely give to me.*

In what areas have I grown in my obedience to the Lord? In what areas do I need to cultivate obedience to the Lord?

# GIVING GRACE
## Proverbs 14:21–31

Let no unwholesome word proceed from your mouth
. . . so that it will give grace to those who hear.

Ephesians 4:29

R eceiving grace is much easier than giving it. Although we don't deserve it, we are more than happy to receive the grace God offers.

However, as much as we enjoy being recipients of His love and mercy, treating others with the same grace does not come easily. We chafe at showing people kindness they don't deserve. We complain about a lack of fairness when others seem to be getting away with sin or when we have not been treated as well as we think *we* deserve.

The writer of Proverbs provided several examples of ways to show grace to others: We can respond to the needs of those around us who are less fortunate (see 14:21, 31). We can speak words of kindness and truth (see 14:25). We can restrain quick tempers (see 14:29).

God calls us to treat others with the same grace He gives us. They do not deserve it . . . and neither do we.

*Lord, help me respond with grace to the difficult*
*people You have allowed in my life.*

In what specific way is God calling me to respond with grace to someone who does not deserve it today?

# SOUL GUARD
## 2 Timothy 1:7–14

For you were continually straying like sheep, but now you
have returned to the . . . Guardian of your souls.

1 Peter 2:25

The apostle Paul was familiar with guards. He wrote his second
epistle to Timothy while chained and imprisoned, his death
imminent. Roman guards were a part of daily life.

Yet even in prison, Paul knew his faith was not misplaced. He
confidently wrote that God had carried him this far and would guard
his soul until the day Paul met his Lord face-to-face. The Roman
guards belonged to a mighty empire, but Paul belonged to the One
who causes empires to rise and fall. Knowing to whom he belonged,
Paul could encourage Timothy to rely on the indwelling Holy Spirit
as his guard as well.

We have many enemies today working to undermine our relationship with the Lord. The devil, the world, and our own flesh all seek
to spiritually derail us. However, the Guardian of our souls never
leaves His post. Speaking of believers, Jesus said, "I give eternal life
to them, and they will never perish; and no one will snatch them out
of My hand" (John 10:28).

Rest in the assurance that our God is always on guard.

*Heavenly Father, help me to rest in the assurance
that what You guard is truly safe.*

What can I do today to yield to the Holy Spirit as He guards
my soul?

# MOUTH GUARD

## James 3:3–12

Set a guard, O LORD, over my mouth;
Keep watch over the door of my lips.

Psalm 141:3

You might remember your mother telling you to "think before you speak." Easier said than done. Most of us unbridle our tongues more readily than we hold them.

The difficulty of the tongue is not a new one. James wrote of the same problem to the early church. We can still attest to the accuracy of his illustrations. How many relationships have we burned with our words? How many hearts have we poisoned with words that cannot be retrieved? How often have we tried to tame our tongues, only to fail again and again?

James recorded what appears to be a hopeless statement. "No one can tame the tongue" (3:8). No *human*, that is. The psalmist, King David, knew the One who could. He asked the Lord to "set a guard" over his mouth and to "keep watch" over his lips.

God can do what we can't. When we surrender to the control of His Holy Spirit, He enables us to resist speaking words that hurt others and dishonor Him.

James is right—no one can tame the tongue. That's why we need the Guardian of our souls to set a guard over our mouths.

*Lord, I confess my feeble attempts to control what
only You can guard by Your Spirit.*

In what circumstances do I tend to use unkind words? How can God help me to guard against such words today?

# THE FRUIT TEST
## 2 Timothy 4:9–16

Be on guard.
2 Timothy 4:15

The influence of others can cause us to do things we would never do alone. The danger is serious enough that the book of Proverbs is replete with warnings against associating with evil or foolish people.

The apostle Paul's final words to Timothy also included a warning about guarding against certain people. Alone in his prison cell, Paul had time to consider the behavior of various individuals. Although Paul named several people still faithfully serving the Lord, he also included the names of men such as Demas and Alexander, who had either fallen away or were actively working against the gospel.

Jesus warned His followers to use the "fruit" test in their relationships: "Each tree is known by its own fruit" (Luke 6:44). The apostle Peter also urged believers to be on guard.

Do we choose our relationships according to the popularity contests of our culture, or are we developing relationships with those who will influence us for our good and God's glory?

*Lord, help me be discerning in my relationships and to guard against wrong influences.*

Have I been discerning in my relationships? Do my close friendships pass the "fruit" test?

# Holy Is He
## Psalm 99:1–9

> Then I will praise you . . . O Holy One of Israel.
>
> Psalm 71:22 NLT

Israel's God, Yahweh, was not like other gods. His holiness separated Him from sinful people, and He did not accept the common practices of ancient worship.

Yahweh forbade images representing Him. His worship did not include human sacrifice or sexual promiscuity. He restricted sacrifices to one location. Although He took Israel as His own people, Israel's geographic boundaries did not limit His power. Because the Lord is holy—set apart—He expected His people to reflect His holiness, even as the moon reflects the sun's light.

God's actions cannot be separated from His holy nature. His holiness is mirrored in everything He does. Several times in Psalm 99, the psalmist recounted the Lord's wonderful works and came to one firm conclusion: "Holy is He."

As we read about God's tremendous works on the pages of Scripture and see His Hand at work in our lives today, our conclusion must also be, "Holy is He."

> *Lord, You are holy, and everything You do affirms*
> *Your holiness. Use my life as another way to reveal*
> *Your holiness to the people around me.*

How can my thoughts, words, and deeds reflect God's holiness today?

# CALLED TO BE HOLY
## Genesis 39:1–10

For he himself has said, "You must be holy because I am holy."

1 Peter 1:16 NLT

God gave the Law to Israel because He is holy and they were not. He could not be in the midst of a sinful people or they would be destroyed.

To be His people, they needed to confess and turn away from their sin, atoning for it according to the sacrificial system He established. Belonging to Yahweh meant discerning the holy from the unholy, the clean from the unclean. Yet the Lord wasn't teaching them the holiness of things or places. Instead, He communicated what it meant to be separated *from* a pagan, immoral world, and *to* a holy God.

Today, we justify sin—"If you only knew what he did to me, you'd understand." We rationalize it—"I took the office supplies to make up for the extra hours I worked yesterday."

However, the Lord said, "You must be holy because I am holy." All sin is ultimately against God Himself. This knowledge strengthened Joseph in Genesis 39 to stand against the temptation to sin with his master's wife.

No sin, no matter how small or how much we justify it, can stand before God's holiness.

> *Holy Lord, show me where I need to see sin as You*
> *see it and call it what You call it.*

What will I do today about the sin that I have tolerated or rationalized in my life?

# INSIDE AND OUT
## Mark 7:1–15

These people honor me with their lips,
but their hearts are far from me.

Mark 7:6 NIV

Have you ever looked up to a pastor or teacher, wishing you could be as good a Christian as they appeared to be? Perhaps *you* are the one others admire, hoping to be more like you in their Christian walk.

In Jesus's day, people admired the Pharisees as being highly spiritual. Jesus knew better.

The Pharisees did not start out as bad guys. When Israel returned to her land after the Babylonian captivity, the religious leaders determined not to give God another reason to displace them. The Pharisees taught the people the dangers of idolatry and the need to obey God's Law. As the years passed, their desire to be seen doing right things became more important to them than being in a right relationship with Yahweh.

It's tempting to reduce the Christian walk to a list of dos and don'ts. After all, the Lord is holy and requires His people to be holy. Still, holiness is not about *doing*; it is about *being*. It begins on the inside. A life of holiness is not a performance; it is our "thank You" to Yahweh.

*Holy Lord, show me where my Christian walk has become a performance for others. Help me walk with integrity before You and others.*

How have I been trying to impress others with my holiness?

# UNCHANGING STANDARD
## Micah 7:14–20

I, the LORD, never change.

Malachi 3:6 GW

Sin isn't sin anymore. That's what the world tells us. Behaviors once thought shameful are now practiced openly and defiantly. The subjects of judgment and eternal punishment are relegated to fairy-tale status or completely avoided even in some churches. Has God changed His standards? Does He now accept the things once named sinful in His Word?

God is immutable. That means He does not change. Since God is unchanging, so are His standards. Sin is still sin, and right is still right. Judgment may be delayed, but it will come.

Judgment for sin isn't the only thing we can count on as unchanging. God's grace and mercy also do not change. The prophet Micah tells us God "delights in unchanging love" (Mic. 7:18). His forgiveness is always available to us. We need only receive the salvation He provides.

Don't despair that our society embraces right as wrong and wrong as right. The day will come when our immutable God will make all things right.

*Immutable Lord, help me obey all of Your Word as I rely on Your unchanging nature.*

What moral principles have I been tempted to compromise because the world has painted God's standards as archaic?

# ALWAYS RELEVANT
## Hebrews 13:7–14

But you remain the same,
and your years will never end.

Psalm 102:27 NIV

How do you listen to your favorite music? Remember when the only option was a live concert? Then came radio and vinyl records, followed by eight-tracks and cassette players. Soon we listened to our favorite songs on CDs, then on MP3 players. And who knows what's next!

Our world keeps changing, and we have to adjust to keep up. All this change may cause us to wonder about God. The Bible says He does not change—ever. Does that make Him irrelevant in our changing world?

Rather than being irrelevant, God's immutability becomes our anchor in a stormy sea. When nothing else is certain in our lives, we have the assurance that our God is the same, "yesterday and today and forever" (Heb. 13:8). What He said in His Word is as true today as it was two thousand years ago. The Savior He sent then is the same Savior we need today.

No matter how much our world changes, we know we can rely on God as the one unchanging, constant reality.

*Immutable Lord, thank You that I can depend on Your unchanging nature to meet my unchanging need for a Savior.*

How does knowing that God is unchanging help to ground me in my present situation?

# BAD NEWS, GOOD NEWS
## Psalm 33:1–22

God, desiring even more to show . . . the
unchangeableness of His purpose.

Hebrews 6:17

L istening to the news can be fearful. Discouraging reports of wars, famines, droughts, terrorism, epidemics, and economic crises are the daily norm. What is worse, the more humanity tries to resolve these problems, the more new problems seem to arise.

Our immutable God is not impressed with society's plans to solve the world's troubles. Blueprints for world peace, plans to eradicate illness, and projects to eliminate hunger will ultimately fail when they lack one crucial factor: they leave God out of the equation.

That does not mean we should stop working to help others in need. It does mean, however, that our plans should include our unchanging God. He has always been the first and only answer to the problems of the world *and* the problems of the individual heart. His purposes are unchanging, and in the end, His plans and purposes will always prevail.

The immutable God is the only antidote to the fear caused by the bad news in our world. Speak up and share His good news today.

*Lord, help me look beyond the bad news to see and
share Your unchanging purposes.*

Who do I know who is fearful because of the bad news of current events today? How can I encourage them with the good news of my immutable God?

# NO APPEALS
## Romans 2:1–16

For there is no partiality with God.

Romans 2:11

The principle of *blind justice* emphasizes that decisions are made without prejudice or bias. In our system of justice, verdicts can be appealed if a judge's personal opinions appear to have interfered with the neutral performance of his duties.

When God judges the world, there will be no appeals. His determinations will be completely impartial. He will judge each person according to the objective standards of His Law, and everyone's own actions will either accuse or defend them.

Regardless of whether people are familiar with the Bible, they still live out the knowledge of right and wrong written in their hearts and on their consciences. We all stand condemned under the Law, and no one will have the slightest basis for complaint or appeal.

Yet God did not leave us condemned. He provided His Son as the answer to our predicament. We cannot change our standing under the Law, but Jesus Christ changes it for us.

God's Law and judgment are both impartial, but His salvation is available to all.

*Holy Lord, thank You for offering salvation without restriction or partiality.*

Have I been hoping God will make an exception for an unsaved loved one? How does God's impartiality motivate me to share salvation with this person?

# NEVER TOO BAD
## Acts 10:9–23

I most certainly understand now that God
is not one to show partiality.

Acts 10:34

Is there someone in your life so sinful that you believe they are
beyond salvation? Perhaps you've thought sharing the gospel with
certain people would be a waste of time because they would not
be interested?

That's how some Jewish believers felt about the Gentiles in New
Testament times. Jews considered Gentiles unclean and refused to
associate with them. Besides, the Jews believed the Messiah had come
for the nation of Israel, not for the Gentiles.

God taught the apostle Peter that no one was beyond the hope of
salvation. In His impartiality, God did not care if they were Jewish
or Gentile. What mattered was their universal need to be released
from the bondage of sin.

Today, we may conclude there is no point in "wasting our time"
because a person refuses to read the Bible or is too deep in sin. Maybe
we have given up on some people after praying for them for years.
From God's impartial perspective, however, there are no good or bad
candidates for salvation. Everyone has the same need to be restored
to Him.

> Lord, help me see those around me through Your
> impartial perspective.

Whom have I given up on as hopeless? How can I reach out to
this person today?

# PLAYING FAVORITES

## James 2:1–13

If you show partiality, you are committing sin.

James 2:9

Should people receive preferential treatment based on their ability to donate money to the church? Some might say yes. If special treatment encourages people to give more, then why not treat them better? Besides, the entire church body benefits from the increased giving, doesn't it?

In his letter to the early Christians, James warned believers not to practice such favoritism. Rich or poor, we are all the same in the eyes of our impartial God. James wrote, "The brother of humble circumstances is to glory in his high position; and the rich man is to glory in his humiliation, because like flowering grass he will pass away" (James 1:9–10).

When we play favorites, we imply that external factors make some people better than others. We also forget that the things we are impressed with will not last, and the things that will last are not found in clothes and bank accounts.

The Lord calls us to resist the urge to treat other believers with partiality. God sees the heart. When we view people as our impartial God sees them, we will cease to be impressed by things that quickly fade. Instead, we will focus on what lasts for eternity.

*Impartial God, help me look past external trappings*
*to see the hearts of Your people.*

How might I be treating people differently because of their position or wealth?

# NO EXPLANATIONS
## Isaiah 40:21–31

His understanding no one can fathom.

Isaiah 40:28 NIV

Have you ever heard someone say, "I could never believe in a God who allows suffering, or who doesn't let everyone go to heaven, or ___"? Fill in the blank with a variety of objections. What they are actually saying is they refuse to believe in a God they do not understand.

Is it possible to understand God completely? His Word tells us no, and for that we should be glad. If we could understand everything about God, He would not be God; He would merely be an exalted human being.

Can we understand *some* things about God? Absolutely. He reveals His nature and His ways in Scripture. It is there we also learn who we are in relation to who He is.

The day will come when all our questions will be answered. Paul tells us in 1 Corinthians 13:12, "For now we see in a mirror dimly, but then face to face; now I know in part, but then I will know fully just as I also have been fully known."

Until that day, we believe in and worship a God who does not owe us any explanations.

*Lord, thank You that who You are does not depend on my understanding.*

Is there something I don't understand about God that has interfered with my worship and obedience to Him? What will I do with this question today?

# OBEY WHAT YOU KNOW
## Psalm 119:33–40

Give me understanding, and I will keep your
law and obey it with all my heart.

Psalm 119:34 NIV

There are many parts of the Bible I don't understand. Several verses have me wondering if *anyone* could understand them. It also does not help when five different Bible commentaries suggest six interpretations of the same passage!

Some people won't study the Bible because of their inability to understand what they are reading. While I appreciate the frustration this brings, two pieces of wise advice have helped me when I read Scripture. First, always ask the Holy Spirit to give you understanding as you read His Word. After all, who better to ask than the Author Himself? Second, don't let the parts of the Bible that are unclear prevent you from obeying the parts that are perfectly clear.

The more we apply and obey the Scripture passages we do comprehend, the more God gives us greater understanding of His Word.

> *Lord God, thank You for helping me to understand
> and obey Your Word by the power of Your Holy
> Spirit.*

Is there something in the Bible I understand, but have not yet applied to my life? How will I begin to obey His Word in this area today?

# FOOLISHNESS
## 1 Corinthians 2:6–16

"My thoughts are completely different from yours," says the LORD.
"And my ways are far beyond anything you could imagine."

Isaiah 55:8 NLT

I used to be surprised when people who are not Christians expressed confusion or hostility to the things of God. But when we think about it, how else should they behave?

Our ability to understand how God reveals Himself in His Word depends on the Holy Spirit living in each Christian. Apart from the Spirit of God, the things of God will not make any sense. Those who are not believers view God and His Word as foolishness because they cannot understand spiritual things. They are unable to appreciate the solution to their own need.

People can "clean up their act," but a change in behavior is not a substitute for a change of heart. As we share the Lord with those who need Him, we must pray that God would open their eyes to the truth of who He is. Every man, woman, and child needs to be restored to the Lord—a need that can be filled only by God Himself.

Christianity may be foolishness to a hostile world, but it is life to those who believe.

*Lord, I confess I have expected others to behave like Christians without the heart change that comes from You opening their eyes.*

For whom can I pray that God would open their eyes to the truth of the gospel?

# NO END IN SIGHT
Job 36:24-33

His years are without number.

Job 36:26 NLT

Our finite minds have always been fascinated with the infinite. Some may recall studying geometry and learning the value of pi. Pi is the ratio of a circle's circumference to its diameter. It begins with 3.14159 and continues in an infinite sequence of digits. Mathematicians have calculated its continuing value to a trillion digits with no end in sight, but still they try.

Our finite minds also struggle to grasp the concept of an infinite God. Yet we continue to try. We speak of God in superlative terms, hoping to describe His nature. We use words such as omnipotent— all-powerful; omniscient—all-knowing; omnipresent—existing every- where at all times. We employ names such as the Most High God to affirm there is no one higher. Still, these terms only begin to approach the extent of His attributes.

God's infinite nature makes the incarnation of Jesus Christ amazing to consider. The infinite God of the universe voluntarily and temporar- ily limited Himself to the finite, frail body of a man. More astounding, He did it for us, so we could share eternity with Him.

*Lord, thank You that I do not have to understand*
*Your infinite nature to enjoy Your infinite love.*

How has God revealed His infinite nature to me this week?

# HOW MANY SINS?
## Romans 5:12–21

Through the obedience of the one man the
many will be made righteous.

Romans 5:19 NIV

How many sins did Jesus Christ die for? A billion? A trillion? A quadrillion? More?

Sin entered humanity through one man—Adam. Because of that sin, spiritual and physical death also entered the world. Every human born after Adam has been born with a sin nature. Our natural bent toward sin shows in our thoughts, words, and deeds. Not a day goes by that every one of the six billion people in our world does not sin in at least one of these areas. Add in the people who have lived throughout history, and that totals more sins than we can count.

If Jesus had been only a finite human being, He would not have been able to pay for the sins of the whole world. However, Jesus was not only human, He was fully God *and* fully human. Infinite God in finite man. As infinite God, He could pay for an infinite number of sins, from the first sin in the Garden of Eden to the last sin committed prior to the final judgment.

How reassuring to know our infinite Savior paid for our infinite sins and extends infinite forgiveness.

*Heavenly Father, thank You for the assurance Your
infinite forgiveness brings me.*

When my sinfulness overwhelms me, how does the infinite nature of Jesus's forgiveness bring me comfort?

# HOW MUCH IS ENOUGH?
## Matthew 18:21–35

Jesus answered him, "I tell you, not just seven
times, but seventy times seven."

Matthew 18:22 GW

God's attributes reflect His nature, including His infinite forgive-ness. Since we are finite, God could not expect us to extend infinite forgiveness as well, could He?

In New Testament times, the rabbis taught that one could stop forgiving after three times. The apostle Peter probably considered himself quite noble in offering forgiveness to the same person seven times. He doubled the rabbis' number and added one, bringing the total to seven, a number associated with completion in the Bible. Surely Jesus would compliment him for his generosity.

Jesus's answer must have shocked Peter. Not seven times, nor seventy times should he forgive, but seventy times seven. Jesus did not mean for us to keep an account of forgiving someone up to 490 times. Even with the advantage of technology, imagine trying to maintain a running total of forgiveness for everyone we know! Rather, "seventy times seven" illustrated how we should continually forgive long after we lose count. This is what God does for us.

We may be finite, but God expects us to reflect the infinite forgiveness we have received.

*Lord, help me freely forgive others without keeping
an account of the wrong done to me.*

Have I kept a count of wrongs done to me? How can God help me to endlessly forgive?

# GOD WITH SKIN ON
## Exodus 32:1–8

He is the image of the invisible God, the firstborn of all creation.

Colossians 1:15

The nation of Israel arrived at Mount Sinai three months after their deliverance from Egypt. For an additional forty days, Moses remained in the Lord's presence on the mountain. The people grew restless; not only was their God invisible, now Moses had disappeared.

They responded by creating a god that appealed to their physical senses. They made a golden calf and called it by the name of the living, invisible God, Yahweh (Exod. 32:4–5).

We are quick to fault Israel for her idolatry, but human nature has not changed much. We're like the boy who cried to his father because he feared the dark. When his dad reassured him that God watched over him, the child responded, "I want someone with skin on!"

Jesus Christ came to earth as the physical image of the invisible God. His birth, His earthly ministry, even His death, revealed God in human form.

We do not need to create substitutes for God that appeal to our physical senses. God has already sent His Son, Jesus. The historical reality of His life, death, and resurrection gives us the assurance we need that He is, indeed, God "with skin on."

*Invisible God, thank You for sending Your Son to show me who You are.*

In what area am I depending on my physical senses instead of trusting the invisible God?

# HIS INVISIBLE HAND
## Job 9:1–11

Faith assures us of things we expect and convinces
us of the existence of things we cannot see.

Hebrews 11:1 GW

What do you do when everything you know to be true and right disappears, and all you can see is a lie?

To say that Job was having a difficult time would be a gross understatement. It appeared the God he worshiped and served had turned against him. Prayers for relief went unanswered as he suffered wave upon wave of traumatic hardship. Where was the visible hand of the invisible God when Job needed Him?

Although God's hand seemed against him, Job refused to abandon his faith in everything he knew to be true about the heart of God. He held fast to his trust despite his situation.

When the circumstances we *can* see pressure us to lose faith in the God we *cannot* see, what do we do? Do we lose our faith because the hand of God is not working the way we think it should, or do we seek the heart of God as we draw closer to Him?

Our response will reveal our priority—His hand or His heart.

*Dear Lord, help me remember You are always at work, whether I see Your hand or not.*

When I face difficult circumstances, what do I seek first: God's hand or His heart?

# WITHOUT EXCUSE
## Romans 1:18–25

Since the creation of the world His invisible
attributes . . . have been clearly seen.

Romans 1:20

Since God is invisible, what happens to the people who have never heard of Him? How can God hold them accountable for not believing in Someone they cannot see?

The apostle Paul explained that God may be invisible, but His creation reflects His attributes. Towering mountain ranges demonstrate His majesty. The growth of a huge oak tree from a tiny acorn reveals His patience. His tenderness is reflected in the way a mother holds her newborn baby. His power is unleashed in a Category-5 hurricane. The twinkling universe reflects His infinite nature.

Communicating the existence of God to an unbeliever doesn't always begin with opening the Bible. Sometimes we can start with an observation about the incredibly complex and beautiful world around us, associating God's invisible attributes with the visible world.

Our invisible God has always been evident to anyone who wants to find Him . . . and we can help. Let's use the opportunities we have in the natural, visible world as a starting point to direct others to our invisible God.

*Lord God, thank You that You can be clearly seen*
*when I seek You.*

How can I encourage someone today to see God's existence evidenced in His creation?

# WITHOUT EXCEPTION
## Psalm 37:28–34

The LORD is a God of justice.

Isaiah 30:18 GW

We long for justice. We see that desire all around us. We refer to our court systems as the Halls of Justice. Children read comic books filled with superheroes fighting for truth, justice, and the American way.

Our desire for justice did not occur by accident. We are made in God's image, and He is a just God. Our anger at injustice reflects God's anger at injustice.

Still, because of sin, we often want God to apply His justice selectively. We ask for leniency when we do wrong, but when we are wronged, we want—no, we demand—justice!

God's holiness, however, requires His justice be applied without exception. *All* sin offends His holiness and must be judged.

The psalmist David found comfort in knowing a day would come when God would execute justice for everyone. The wicked will be judged, and God's people will receive His reward. David did not know Christ's crucifixion would be the way God would provide perfect justice and salvation. He simply knew that God is a God of justice, and that was enough for him.

*Holy Lord, thank You that Your Son paid the price*
*of my sin to satisfy Your justice.*

When I get discouraged, how does the knowledge of God's justice encourage me?

# NOT FAIR
## Matthew 20:1–16

God made him who had no sin to be sin for us, so that
in him we might become the righteousness of God.

2 Corinthians 5:21 NIV

Siblings know how to keep score. At the slightest hint of disparity in toys or rules, parents will hear a loud, "That's not fair!"

We are not much different in how we respond to our heavenly Father. When we compare ourselves to other Christians, we are apt to say, or at least think, "That's not fair!"

God is just, but He is *not* fair. Jesus told a parable to prove it. A vineyard owner hired several groups of workers. Each group agreed to their wages beforehand, but several became disgruntled to learn they had received the same pay as others who worked fewer hours.

Before you and I demand that God be fair, we should remember that it was not fair for His Son to die for our sin. He did not deserve our punishment, yet God poured out His full wrath against sin on Jesus as Jesus hung on the cross for you and me. He satisfied God's justice and secured our salvation, but there was nothing fair about it.

*Heavenly Father, thank You for the unfairness that
satisfied Your justice and purchased my salvation.*

Do I compare myself to others? How does that lead to dissatisfaction with God?

# JUSTICE FOR ALL
## 2 Samuel 12:1–10

"He must make restitution." . . . "You are the man!"

2 Samuel 12:6–7

You know the expression, "You can't fight city hall." It means we cannot take on governmental bureaucracy and hope to win. For the prophet Nathan, city hall was located in the palace of the king of Israel.

King David had Uriah the Hittite killed so he could marry Uriah's wife. God used Nathan to confront David. Nathan described an anonymous abuse of power, arousing the king's passion for justice. When Nathan challenged David about his own sin, David repented.

It is always easier to recognize injustice perpetuated by others than it is to recognize the injustice for which we may be responsible. Injustice can sneak into our relationships in subtle and understated ways. We may speak out against racism but then laugh at ethnic jokes. We may claim to respect others but then make belittling remarks about the opposite sex.

Before God sends us a "Nathan," let's root out injustice wherever we find it, especially if we find it in ourselves.

*Lord God, forgive me for the times I have allowed injustice to taint my relationships.*

If God sent me a "Nathan" today, what might he tell me about injustices I am displaying in my relationships?

# DOING WHAT COMES NATURALLY
## Exodus 20:1–17

The law of the LORD is perfect,
reviving the soul.

Psalm 19:7 NIV

People rarely have to be told to do what they enjoy or what comes naturally. That may explain why God's Word always commands us to do what does *not* come naturally.

Consider the Ten Commandments, for example. Before we congratulate ourselves on never having committed murder or adultery, remember Jesus's words, "Everyone who is angry with his brother shall be guilty," and, "Everyone who looks at a woman with lust for her has already committed adultery with her in his heart" (Matt. 5:22, 28).

God's holiness requires our total obedience to His law, something our sinful nature cannot do. However, God did not give us the law to set us up for failure. He gave the law so that His people—Israel then, and us today—would understand the height of His holiness and the depth of their depravity. God gave the law to prepare His people for grace.

Unless we realize our inability to be holy apart from Christ, we will never recognize our need for a Savior.

*Lord, thank You that the law shows me Your holiness, and Jesus gives me His holiness.*

Which of God's laws do I find most difficult to obey? Why? What can I do today to obey this specific law?

# LESSONS FROM A FRUIT TREE
## Psalm 1:1–6

But his delight is in the law of the LORD.

Psalm 1:2 NIV

There are times when I obey God's law grudgingly. Yet His Word promises blessing when we love His law, meditate on it, and take delight in obeying it. The psalmist compares us to a well-planted fruit tree as he details three blessings we can depend on.

First, we will be fruitful. A fruit tree that yields little or no fruit does not fulfill its purpose. When we meditate on God's Word and delight in obeying His law, we place ourselves in a position to yield great fruit for His kingdom and fulfill His purposes for us.

Second, we will be filled with life. Just as healthy leaves convert sunlight to nourish the tree, we will be energized to accomplish everything God has purposed for us to do.

Third, we will be prosperous. This does not necessarily mean a seven-figure bank account or a luxury sports car in the driveway. We may prosper in other ways, such as in our relationships, our physical or spiritual health, or in sharing the gospel. God will determine the kind of prosperity that is best for our ultimate good and for His glory.

Fruitfulness, life, and prosperity . . . all are produced when we love and obey God's law.

*Lord, give me a desire to meditate on Your Word*
*and to delight in obeying Your law.*

What does God want me to apply from His Word as I meditate on it today?

# CIVIL AUTHORITY
## Romans 13:1–10

I encourage you to make petitions, prayers, intercessions, and
prayers of thanks . . . for everyone who has authority over us.

1 Timothy 2:1–2 GW

Only a few weeks after each of the last several presidential elections, bumper stickers touted, "Don't blame me, I voted for the other guy!"

The apostle Paul wasn't interested in whether the early Christians liked or disliked government officials. Christians in New Testament times had to submit to the civil laws of the Roman Empire. Although the believers frequently encountered persecution and suffering, Paul exhorted them to obey the government and pray for those in authority.

Today, Christians are to submit to the laws of the nation in which they live. We may disagree with some laws, but we are still told to obey them unless obedience to the civil law requires disobedience to God. Equally important, we are to pray for those in authority, regardless of their political party or whether we voted for them.

To influence our culture for eternity, we must begin by being good earthly citizens.

> *Lord, help me remember to pray for those in authority over me. Forgive me for the times I have used political differences as an excuse not to pray for elected officials.*

Will I begin today to pray daily for those in civil authority over me, regardless of their political affiliation?

# BENEFITS OF RELATIONSHIP
## Psalm 136:1–26

Give thanks to the LORD, for He is good,
for His lovingkindness is everlasting.

Psalm 136:1

Being in a relationship with the one, true, living God has its benefits. One of those benefits is God's lovingkindness.

Of all the words used to describe God's interaction with His people, *lovingkindness* is one of the most unusual. This word has been translated as love, mercy, kindness, steadfast love, or faithful love.

While God is all these and more, the word *lovingkindness* comes closest to reflecting the original Hebrew. It is what God extends to those in a relationship with Him. Israel's covenant relationship with the Lord gave the people an assurance that He would respond to them in certain ways. God would always be faithful to His covenant, and He would always be faithful to His people. They could depend on this loyalty, regardless of their faithlessness.

Christians also have a covenant relationship with the Lord. Because of Jesus Christ, we can rest on the assurance that God will always extend His lovingkindness to us.

> *Lord, thank You for the gift of Your lovingkindness.*
> *Help me rely on and trust Your lovingkindness each*
> *day.*

What specific expressions of God's lovingkindness have I experienced this week?

# DEPENDABLE RELATIONSHIP
## Psalm 52:1–9

I trust in the lovingkindness of God forever and ever.

Psalm 52:8

Have you ever depended on family members or friends, only to have them let you down when you needed them most?

People will disappoint us. Whether they intend it or not, their priorities may change, circumstances may interfere, or they may simply change their minds. In any case, all too frequently, we react with disappointment and disillusionment. We might also decide never to depend on anyone again to keep from being hurt.

The Lord does not respond like human beings. He extends His lovingkindness to us based on the relationship that He initiated and He sustains. God will always respond in the best way possible for our good, even when our good requires loving correction or discipline.

No matter what the situation, we can freely and confidently depend on the Lord's lovingkindness, because that is what a relationship with Him guarantees.

*Lord, Your lovingkindness is more than I deserve,*
*yet You have promised it to me anyway. Help me*
*to trust Your lovingkindness even when it comes in*
*the form of correction.*

What am I facing today for which I need God's loving-kindness? How can depending on His lovingkindness help in this situation?

# SPEAK UP
## Psalm 57:1–11

I will sing praises to You among the nations.
For Your lovingkindness is great to the heavens.

Psalm 57:9–10

When people are angry with God, they usually don't keep it to themselves. Everyone around them hears how God did not do what they thought He should have done.

Christians can be as vocal in communicating disappointment with God as anyone else. How often, though, do we tell others about the lovingkindness God has extended to us?

When David wrote this psalm, he was running for his life from King Saul. He began the psalm with a prayer for God to be gracious and to provide refuge in the midst of danger. Then he asked God to save him from his enemies. He closed the psalm expressing assurance that God would respond with lovingkindness. Then he committed to speak of God's lovingkindness to the world.

When and how has God responded to your needs? Follow David's example and speak up. God's lovingkindness is not something we should keep to ourselves.

*Dear Lord, forgive me for the times I have been
quicker to tell others of my disappointments than
of Your lovingkindness to me.*

What specific act of God's lovingkindness can I speak of today, and whom will I tell?

# THE PRICE OF MERCY
## Leviticus 16:11–16

He shall take some of the blood . . . and
sprinkle it . . . on the mercy seat.

Leviticus 16:14

The Bible describes God as merciful, but have you ever wondered why the cover of the ark of testimony is called the mercy seat?

God's mercy and forgiveness of the Israelites' sin was contingent upon a system of sacrifices. Annually, on the Day of Atonement, the high priest would enter the Holy of Holies and sprinkle the blood of the sacrifice on the cover of the ark, which contained the Ten Commandments.

When God "looked down" from heaven, He would see the stone tablets inside the ark, a reminder that His people continued to break His law. However, the blood on the cover stood between God and the broken law. Based on that shed blood, year after year, God extended His mercy to His people.

God's mercy is still dependent on the shed blood of sacrifice. Instead of animal sacrifice, however, our sin is covered by the once-and-for-all sacrifice of His Son, Jesus Christ.

*Merciful God, thank You that Jesus's shed blood
enables me to receive Your mercy.*

When God "looks down" at me, does He see His broken law or the blood of His Son? How can I thank Him for His mercy today?

# THE PRACTICE OF MERCY
## Luke 6:27–36

Be merciful as your Father is merciful.

Luke 6:36 GW

Extending mercy is not an easy thing to do. One reason is that, instead of focusing on the other person's need, we focus on ourselves.

When our rights are violated, a family member is hurt, or our needs have gone unmet, we think about how *we* are affected. We withhold mercy because we are too busy feeling sorry for ourselves, comforting loved ones, or determining how to correct the situation. The last person we are concerned about is the person who caused the problem. If we think of them at all, it is usually to ask God to judge them for how they have hurt us.

However, God teaches us to look beyond our offense. He wants us to see the offender as He does: someone who has the same need for mercy as we do. He tells us repeatedly in His Word that it is not about us. It is not about our pride, our rights, or our hurts. Instead, we are to focus on sharing the same mercy we receive from God with those around us.

God extends His mercy to us although it cost the life of His Son. Extending mercy to others does not cost us nearly as much.

*Merciful Lord, help me look past my pain to the need others have for Your mercy.*

To whom have I been reluctant to extend mercy? In obedience to God, will I do it today?

153

# OUR TURN
## Jude 17–25

Have mercy on some, who are doubting . . .
and on some have mercy with fear.

Jude 22–23

In His mercy, God saves the lost. Salvation is His job, not ours, right?

Yet Jude said in his letter to the early Christians, "Have mercy on some, who are doubting; save others, snatching them out of the fire; and on some have mercy with fear, hating even the garment polluted by the flesh" (vv. 22–23).

God uses those who have *received* His mercy to reach out to those who *need* His mercy. Unfortunately, as Jude pointed out, those in need of God's mercy can be the most difficult, hostile, ungodly people we will ever meet.

Still, the One who extends mercy to us urges us to persevere in reaching others for Christ. No matter how deeply they are enmeshed in sin, or how coarse their lifestyle, Jude exhorted us to share God's mercy with love for the sinner, even while we hate the sin.

Someone told us about God's mercy. Now it is our turn to share it with others.

*Merciful God, I confess my desire to isolate myself*
*from those who need You most. Help me extend*
*Your mercy just as I receive Your mercy.*

Who will I begin praying for today, asking God for an opportunity to demonstrate His mercy?

# TOO DIFFICULT?
## Psalm 145:1–13

Ah Lord GOD! . . . Nothing is too difficult for You.

Jeremiah 32:17

Occasionally, someone will try to challenge God with a seemingly unsolvable problem, such as, "If God can do anything, can He create a boulder too heavy for Him to lift?"

The power of God is not some tool we take out of a box when we need a job done, only to place Him back in storage until the next time we need Him. God does not just *have* power, He *is* all-powerful, along with all His other attributes such as love, grace, truth, holiness, justice, and mercy.

Some people underestimate God's power because He does not use it the way they think He should. However, when God exhibits His power, it is always to accomplish His purposes.

No matter how impossible the situation, no matter how insurmountable the circumstances, we can rest confidently in the assurance that, indeed, nothing is too difficult for our omnipotent God.

> *Lord God, forgive me for the times I doubted Your power because You did not work the way I wanted. Help me trust that Your power always accomplishes Your purposes.*

What situation am I praying for God to change today? If He does not reveal His power in the way I would like, how will I choose *now* to respond?

# CONTRADICTIONS
## 2 Corinthians 12:1–10

[The Lord] told me . . . "My power is strongest when you are weak."

2 Corinthians 12:9 GW

The Christian life is one of contradictions. We humble ourselves to be exalted, the first shall be last, and power is perfected in weakness. It should not make sense, yet it does.

The apostle Paul had an impressive ministry, and God used him in mighty ways. Still, one mysterious burden plagued him, and he asked God to remove this "weakness." After three requests, God's answer remained *no*, because He had something better for Paul.

Depending on our own strength is similar to relying on battery power. Everything seems to work fine for a while, then . . . nothing. We run out of energy, usually at the worst times. We think we are strong only to discover that we are not.

When we acknowledge our weakness, however, we stop drawing on our own limited power and strength, and turn instead to our omnipotent God.

It may not sound logical, but it is true every time: when we are weak, then we are strong.

*Omnipotent Lord, I confess that I frequently depend on my own strength instead of relying on Yours. Help me see that it is only when I am weak that I am truly strong.*

How has God shown Himself strong in my weakness? How will I trust Him today to provide the power I need to respond to my circumstances?

# FORM WITHOUT SUBSTANCE
## 2 Timothy 3:1–13

Holding to a form of godliness, although they have denied its power.

2 Timothy 3:5

Sometimes the greatest danger to the Christian church comes from within.

In today's passage, the apostle Paul described certain people as "holding to a form of godliness, although they have denied its power." Yet they might easily have been part of the early church.

We see the same thing today. People identify with Christianity because it is the social thing to do, or it is the way they were raised, or they want to impress others with their spirituality. They go through the motions of worship without the power of being in relationship with the omnipotent God. Their influence causes churches to struggle with divisions, discard biblical doctrines as archaic, and dismiss wide portions of Scripture as irrelevant.

Paul warned us to avoid these imposters. His advice may seem harsh, but it is a necessary defense against deception and protects our relationship with our omnipotent God.

> *Lord God, help me discern those who hold to a form of godliness but deny its power. Keep me from being deceived as I rely on Your power for true godliness.*

Have I been "going through the motions" in my quiet time with the Lord or during worship services? How can I reconnect with my omnipotent God today?

# NO SURPRISES
## Psalm 139:1–6

Before I shaped you in the womb,
I knew all about you.

Jeremiah 1:5 Message

I hate surprises—at least the bad ones. Sometimes I wish I knew all the bad stuff that will occur, so I could prepare for it. Then again, if I knew about every bad thing that will happen, I would probably go into hiding and never come out!

However, God *does* know. He is omniscient, which means He is all-knowing. Not only does He know every detail of world events before they occur, He knows every detail of our lives—past, present, and future, good and bad.

He knew about your crisis before it occurred, whether it is a cancer diagnosis, a foreclosure, an accident, a job loss, or anything else. The important thing to remember is that while people and circumstances may surprise us, they never surprise God.

How comforting it is to realize that, although we do not know the future, we belong to the One who *does* know.

*Omniscient Lord, Your knowledge is too wonderful for me to understand. Thank You for the comforting assurance that nothing ever takes You by surprise.*

What news has recently surprised me? How does knowing that God is omniscient change the way I view this information?

# WHO KNOWS BEST?
## Isaiah 40:12–17

God is greater than our hearts, and he knows everything.

1 John 3:20 NIV

*od doesn't know everything.* Few people would be brave
enough—or foolish enough—to say these words to the Lord.
Still, although we don't say the actual words, our actions
broadcast this message almost every day.

Every time we choose what God has forbidden, or choose not to
do what God has commanded, we are telling Him, in effect, that we
know more than He does. We are saying that His rules might be okay
for everyone else, but extenuating circumstances require different
standards for us. Do we really think we need to educate God about
what is best for us?

The prophet Isaiah asked several questions to make it clear that
God's omniscience does not need our help. Do we know how much
the mountains weigh? Have we measured the earth's dust? Does God
consult with anyone to add to His knowledge or to teach Him justice?
No!

The next time we are inclined to choose our own way, let's remember the message we send by our actions. Obedience declares that our
heavenly Father always knows best.

> *Omniscient Lord, forgive me for the times my dis-*
> *obedience proclaims that I know better than You*
> *about what is best for me.*

In what area have I been reluctant to obey what God has determined is best for me?

# ARROGANT KNOWLEDGE
## 1 Corinthians 8:1–13

Knowledge makes arrogant, but love edifies.

1 Corinthians 8:1

D o you know any experts? Perhaps you are an expert in your vocational field or hobby.

The early church included a number of believers who were experts on the subject of animals sacrificed to idols. They knew the idols were not really gods. They also knew that buying this discounted meat enabled them to be wise stewards of their limited funds.

However, not all the early Christians possessed the same knowledge. Some Christians were recent Gentile converts, disturbed by reminders of their previous pagan worship. Eating meat sacrificed to idols was a sensitive issue for them.

The knowledgeable Christians had a choice. They could enjoy their liberty at the expense of their Christian brothers and sisters, or they could be sensitive to their fellow Christians and forego a bargain. The apostle Paul reminded them that only arrogant people permit superior knowledge to hurt a weaker brother.

We are to be experts on God's Word, but not to boast about our knowledge at the expense of others. Rather, we are to use our knowledge to build up our brothers and sisters in Christ.

*Omniscient God, help me not to be arrogant as I grow in the knowledge of Your Word.*

How can I use my growing knowledge of God's Word to encourage someone else today?

# ORDER IN THE WORLD
## Genesis 1:14–19

Let them serve as signs to mark seasons and days and years.

Genesis 1:14 NIV

Rhythm and order permeate creation. We see it in the orbit of the earth around the sun, and the hatching of baby birds in their nests each spring. We find it in the cycle of high and low tides, and in our routine of waking and sleeping. We see it in scientific laws such as the laws of gravity and thermodynamics. There is a certain order to everything in life.

Creation's order reflects its orderly Creator. Imagine a man who finds a pocket watch on a desert island. With no one else in sight, he opens the watch to reveal its inner workings. It would be unreasonable for him to conclude the intricate mechanisms of the watch just happened to develop on their own. In the same way, it is unreasonable for us to assume the universe just happened to develop on its own. Both bear the mark of an intelligent and orderly Creator.

No matter how chaotic our lives may become, the God of order is still in control. When we rest in His care, He brings order out of chaos.

*Creator God, thank You that I do not have to be a victim of chaotic events in my life. Help me trust You to bring order in every area of my life.*

What issue or event is bringing disorder into my life today? How can knowing that I belong to the God of order help me in this situation?

# ORDER IN THE CHURCH
## 1 Corinthians 12:1–11

For God is not a God of disorder.
1 Corinthians 14:33 NLT

Different does not always mean better. I remind myself of that when I see how God has gifted other Christians differently than me. I appreciate our church worship leader, knowing my croaking would only scare away worshipers. I admire the cheerful murals in the nursery, aware that my stick-figure drawings are indecipherable. I respect the person who repairs the church van, mindful that my mechanical skills are limited to kicking the car if it doesn't start.

God gave each of us different gifts to bless the body of Christ. When we long for someone else's gifts and abilities, we neglect to use the ones we have been given. When we bury our gifts and talents, nobody benefits.

Our orderly Lord placed just the right gifts in each of us. Then He placed each of us in just the right place to use them.

*Father, You gifted me in a unique way to fulfill the*
*role You have for me within the body of Christ.*
*Help me not to hide my gifts, but to use them for*
*Your glory.*

Which of my gifts have I not been using because I long for other abilities instead? How can I begin using my gifts today to benefit the body of Christ?

# ORDER IN RELATIONSHIPS
## Ephesians 5:21–33

The husband is the head of the wife, as Christ
also is the head of the church.

Ephesians 5:23

Follow the leader" has been a favorite child's game for generations. Children choose a leader and follow the leader's every move. The most successful follower then takes a turn as leader.

Leadership is not as simple when we become adults, perhaps because we may struggle against God's model for orderly leadership. Pride can cause us to resist what God has ordained.

The apostle Paul told the early church that we are to submit to one another. The Greek word for submission did not have the negative connotations it has today. It simply means we are to arrange our lives in order under a particular authority, much as a soldier orders his life under the authority of a higher-ranking officer.

Paul went on to explain how we are to do this: husbands are to be subject to Christ, and wives are to be subject to husbands. He also spoke of the child-parent relationship, and the slave-master relationship that we apply to employee-employer relationships today.

When we honor and submit to the authorities God has placed in our lives, we honor Him.

*Lord, help me honor You by honoring the authorities You have placed in my life.*

Who are the authorities God has appointed me to arrange my life in order under? Would those authorities say that I resist them or honor them?

# CREATIVE PLANS
## Jeremiah 18:1–12

"Can I not . . . deal with you as this potter does?" declares the LORD.

Jeremiah 18:6

It can be an inspiring experience to produce something from raw material. Whether we use colors to paint a landscape, words to weave a story, or clay to fashion pottery, the final product brings substance to what first appeared in our mind's eye.

God used the illustration of a potter to teach us something about our relationship with Him. The clay does not always cooperate. It may be too dry or wet, failing to form the desired shape. The potter may choose to add a little moisture or a little more clay, or he may discard the entire batch.

Our Potter fashions His vessels according to His creative plans and purposes. In our particular situations, He may choose to add or remove something, but He never discards His people. He is continuously working in us to create vessels that will glorify Him.

We may not always understand what He is doing or why, but then why should we expect to? You and I are not the Potter.

*Lord God, thank You for being my perfect Potter.*
*Help me to trust Your creative purposes as You*
*make me all that You intended for me to be.*

What puzzling thing is the Potter doing in my life? How can I show Him my trust today?

# THE CLAY
## Isaiah 45:9–12

Does the clay say to the potter,
"What are you making?"

Isaiah 45:9 NIV

"You can be anything you want to be, if you set your mind to it." This may be motivational, but it's not true. What if I wanted to be a mountain lion or an eagle?

Our Potter has fashioned each of us to be precisely what He wants us to be for His purposes. We don't know why God made some of us men and some women, but He did. We don't know why He made some of us with dark features and some light, but He did. We don't know why He made some of us extroverted and some introverted, but He did.

While we may not know anyone who has told God they would rather be a mountain lion or an eagle, we all know people who have decided the Potter made a mistake. They think they know better than He does as to what is best for them. The clay tries to mold itself. In extreme cases, we see men and women even changing genders. The clay refuses to admit it does not know better than the Potter.

Our greatest satisfaction comes from being exactly what our Potter created us to be.

*Creator God, forgive me for the times I try to usurp
Your role as my Potter. Show me where I have tried
to mold myself instead of trusting Your skill.*

How have I tried to force a change in my life that the Potter has not intended?

# THE VESSELS
## 2 Corinthians 4:1–7

We have this treasure in earthen vessels.

2 Corinthians 4:7

I usually bring out the fancy dishes when company comes for dinner. Everything looks nicer than if the table had been set with my everyday, chipped set that's missing a few pieces. The food even seems to taste better on the good dishes.

We might expect that our Potter would prefer to use the fancy "dishes" to accomplish His work. You know the type: people who have it all together, don't struggle with sin, and confidently serve in multiple ministries while working and raising a family. Instead, God uses you and me. We may be more like worn dishes, flawed and cracked. We labor against sin and struggle to find time for all the pieces of our lives as we balance the demands of work, family, and ministry, along with other worn, chipped, and cracked "dishes" doing the same thing.

God prefers to use earthen vessels because that is how He gets all the glory. When we depend on our own strengths and embellishments, we glorify ourselves. When we work together, depending on His power to fulfill His work in us and through us, we glorify our Potter.

We may be mismatched pieces, but together we become a set of God's best dishes!

*Father, thank You for opportunities to work with*
*Your other vessels for Your glory.*

How can I display God's power today by working together with other "earthen vessels"?

# PRESERVED FROM AND FOR
## Psalm 97:1–12

The LORD . . . preserves the souls of His godly ones.

Psalm 97:10

Homemade preserves are a tasty treat. With a little preparation, we are able to preserve fresh fruit *from* decomposition and *for* later enjoyment.

The Bible tells us God is our Preserver. He also preserves us *from* something and *for* something else. He preserves us from eternal judgment and for eternal life in His presence.

However, God does not save us and then leave us on our own. He saves us and continues to keep us preserved for Him. Jesus said of us, "No one is able to snatch them out of the Father's hand" (John 10:29).

Not only does the Lord preserve us for eternal life, He also preserves us in this life. The Bible contains repeated references to God's preservation from troubles in the here and now. We rest on His promises to bless us and protect us.

What a blessing to know God has preserved, is preserving, and will continue to preserve us for intimate fellowship with Him.

> *Dear Lord, thank You for preserving me in my relationship with You until the day I will be with You for all eternity.*

How have I experienced God's preservation this week? Have I taken time to thank Him?

# RELEASE TO KEEP
## Genesis 19:1–26

Whoever tries to keep his life will lose it, and
whoever loses his life will preserve it.

Luke 17:33 NIV

Poor Mrs. Lot! She wanted so desperately to keep the life she
had. Instead, she had to leave her home and move away from
the only life she knew. She must have wondered why she had to
lose her lifestyle simply because a few strangers arrived in town with
a message of doom.

We hear similar objections today. "I won't give up my life for a
threat of hell or a pie-in-the-sky promise of heaven," or "My life
belongs to me and no one else. I'm my own person."

However, the alternative to Christianity really is death and destruction, no less than what Sodom and Gomorrah experienced years ago.
Lot's sons-in-law tried to keep what they thought belonged to them
and lost everything. Mrs. Lot reluctantly followed her husband, but
her heart remained with her old life. Because she would not let go,
she lost both her past and her future.

God offers to preserve our lives if we give ourselves up to an intimate
relationship with Him. We can accept His preservation, or keep our
lives now and lose everything in the end.

*Heavenly Father, forgive me for the times I hold on
to what will not last, instead of seeking the best
You have preserved for me.*

What things or people do I struggle with releasing? Why is it so
difficult to release them?

# BE SALTY
## Matthew 5:1–13

You are salt for the earth. But if salt loses its taste. . . . It is
no longer good for anything except to be thrown out.

Matthew 5:13 GW

Preservatives have developed a bad reputation. Healthy lifestyles now include foods with fewer chemical additives. In ancient times, however, they used natural preservatives such as salt to retard decay and protect the food supply. That made salt a valuable commodity.

When Jesus called His followers "the salt of the earth," He meant for them to exhibit in their culture the qualities associated with salt. While pure salt does not go "bad," the salt in the Dead Sea area also contained other minerals, diluting its effectiveness and longevity.

God has always called His people to act as preservatives in their culture, and today is no different. Jesus described the marks of a true Christian in the Beatitudes. Those who belong to Him will influence others with characteristics such as humility, gentleness, and righteousness.

We need to be careful, however, in how we distribute our salt. We must not dilute it with worldly values. And if we pour too much at once on those around us, we will burn them. Our heavenly Father calls us to season our world carefully with His preserving influence.

*Lord God, use me to preserve and influence my*
*world to draw others to You.*

Have I had a preserving effect in my culture or has the world diluted my saltiness?

# DOUBLE PROTECTION
## Psalm 121:1–8

The LORD will protect you from all evil;
He will keep your soul.

Psalm 121:7

If God protects His children, then why do bad things happen to us?

Misconceptions about God can cause us to doubt Him and His Word. We may think God selectively dispenses His protection based on whether we prayed long enough. We may fall into the trap of thinking God is not always *able* to protect us from the enemy's attacks, or that He sometimes "sleeps on the job." Wrong on all counts!

To understand God's protection, we need to view our lives from His perspective. God protects us from evil in two ways. First, He protects us in this life from any evil that would disrupt His plans for us. Bad things may happen, but God will permit His children to experience only what He will use for our ultimate good and His ultimate glory.

Second, God keeps our soul. He protects our eternal life in Him from evil. Someday in heaven, we will be free from the presence of sin and temptation. He will eradicate all evil.

Until then, trust God's protection. The safest place for us to be is in the palm of His hand.

> *Lord, thank You for Your protection. Help me rest in the palm of Your hand.*

What am I experiencing today that is causing me to doubt God's protection? How can I rest in His protection in the midst of this circumstance?

# KEPT FOREVER
## 1 Peter 1:1–5

Protected by the power of God through faith
for a salvation ready to be revealed.

1 Peter 1:5

Can we lose our salvation? Some people think we can.

If we could earn our salvation, it would follow that we could lose our salvation. However, if we have done nothing to earn it and we do not deserve it, then how could we do anything to lose it? God's grace both saves us and keeps us protected in Him.

This assurance of salvation does not mean we have a license to sin. The apostle Paul said, "Are we to continue in sin so that grace may increase? May it never be!" (Rom. 6:1–2). If we are truly in relationship with God, we do not *want* to go on sinning. He changes the desire of our heart to please the One who protects our soul.

God is not only our Protector in this life, He protects the salvation we have in Him until we are with Him for all eternity.

> *Heavenly Father, thank You for protecting my relationship with You. Help me not to view Your protection as a license to sin; instead, give me a desire to please You continuously.*

How have I begun to take my relationship with God for granted? How does God want me to view His protection today?

# The Least of These
## Psalm 146:1–10

The Lord protects the strangers;
He supports the fatherless and the widow.

Psalm 146:9

One of the marks of a civilized society is that it takes care of those who cannot take care of themselves. In ancient Israel, God placed a priority on caring for widows and orphans—the most vulnerable members of society.

Today, we expect the government to provide the answer to all our social ills. Christians—and everyone else—can easily evade the inconvenience of caring for the less fortunate by deferring to an abundance of government programs.

However, when we avoid the people who most need our help, we are avoiding those whom God has personally declared He protects and supports. Christians are often the means He uses to provide for those who cannot care for themselves. To reflect the heart of God, we need to reflect His treatment of those who most require His protection.

If we belong to Him, how can we do any less?

> *Heavenly Father, I confess I have too often ignored those whom You have promised to protect and support. Help me respond as Your hands and feet to those in need.*

Who has God placed in my life for me to demonstrate His protection and support?

# ETERNAL PURPOSE
## Ephesians 3:1–13

In accordance with the eternal purpose which
He carried out in Christ Jesus our Lord.

Ephesians 3:11

What is God's "eternal purpose"? Can we know what it is, or is it a secret?

God is not purposeless. There is nothing pointless or meaningless about Him. Everything He does and everything He allows is for one purpose. Creating the universe, allowing man to follow free will into sin, choosing Israel as His possession, sending the Messiah—it all happened so that the one, true, living God would receive the glory and honor due Him.

We have the added blessing of participating in this process. When we surrender to His authority in our lives, He is glorified by the revelation of His grace, mercy, and forgiveness. For those who refuse to receive His Son as Savior, God will reveal His glory in His holiness, justice, and judgment. Either way, He will be glorified.

God was working, is working, and will continue to work for the purpose of glorifying His name. His eternal purpose will always be realized.

> *Lord God, thank You for the blessing of participating in Your eternal purpose. Help me to glorify You in all that I am and in all that I do.*

How does God's eternal purpose affect the choices I make today?

# Purpose We Can Live With
### Jeremiah 29:1–14

I know the plans that I have for you, declares the Lord.

Jeremiah 29:11 GW

Most parents have hopes and plans for their children—education, career, marriage. Parents usually have definite ideas as to what they would like their children to pursue and how they should pursue it.

Our heavenly Father also has plans for us. Plans for our earthly life and plans for life into eternity. Plans filled with hope and a relationship with Him. Plans to glorify Him.

The plans of our earthly parents may be faulty, because they do not always know what is best for us. However, God is the One who holds the future. He guides us in the absolute right direction; therefore, it is the direction that brings us the greatest joy. Refusing to follow His path for our lives is worse than foolishness—it is self-sabotage.

God's eternal purpose is to be glorified. His purpose for each of us is to be a vessel by which He reveals His glory. At the same time, He is working to give us a glorious future. That is a purpose we can live with.

*Heavenly Father, forgive me for the times I have*
*disregarded Your purpose for my life.*

How can studying God's Word develop my understanding of His specific purpose for me? What new portion of Scripture can I begin studying today?

# APPEALING PURPOSES
## Daniel 1:8–16

He sought permission . . . that he might not defile himself.

Daniel 1:8

We all answer to various God-ordained authorities, such as family members, employers, the government, or pastors. These people may have definite ideas as to what we should be doing. What happens, though, when our earthly authorities ask us to violate God's purposes for us?

The prophet Daniel provided a step-by-step illustration of how to make an appeal. First, he resolved to obey God's Word (1:8). He also maintained a good relationship with his authority (v. 9). When the overseer denied Daniel's request, Daniel sought to achieve his authority's purpose in a way that would not cause him to violate God's commands. The overseer had a job to do; he was responsible for ensuring that Daniel and his friends remained healthy and strong. Daniel offered an alternative that would accomplish his authority's purpose without causing Daniel to compromise his own convictions (vv. 12–13).

If our desire is truly to glorify God, He will always provide us a way to do it.

> *Dear Lord, give me Your creativity in responding to the authorities in my life so I may continue to fulfill Your purpose for me.*

Have I been asked to violate the Word of God? How can I appeal this request in a way that honors God, while also honoring my earthly authority?

# RUN AND HIDE
## Numbers 35:9–28

The cities shall be to you as a refuge from the avenger.

Numbers 35:12

Have you ever felt the urge to run from your own sin? No matter how far or how fast we run, our sin always follows us. We can run, but we cannot hide.

In ancient Israel, God established the death penalty for murderers. To ensure the victim's family did not execute a death sentence for an innocent man, God provided the nation with cities of refuge. In the case of an unintentional death, the accused ran to the nearest of these cities. Family members seeking vengeance then had to wait for a proper trial to be held.

Our God is a God of refuge, providing a safe haven for us from sin. All we have to do is run to Jesus. The trial has already been held, and although a guilty verdict has been rendered, the One who is our refuge has already paid our death sentence.

We can run *and* we can hide—in Him, safe from the sin that accuses us.

> Lord God, thank You for providing the refuge I need
> from sin. Help me never to take for granted the price
> You paid for my freedom.

How have I tried to run or hide from my sin? What does having Jesus as my refuge mean to me today?

# FEATHERS
## Psalm 91:1–9

He will cover you . . . and under his wings you will find refuge.

Psalm 91:4 GW

I will never forget the first time I saw a chick hiding under his momma's wings. The plump hen appeared to be a large ball of feathers. A closer look revealed a tiny head poking out of his refuge. All that showed of the chick was his beak and his eyes. The rest of him was buried under her feathers, and he was staying put. Momma hen's stance made it clear she would do whatever was necessary to keep her baby safe.

This is the image the writer of Psalm 91 must have had in mind when he described the refuge found under God's wings. God longs for us to do more than run to Him for refuge. He also wants us to remain there. The psalmist spoke of the security of dwelling and abiding (v. 1) and making God our dwelling place (v. 9).

Some days we feel like that little chick. The world can be a scary place. What a comfort to know we have a refuge to run to and abide in, regardless of our circumstances.

> *Heavenly Father, forgive me for the times I run to*
> *You but do not remain with You. Teach me to make*
> *You my dwelling place.*

When I run to God as my refuge, what discourages me from remaining there?

# WHERE DO I RUN?
## Isaiah 30:1–5

It is better to take refuge in the LORD
than to trust in man.

Psalm 118:8 NIV

The king of Judah was in a bind. When the powerful Assyrians threatened his kingdom, King Hezekiah had two options. He could consult the Lord, or he could listen to his advisers. They counseled him to defend against the invasion by seeking help from Egypt.

But God used the prophet Isaiah to deliver a warning to King Hezekiah. The message was simple and direct: do not depend on other people for a refuge.

Most of us will not encounter the life-threatening predicament that King Hezekiah did. Still, we all have a tendency to run to people, things, or habits for a refuge, only to be disappointed or hurt when these refuges fail us. Friends and resources are never meant to substitute for God.

God is the only refuge that will never fail. Our first choice should be to run to Him. No matter how difficult our situation, He will carry us through with the grace and strength that only He can provide.

*Dear Lord, forgive me for the times I run to shelters other than You. Help me remember You are the only refuge I will ever need and the only One who provides true safety and peace.*

What circumstance is causing me fear or stress today? How can I run to God as my refuge in this situation?

# BETTER THAN NEW
## Psalm 23:1–6

He restores my soul.

Psalm 23:3

A few years ago, I came across an eighty-year-old sepia photograph. Torn edges, a diagonal crack through the center, and water spots marred the picture. Still, it was the only photo our family had of my husband's great-grandmother. A trip to the photo restorer gave me back the picture, better than new.

You and I can be much like that old photograph. We come to God tired, worn, and sin-damaged. We have cracks from being mistreated, and we are marred from going where we should not have gone. We come longing for a little rest and a little love, hoping He can patch us up so we can keep going. Anything would be an improvement over our current condition.

Then God comes with His deft, restoring touch. First, He declares us righteous before Him, removing the penalty of sin. Then, He gives us rest and refreshment. He guides, comforts, protects, and provides. When we spend time in His presence, we overflow with His blessings.

When God restores us, He does not just make us better. He makes us better than new.

*Lord, thank You for Your restoring touch. Help me to make time with You a daily priority.*

How has God's restoring touch in my life exceeded my expectations? What obstacles get in the way of my daily time with Him?

# RESTORED AGAIN AND AGAIN
## Psalm 51:1–12

Restore to me again the joy of your salvation.

Psalm 51:12 NLT

Few things compare to the feeling of a long, hot shower. Scrubbing away dirt can be both invigorating and therapeutic.

Think back to when you first surrendered to the Lord and allowed Him to make you truly clean on the inside. Remember the wonder of learning for the first time that God sacrificed His Son to spare you sin's eternal penalty and to restore your relationship with Him. Recall your joy as He removed the burden of sin from your shoulders and sponged away your guilt and shame.

It may have been weeks, months, or years since that precious day when God made you truly clean. But what about today? Like physical dirt, sin creeps in unannounced. Just as we may not notice the film of dirt behind our ears or under our nails, we ignore the buildup of wrong attitudes or inappropriate words. Once God has made us clean, we need to regularly confess our sin to stay clean. Then He restores the joy of an unobstructed relationship with Him.

*Father, forgive me for when I have been careless about sin in my life. Help me to be aware of things that obstruct my relationship with You as You restore the joy of Your salvation.*

In what area do I need God's restoring touch? How can I yield to His touch in this area today?

# RESTORED AND RESTORING
## Galatians 6:1–5

Restore such a one in a spirit of gentleness.

Galatians 6:1

When you see someone caught in sin, is your initial reaction, "Serves him right for playing with fire," or "Been there, done that, bought the T-shirt"?

You might think we would have a soft spot in our hearts for other Christians who fall into sin. Frequently, though, we either look the other way or condemn them for their failures. It has been said that Christians are one of the few groups that shoot their wounded. That may be why God commands us to focus on restoration instead of condemnation.

A warning accompanies this command. Not only are we to restore others, we must do it gently, knowing our own tendencies to fall. This warning for gentle restoration is as much for our benefit as for the other person's benefit. We are most vulnerable to sin when we think we are immune to it.

We all have a yearning to be restored to God and to each other. If we refuse to extend restoration to others, we will discover that we are actually shooting ourselves.

*Heavenly Father, help me restore others with the same gentleness You have used in restoring me. As I do, cause me to be aware of my own vulnerability to sin.*

How can God use me today to help restore someone who has fallen into sin?

# DON'T LEAVE WITHOUT HIM
## Psalm 28:1–9

The LORD is my strength, my shield from every danger.

Psalm 28:7 NLT

Fighting battles in ancient times was cumbersome at best. In addition to wearing armor, soldiers carried a heavy sword or spear in one hand and a shield in the other. They needed the offensive *and* defensive equipment to be effective. A good soldier would never think of leaving home without both his sword and shield.

As Christians, we are engaged in a different kind of warfare. Our adversary does not fight fair, and we need all the help we can get to live victoriously. God has proclaimed Himself our shield. He is the One who deflects the enemy's attacks and protects us from injury. He is our defense when we cannot defend ourselves.

Although God refers to Himself in Scripture as our shield, we don't always remember to rely on Him in this preventive way. Of course, God wants us to come to Him at all times. Too often, though, we ask Him to fix a situation that has already exploded, instead of coming to Him to defend and protect us beforehand.

God has promised to be our shield. Don't leave home without Him.

*Lord God, thank You for being my shield in both
my physical and spiritual battles.*

In what situation am I exposed today because I have not relied on God to be my shield?

# SHIELD OF FAITH
## Ephesians 6:10–17

Take up the shield of faith, with which you can
extinguish all the flaming arrows of the evil one.

Ephesians 6:16 NIV

Christians need one shield, and that shield is God Himself. If this is true, then what shield is the apostle Paul speaking of in this passage, when he urged us to "take up the shield of faith"? The apostle Paul is not talking about faith in just anything. All faith must have an object, and the object of a Christian's faith is the living God. Even then, faith is more than merely believing in God. Faith is believing God and *acting* on that belief.

When we take up the shield of faith, we are saying in effect, "Lord, I believe that You are who You say You are, that You have done what You said You did, and that You will do what You said You will do. I take You at Your Word and I will hold up that Word as my shield against the enemy's attacks." Those attacks might be temptation, blasphemous thoughts, or doubts. The flaming arrows could come in the form of depression, discouragement, or failure.

Whatever the attack, our faith in the character and ways of God is our defensive shield.

*Heavenly Father, forgive me for the times I have
placed my faith in myself or in other people. Help
me take up the only shield that can defend me, the
shield of faith in You.*

How can I express my faith in the character and ways of God throughout my day today?

# FEARLESSLY SHIELDED
## Psalm 3:1–8

You, O LORD, are a shield about me. . . . I will not be afraid.

Psalm 3:3, 6

Does someone in your life view you as an enemy? Perhaps you work with an insecure supervisor who is threatened by your ability, or you live near an aggressive neighbor who battles over parking spaces. Maybe the person who is hostile to you is a member of your own family.

We can respond to such people in several ways. We can ignore them, hoping they will go away; we can confront them, hoping they won't resort to violence; or we can appease them, hoping their demands won't become excessive.

The Bible offers us one more option. Knowing that God is our shield frees us from fear, enabling us to ask, "How can God use my interaction with this person as a blessing?" Perhaps He will use such people to teach us something about ourselves we might not learn any other way. Or maybe God will use us to touch something deep within them to draw them to Him.

When the Lord is our shield, we need not fear the fiercest enemy.

> *Lord God, help me rightly respond to those who consider themselves my enemy. Give me the confidence that comes from knowing that You shield me.*

Has someone in my life declared himself my enemy? How does knowing that God is my shield change the way I will interact with this person?

# GOD'S CHOICE
## Romans 9:14–29

So then He has mercy on whom He
desires, and He hardens whom He desires.

Romans 9:18

*S*overeignty is a term associated with rulers and kings. It is not something we commonly talk about today. It is, however, an attribute of God. God is sovereign. This means He can do whatever He wants, whenever He wants, wherever He wants, with whomever He wants. Does that sound unreasonable to you? It did to some of the apostle Paul's readers.

In this passage, Paul wrote of the Gentiles' opportunity for salvation because of Israel's rejection of their Messiah. Paul anticipated and addressed several objections to God's sovereignty, including the concept of *election*—the idea that God chooses whom He chooses.

Is salvation based on God's choosing us or on our choosing God? Although we may not fully understand, the Bible says both are true. Paul speaks of God's choosing us in Romans 9, and then speaks of our responsibility to choose God in chapter 10. Through His Son, God reaches out to us in our sinfulness and gives us the opportunity to reach out to Him.

The next time you struggle with the sovereignty of God, consider this: the question is not why God chooses *some* people; the question is why God chooses *anyone*.

*Lord, I don't always understand Your sovereignty,*
*but I thank You that I don't have to understand it*
*to submit to it.*

What other attributes of God do I not understand? Does this impede my worship of Him?

# OUR CHOICE
## Habakkuk 3:1–19

Though the fig tree does not bud . . . yet I will rejoice in the LORD.

Habakkuk 3:17–18 NIV

The Bible tells us to praise the Lord, regardless of what happens. That may be our desire, but what if . . . ? What if your husband has an affair, or your wife leaves you, or your child is killed in an accident? What if a tornado tears the roof off your home, or a fire destroys all your possessions? What if the diagnosis is cancer and you have no health insurance, or you've lost your job after thirty years with no prospects for a new one? Will we still praise the Lord when His hand appears to be working *against* us instead of *for* us?

We love God's sovereignty when He overrides the natural course of events to intervene on our behalf. Then we praise Him and tell of His great mercies to all our friends and family. When He does not choose to override events, however, we are not always as fast with our praise.

The prophet Habakkuk made a decision, in advance, to praise God no matter what happened. Even if the most basic and necessary events failed to occur, he chose, and would continue to choose, to praise God. Will we do the same?

*Heavenly Father, I choose to praise You no matter
what happens in my life.*

What has God's sovereignty allowed or not allowed in my life that concerns me? How does my opinion of my situation affect my opinion of God?

# DON'T FIX IT

## 1 Samuel 3:1–18

I told him that I would judge his family forever
because of the sin he knew about; his sons made themselves contemptible, and he failed to restrain them.

1 Samuel 3:13 NIV

A friend had a son spiraling out of control. When he developed massive debt problems, she paid his bills. After his arrest for fraud, she paid his victims to discourage them from pressing charges. She repeatedly fixed his problems, not realizing the new problems she created. The young man never learned to be accountable for his actions.

The Bible says Eli knew of his sons' evil activities but failed to hold them accountable. Because Eli spared them the consequences of their actions, God Himself judged them.

Some of us become enablers when family or friends make wrong choices. We interfere with God's sovereign activity in their life. By becoming their safety net, we prevent things from getting so bad that they have to look to God alone. This does not mean we should abandon them. We can encourage them without fixing their situation, leaving the outcome to our sovereign God.

*Sovereign Lord, forgive me for the times I get in the way of what You are doing in the lives of others. Help me get out of the way and point them to You.*

How have I interfered in others' lives with well-meaning activity that hinders God's sovereign orchestration to get their attention?

# PROVEN RELIABILITY
## Psalm 9:1–10

Those who know your name trust you, O LORD.

Psalm 9:10 GW

Advertisements are often used to encourage us to buy expensive products such as vehicles or appliances by touting the products' proven reliability. Then when we make the purchase, the sales staff try to sell us extended warranties. What happened to the reliability?

Trusting others is not easy in today's culture. We are conditioned to expect the worst from people. We don't trust strangers because we don't know them well enough, and we may not trust those we know because we know them too well!

The more we learn about God, however, the more we are convinced He can be trusted. We trust His Word because it has proven reliable. We trust His love because He offers it to us unconditionally. We trust His justice because He satisfied it with the death of His own Son.

The world offers a variety of options in which to place our trust. God offers Himself, and He shares His names and attributes so we might know that the One we trust is trustworthy.

*Lord God, thank You for the assurance that I can trust You because You have proven Yourself trustworthy.*

How has God revealed Himself trustworthy in my own life? With whom can I share His trustworthiness today?

# THE NEXT FIVE MINUTES
## Psalm 56:1–13

In God I trust; I will not be afraid.
What can mortal man do to me?

Psalm 56:4 NIV

Can God be trusted for the next five minutes?

For years, I suffered anxiety attacks while working as a corporate executive in New York City. My position required extensive travel to destinations such as Mexico City, London, Caracas, or cities across the United States. My desire to be in constant control, including control of my surroundings, produced bouts of severe anxiety. Alone in an unfamiliar hotel room, waves of fear would engulf me late at night as I fought to maintain calm.

I finally asked myself one question: if the God of the universe is trustworthy enough for me to place my eternal soul in His hands, how could I not trust Him for the next five minutes, and the five minutes after that, and then the five minutes after that?

The anxiety attacks diminished, and finally disappeared, as I rested in the realization that the God of creation can be trusted for eternity *and* for today.

*Heavenly Father, teach me how to trust You, one
minute at a time, regardless of my circumstances.*

In what areas does anxiousness or worry indicate that I am not trusting God? How can I release those areas to Him today?

# AM I TRUSTWORTHY?
## Proverbs 20:6–10

Who can find someone who is really trustworthy?

Proverbs 20:6 GW

If you asked ten of your closest family and friends to describe you in one word, would that word be *trustworthy*?

Finding a trustworthy person is not easy. Even the Greek philosopher Diogenes supposedly failed to find an honest man in his lifelong search of ancient Athens.

The more anonymous our communications become, the easier it is to dodge responsibility for our words and actions. We rely on ever-increasing voicemail, email, and text messaging, and we almost never talk face-to-face. As we deal with the bureaucratic systems of government agencies and corporations, it becomes more and more difficult to find an individual who will take ownership of a problem and correct it.

We are to be trustworthy as God is trustworthy. It doesn't matter if we work in a large bureaucracy, run our own small business, or if we like the other person or not. If those who belong to the Lord are not trustworthy, how will others learn that they can trust Him?

> *Lord God, help me be trustworthy in all my relationships as I represent You.*

Have I given anyone reason to consider me untrustworthy? How can I correct this impression today?

# KNOWLEDGE APPLIED
### Proverbs 3:7–20

By Wisdom the LORD laid the foundation of the earth.

Proverbs 3:19 GW

I enjoy solving puzzles. Jigsaws, crosswords, Sudoku—the solutions lie in more than an accumulation of knowledge. They also require an ability to apply that knowledge in practical ways to arrive at the correct conclusion.

When God formed the universe out of nothing, He applied all of His perfect knowledge in His creation. His wisdom—the application of knowledge—was exhibited as He employed astronomy, biology, geology, and all the other sciences. The result is the creation of a world where the pieces and processes fit together better than the finest jigsaw puzzle.

Consider the interaction between the moon's gravitational pull and earth's ocean tides. Ponder the impact of the monarch butterfly's migratory pattern on the food supply chain. Think about the relationship between the earth's precise rotation axis and the support of life on our planet. Pieces of a puzzle that all fit seamlessly together.

Our incredibly complex world reveals the amazing wisdom of our very wise God.

> *Lord, thank You for revealing Your wisdom in all
> You do. Help me to live in a way that acknowledges
> Your wisdom in all I do.*

In what ways has God revealed His creative wisdom to me this past week?

# JUST ASK

## James 1:5–8

If any of you lacks wisdom, he should ask God.

James 1:5 NIV

Some things come to us through a natural progression. The fruit of the Spirit—love, joy, peace, patience, kindness, goodness, faithfulness, gentleness, and self-control (Gal. 5:22–23)—come to us in increased measure as we surrender to the work of the Holy Spirit in our lives. However, wisdom is something God encourages us to specifically seek after and request.

We are not born with wisdom. Quite the opposite. Proverbs 22:15 reminds us, "Foolishness is bound up in the heart of a child." We are born with a sin nature and a bent way of thinking. If we want wisdom, we have to ask for it.

Many spend their lives seeking knowledge without asking for the wisdom to apply that knowledge. They amass headfuls of facts and appear quite educated by the world's standards, but they do not know how to apply what they have learned in a way that will please and honor the Lord. Even worse, much of what masquerades as wisdom in today's world is not wise at all.

We ask God for a variety of things. When did we last ask Him for wisdom?

*Heavenly Father, help me seek Your wisdom, that I might apply knowledge in a way that pleases You.*

In what situation do I need God's wisdom today? Have I specifically asked Him for it?

# SHOW ME
## James 3:13–18

Do you want to be counted wise, to build a reputation for
wisdom? Here's what you do: Live well, live wisely, live humbly.

James 3:13 Message

Missouri is known as the "Show-Me State." The state slogan
originated at the turn of the twentieth century and reflects
an affinity for practicality and common sense.

When it comes to the topic of wisdom, God also says, "Show me."
If we have true wisdom, our behavior will show it—especially in the
way we relate to others.

When James wrote to the early Christians, he related wisdom to
a variety of attributes including humility, gentleness, and mercy. He
also said godly wisdom is *not* associated with such characteristics as
bitterness, jealousy, and arrogance.

Claiming to be wise means nothing if our behavior doesn't match
our claim. People do not want to *hear* about our wisdom, they want
to *see* it.

> Lord, I confess the times I have claimed wisdom but
> not demonstrated it. Help me to ask for wisdom
> and then show it in my relationships.

Which of the characteristics *not* associated with wisdom do I reflect in my relationships? Which of the characteristics associated
with wisdom *do* I reflect in my relationships?

# WORTHY OF WORSHIP
## Revelation 5:1–9

Who is worthy?

Revelation 5:2 NIV

W hy do we worship God?

The simple answer is because He *is* God. There is nothing simple about God, however.

People worship a variety of things, from their bank accounts to their children. Some people worship themselves, believing that no one else is worthy of their loyalty. However, only Yahweh, the one, true, living God is truly worthy of our worship.

The word *worship* is derived from the Old English word for *worth-ship*, designating the recipient worthy of honor and respect. The title, "Your Worship" referred to royalty and other officials to reflect their high position.

Think about God's worthiness to receive our worship. Consider His character and His ways. Reflect on what He has said about Himself and what He has said about us. Ponder what He has promised and how He has fulfilled His promises. God commands and deserves all our worship because He is worthy of all our worship. No one else comes close.

*Lord God, You are truly worthy of all my worship,*
*and I give You all my worship today.*

How has God revealed to me His worthiness to be worshiped? What will be my worship response today?

# WORTHY ENOUGH
## 2 Thessalonians 1:1–12

We pray . . . that our God will count you worthy of your calling.

2 Thessalonians 1:11

What do we have to do to be worthy of God's calling? How many good deeds make up for the bad ones? How many church services make up for going where we did not belong? How many prayers make up for foul speech? When does God consider us worthy enough?

The good news—no, the great news!—is that we will never make ourselves worthy enough because we can't. We become worthy the moment He pours His grace on us and covers our sins with the blood of His Son. Yet if that is true, what does the apostle Paul mean when he writes, "We pray for you always, that our God will count you worthy of your calling"?

Our worthy God has given us *His* worth. Will we walk in the worth He has bestowed on us? Will we continue in the worthiness He gives us, or will we walk away from our high calling and trample the gift we have been given?

Worthiness is never something we earn. It is a gift we cling to by the grace of God.

> *Lord, forgive me for the times I have tried to make myself worthy instead of clinging to Your gift of worthiness.*

Am I trying to make myself worthy of God's grace, or am I walking in the gift of His worthiness? How will I know the difference?

# WHOM DO YOU LOVE MORE?
## Matthew 10:32–39

He who loves son or daughter more than Me is not worthy of Me.

Matthew 10:37

It is common advice that if you want to be a good husband or a good wife, a good father or a good mother, your family must come first in your list of priorities. This sounds like good counsel . . . except it is wrong.

We will only be the best we can be when God has the best possible place in our lives. That best place is always the *first* place. Abraham learned this lesson in Genesis 22, when he had to choose between his son and his God. When he chose to love and obey God above all else, Abraham received his son back as well.

When we love God first, we become better husbands and wives, better fathers and mothers, better sisters and brothers. When our vertical relationship with God comes first in our lives, our horizontal relationships with everyone else will be in balance.

Our worthy God must have worthy worshipers. To be worthy of the privilege of worshiping Him requires that we love no one—not even ourselves—more than we love Him.

*Worthy Lord, help me love You above every person in my life, without exception.*

Who is the most precious person in my life? How would I respond to God if I were to lose that person?

# FERVENTLY DESIRED
## Isaiah 9:1–7

The zeal of the LORD of hosts will accomplish this.

Isaiah 9:7

How eager are you to restore a relationship with someone who is unfriendly or even hostile toward you? What would you be willing to sacrifice to make it happen? Time? Money? How about the life of your beloved, only child?

The prophet Isaiah looked to a day when the Lord would send the Messiah to redeem His people. Isaiah described a time when the light of salvation would dawn across the nation as God's Anointed One took His rightful place to rule over Israel. Isaiah also described God's eagerness to make this happen. "The zeal of the LORD of hosts will accomplish this" (Isa. 9:7).

Zealousness indicates an eager or fervent desire for something. Even if we are eager to restore a broken relationship, however, it is doubtful any of us would be willing to sacrifice one of our children.

God, in all His omniscience, knew exactly what it would cost to redeem His people. Still, He was zealous—eager, fervent—to make it happen, not because He wished pain on His Son, but because it was the only way to restore us to Him. *That* is how much He loves us.

> *Lord, thank You for Your zealous desire to do what
> I could not have done for myself.*

How zealous am I to cultivate the relationship God so willingly provided to me?

# GOD'S REPUTATION
### John 2:13–22

Zeal for your house will consume me.

John 2:17 NIV

A friend of mine is passionate about helping the homeless in our community. She volunteers with an organization that matches homeless people to affordable housing and assistance programs. Another friend is passionate about antique cars. He carefully restores old clunkers, converting them into historical treasures.

When we are zealous about something or someone, that passion becomes a driving force in our lives. People can be passionate about anything—cars, family, jobs, even food. However, how many of us are zealous for God?

When Jesus entered the temple, He was appalled at the things taking place in His Father's house. Instead of the outer courts being a place for Gentiles and women to draw close to the worship of Yahweh, profiteering moneychangers crowded them out. Zeal for God caused Jesus to take action, not for His own sake, but for the sake of His Father's holiness and honor.

God may not be commanding us to clear out a temple, but He *is* calling us to be zealous for Him.

> Holy Lord, give me a heart's desire that is full of
> zeal for You and Your reputation.

Am I zealous for God and for His reputation? How can I act on that zealousness today?

# SINCERELY WRONG
## Romans 10:1–4

They are zealous for God, but their zeal is not based on knowledge.

Romans 10:2 NIV

People can be sincere and still be sincerely wrong. Zeal is not a substitute for truth, as we saw on September 11, 2001. The hijackers who crashed their planes into New York's World Trade Center were zealous, but not in accordance with knowledge of the one true God.

Spiritual zealousness can take a variety of forms. Terrorists are one illustration. Another example is those who profess to be Christians, yet use their zeal to justify murdering abortion providers. Two extreme beliefs, both sincere, yet both sincerely wrong.

How should we respond to zeal that is not based on knowledge of the truth? We can agree to disagree, implying such beliefs are equally valid. We can debate, which may cause us to win the argument but lose the person. Or we can learn all we can from Scripture about who God is, then quietly and persistently live and speak truth in a respectful, yet uncompromising manner.

We must base our zealousness on the accurate knowledge of the Word of God. Anything less will leave us sincerely wrong.

*Lord, may my zealousness always be in accordance*
*with the knowledge of Your Word.*

Am I satisfied that I know God's Word well enough to be able to respond to others' questions or criticisms? If not, how can I begin today to learn more?

199

# A SPECIAL NAME
## Acts 10:36–43

She will give birth to a son, and you will name him Jesus.

Matthew 1:21 GW

Choosing a name for a new baby can be an emotional experience. Parents may select a name based on associations they have with other people of the same name. They may select a name to honor a family member or friend. They may also select a name because it is popular or unusual.

In New Testament times, parents frequently named their babies after family members such as grandparents or great-grandparents. Mary and Joseph, though, did not do this. The Lord instructed them to give their child a special name. They named Him *Jesus*, "because he will save his people from their sins" (Matt. 1:21 GW).

Only Yahweh, the Lord God, can bring salvation, and Jesus is Yahweh. The name Jesus is the Greek form of the Hebrew name Joshua, which means "Yahweh is salvation." This is why the apostle Peter could proclaim, "through His name everyone who believes in Him receives forgiveness of sins" (Acts 10:43).

Only God can bring salvation, and He did it through His Son, Jesus.

*Lord, thank You for the salvation You provide in Jesus. Help me reverence His name.*

How can I honor the name of Jesus today?

# MAGIC WORDS
## John 16:23–28

If you ask the Father for anything in My
name, He will give it to you.

John 16:23

"In Jesus's name, amen." We say the phrase, almost without thought, as if it had magic power. Tack it on the end of any prayer and we are done. God *has* to answer it, because Jesus said so, right? Wrong!

To understand the principle of coming to someone in the name of someone else, we need to remember the etiquette of communication in the days before the telephone and the internet. A king sent a message with his representative, who then spoke "in the king's name." Recipients held the message in the same esteem as if the king himself were standing there delivering it.

When we come to God "in Jesus's name," we are really saying, "Father, this is what Jesus would ask if He were standing here in my place." As we think of the things we have asked of God, can we truly say everything we ask for is what Jesus would ask of His Father?

Jesus never wanted what His Father did not want. His requests to God were always in line with the will of God. When this is our desire, we truly will be praying "in Jesus's name."

*Heavenly Father, forgive me for the times I have*
*come to You invoking the name of Jesus, when I*
*really spoke in my own name.*

What requests have I made of the Father that are not "in Jesus's name"?

# THAT NAME
## Acts 5:17–31

*Didn't we give you strict orders not to teach in Jesus' name?*

Acts 5:28 Message

Our culture tolerates, if not encourages, a spectrum of spirituality. From Native American religion to eastern mysticism, from yoga to Wicca, engaging in a spiritual journey is viewed as reflecting depth of character . . . until we mention the name of Jesus. Then, watch out!

The apostles ran into a similar problem. The religious leaders of their day gave them strict instructions to stop teaching "in this name" (Acts 5:28). Despite the pressure, the apostles did not listen.

Are we intimidated by cultural norms? Do we speak of God, but not of Jesus? Do we talk about spirituality, but not the Holy Spirit? Do we discuss spiritual guidance, but not the Bible? Or are we like the apostles, obeying God rather than men?

The last thing the enemy of our souls wants to hear is Jesus's name, unless it is spoken with hostility or trampled in irreverence. Unfortunately, Christians do equal damage to His name when we try to force the name of Jesus on others. Neither approach honors God.

Jesus. To quote the title of a well-known song, "There's something about that name!"

*Lord, give me discernment to know how to speak of my precious Savior today.*

Am I intimidated into not speaking of Jesus when I am around certain people? How can I share what my Savior means to me without being offensive?

# THREEFOLD SALVATION
## Romans 10:8–13

Whoever calls on the name of the Lord will be saved.

Romans 10:13 GW

The lifeguard's instincts kicked in when he saw the lone swimmer in the surf. He grabbed a life preserver and dived into the waves. When he finally reached the young man caught in a riptide, the first words he heard were, "Can you make it look like I'm saving you? My girlfriend is watching."

Sounds silly, doesn't it? Our human nature does not like us to admit we need saving.

Whether we want to acknowledge it or not, there is one area where we all need saving. No matter how hard we try, we cannot save ourselves from *sin*. That is why God sent His Son, Jesus Christ, to be our Savior. He is the only One who lived a sinless life and could therefore die in our place.

The salvation we have in Jesus touches us in three ways. He saves us from the penalty of sin, which is hell. He saves us from the power of sin by freeing us from its slavery. Finally, when we go to be with Him for eternity, He will save us from even the presence of sin.

The only way to obtain this salvation, however, is to ask for it.

*Holy Lord, thank You for giving me the salvation*
*I could not earn for myself.*

How can my relationship with the Savior change the way I live out my day today?

# FIRE INSURANCE
## 2 Peter 3:14–18

But grow in the grace and knowledge of our
Lord and Savior Jesus Christ.

2 Peter 3:18 NIV

When did you last read your fire insurance policy—*really* read it, from beginning to end? Most of us purchase a policy and then stick it in a file, hoping we will never have to use it.

Some people treat salvation like a fire insurance policy. They walk up to an altar or say a prayer and assume they are covered when they die. On that day, they plan to whip out their "fire insurance policy" to avoid going to hell.

God's gift of salvation does save us from an eternity spent apart from Him in hell, but it does so much more. God saves us from hell because He saves us from *sin*. The salvation we have in Christ breaks the power of sin in our lives and restores us to our holy God. The bonus is that we are also saved from sin's accompanying penalty.

Salvation is a relationship with the Savior, *now*. We have the privilege of experiencing and savoring our salvation every minute of each day as His Spirit works in us to make us more like Him.

Of course, it does provide great fire insurance too!

*Father, forgive me for the times I have treated my salvation as irrelevant to my daily life.*

How can I rely on the Lord for freedom from the power of sin in my life today?

# ARE YOU SAVED?

## Acts 2:14–21

THE GREAT AND GLORIOUS DAY OF THE LORD SHALL COME.

Acts 2:20

Are you saved?" The answer can mean the difference between life and death. Yet this question has become a source of ridicule in the world today.

The world portrays Satan as a comic figure in red leotards with horns and a tail, and Christians as mindless automatons who have lost the ability to enjoy life. God is relegated to one of two roles—either a lovable but doddering grandfather, or an impossible-to-appease, hang-'em-high judge. With all this derision, it is no wonder many believe they don't need saving from *anything*.

People may laugh, but their mockery does not negate the reality of a coming judgment. The salvation God offers through Jesus Christ is the only way to escape the penalty of sin.

We show our love for those around us by our concern for their future. An eternity in hell is no laughing matter. God does not call us to beat people over the head with a ten-pound Bible. He calls us to express our love by gently bringing them to a place where they will face the most important question of their lives: "Are you saved?"

*Lord Jesus, give me a sincere concern for others and*
*help me point them to You.*

Whom can I pray for today, asking God to give me an opportunity to share His salvation?

# HIS TITLE
## Matthew 16:13–20

You are the Christ, the Son of the living God.

Matthew 16:16

Did Jesus have a last name? Many people think it is *Christ*. However, *Christ* is His title. It comes from the Greek translation of the Hebrew word *Messiah*. Both words mean "the Anointed One" or "the Promised One."

By the time of Jesus's birth, the Israelites longed for the coming of their Messiah. Old Testament prophecies declared that the Messiah would be a descendant of King David. He would rule over Israel and restore the nation to her former glory and power. In Jesus's day, they waited expectantly for the Messiah to come and throw off the cruel shackles of their Roman conquerors.

Although the prophets spoke of the coming of God's Messiah, the Israelites did not recognize Him. He first came as a suffering servant to restore the nation to God. Before He could save them from their earthly enemies, He needed to save them from their sin. Most of Israel rejected Jesus because He did not fit their expectations. They wanted their Messiah to be a victorious king, not a suffering servant.

The Messiah was not what they *expected*, but He was everything they—and we—*needed*.

*Holy Lord, thank You for sending Jesus to be my Messiah—the Christ—to save me.*

How might my expectations of Jesus Christ interfere with His work in my life today?

# THE OLD AND THE NEW
## Luke 24:13–35

Then he began with Moses' Teachings and
the Prophets to explain to them what
was said about him throughout the Scriptures.

Luke 24:27 GW

O ccasionally, someone will tell me, "I don't need to read the Old Testament. The new covenant has replaced the old covenant. We're not under law anymore; we're under grace."

Comments like these remind me of Jesus's appearance to the two disciples on the road to Emmaus. He took the time to speak with them about the Old Testament and explain how the Scriptures all pointed to Him. From God's prophetic words to the serpent in the Garden, to the everlasting covenant God made with Abraham in Genesis; from the Passover lamb, to the ceremonial scapegoat recorded in the books of the Law; from the disturbingly accurate description of the crucifixion recorded by David in the Psalms, to the suffering servant described by Isaiah—all of it points to Jesus Christ.

We cannot fully value all Jesus Christ is, and all He did, apart from the Scriptures that pointed to Him. To understand His fulfillment of the law and the prophets, we must learn what the law and the prophets said. We read the Old Testament to appreciate the New Testament.

*Dear Lord, help me to see Jesus Christ on every*
*page of the Old Testament.*

How can I incorporate the Old Testament into my daily Scripture reading and study?

# CHRIST FOLLOWERS
## Acts 11:19–26

The disciples were first called Christians in Antioch.

Acts 11:26

What do you call someone who is a believer in Jesus Christ?

In New Testament times, believers had a variety of names, including *brethren* (Acts 1:16), people of *the Way* (Acts 9:2; 22:4), *disciples* (Acts 11:26), and *saints* (1 Cor. 1:2). The name that stuck was "Christian," which means a follower of Christ. To see a Christian is to see the One he follows. At least, that's how it *should* be.

People do not always have positive encounters with those who claim to be Christ followers. When a Christian missionary asked Indian spiritual leader Mahatma Gandhi why he did not like Christ, Gandhi was quoted as saying, "I like Christ. It is just that your Christians are so unlike your Christ." He is said to have added, "If Christians would really live according to the teachings of Christ as found in the Bible, all of India would be Christian today."

Believers in Jesus Christ bear His name. If the world rejects Christ, let it not be because we have failed to live up to that name.

> *Heavenly Father, I want to live in a way that others will see Christ in me. Help me never to bring shame to the name of Christ.*

In what ways have my thoughts or behavior been inconsistent with the name of Christ?

# WHOSE SON IS HE?
## Luke 1:26–35

The power of the Most High will overshadow you. Therefore, the holy child developing inside you will be called the Son of God.

Luke 1:35 GW

Fully God, yet fully man. Never before in human history had God become man.

Jesus Christ was conceived in the womb of a virgin. Not simply a young girl—a virgin. It was always historically understood that the Messiah would be born of a virgin. More than two hundred years before the birth of Jesus, when Jewish scholars translated the Old Testament into Greek, they used the Greek word for *virgin* in Isaiah 7:14. "Behold, a virgin will be with child and bear a son, and she will call His name Immanuel." This miraculous birth was anticipated for thousands of years, and it brought forth the sinless Son of the Most High God.

Our salvation could be accomplished by no less than God Himself. Only God could live a sinless life to fulfill the Law. Only God could provide the perfect substitutionary sacrifice. Only God had the power to break the stranglehold of sin and death. Only God.

God became man. It had never happened before, because the time had not been right. It will never happen again, because Jesus Christ accomplished our salvation once and for all.

*Holy Lord, thank You for providing my salvation*
*by stepping into human history.*

How can I celebrate the birth of the Son of God in my own life today?

# Worship and Obedience
## Psalm 2:1–12

You are my Son. Today I have become your Father.

Psalm 2:7 GW

Why do some people today work so hard *not* to believe Jesus Christ is God?

The psalmist described people and nations who refuse to yield to the divine authority of the Son of God. God laughs at their feeble attempts to rule themselves apart from Him. He has installed His Son as the eternal King, regardless of whether some people will submit to Him.

Today, many view Jesus as a philosopher, a teacher, or a prophet—anything but God. To acknowledge Jesus Christ is God means admitting accountability to Him. Accountability leads to judgment, and many would rather deny the possibility of judgment than submit to His lordship.

The way Christians live speaks volumes about who Jesus Christ is. If we believe Christ is God, we will do more than worship Him during weekend church services. We will also submit to His lordship and obey Him the rest of the week.

Jesus Christ *is* the Son of God. Our worship *and* obedience communicate the reality of His identity to a world in denial.

> *Lord, forgive me for the times I have dismissed Your authority in my life. Help me live with reverence for You, so others might see what it means to belong to the divine Son of God.*

In addition to my worship, in what area do I need to submit to Christ's lordship today?

# THE EMPTYING
## Philippians 2:1–11

> Who, although He existed in the form of God . . .
> emptied Himself, taking the form of a bond-
> servant, and being made in the likeness of men.
>
> Philippians 2:6–7

F ight for your rights." "Hold on to what's yours." We jealously guard our rights and privileges. Only the weak and pushovers give up what's rightfully theirs.

Yet the Son of God temporarily emptied Himself of His rights as God when He became man. He never stopped being God, but He yielded Himself to be abused by those He created and submitted Himself to receive the full cup of His Father's wrath against our sin.

The apostle Paul told us to have the same attitude as Jesus Christ regarding our rights and privileges. Rather than being motivated by selfishness or a desire to impress others, we should regard others as more important than ourselves, looking out for their interests as well as our own.

Relinquishing rights and privileges to others is not a sign of weakness; it is a sign of Christlikeness.

> *Son of God, You have demonstrated what it means*
> *to lay aside rights and privileges to fulfill the will*
> *of the Father. Help me have the same attitude with*
> *others.*

In what relationship is God calling me to relinquish my rights or privileges today?

# GOD-MAN
## Revelation 1:9–16

And standing in the middle of the lampstands was the Son of Man.

Revelation 1:13 NLT

The title "Son of Man" may bring to mind the image of a gentle, itinerant preacher beaten by the religious leaders of His day. Some may think that as God, He won, but as man, He lost.

Yet the Son of Man was as victorious in His humanity as He was in His divinity. As God, He temporarily set aside His divine privileges to become man. As man, He led a sinless life, obedient all the way to the cross. As God, He could have summoned "more than twelve legions of angels" to defend Him (Matt. 26:53). As man, He allowed Himself to be cruelly executed, submissive to His Father's will.

However, the Son of Man is no longer a person beaten down by His enemies. The apostle John described what he saw. "His head and His hair were white like white wool, like snow; and His eyes were like a flame of fire. His feet were like burnished bronze . . . and His voice was like the sound of many waters. . . . Out of His mouth came a sharp two-edged sword; and His face was like the sun shining in its strength" (Rev. 1:14–16).

Jesus Christ was equally victorious as the Son of God *and* the Son of Man.

*Son of Man, thank You for enduring all that You did to restore me to the Father.*

How is my life different today because Jesus is both the Son of God *and* the Son of Man?

# NOT MY AGENDA
## Mark 8:31–38

He began to teach them that the Son of
Man must suffer many things.

Mark 8:31

What great thing do you want to do for God? Is it the same great thing *God* wants you to do for Him?

Jesus told His disciples about the great purpose God had for His earthly life. "The Son of Man must suffer many things and be rejected by the elders and the chief priests and the scribes, and be killed, and after three days rise again" (Mark 8:31). The apostle Peter did not agree with this agenda, and he rebuked Jesus. Peter's plans for the great thing Jesus was to do did not include suffering and death. However, Peter had not yet set his mind on God's interests.

Today, we can do many great things for God. Teach classes, write books, travel to foreign mission fields—the possibilities are endless. However, what if the plan God has for us is to work in obscurity or glorify Him in suffering? What if His agenda for us is to do a great thing by doing what no one else wants to do?

The Son of Man gave His life to obey God's interests. Are we willing to do the same?

*Heavenly Father, help me glorify You by setting
my mind on Your interests and by following Your
agenda instead of my own.*

How might God's plans for me be different from my own plans to serve Him today?

# NO MORE OBSTACLES
## Hebrews 2:5–10

For it was fitting for Him . . . in bringing many sons to glory.

Hebrews 2:10

Select memberships, whether frequent flyer clubs or country clubs, make us feel special. We like the feeling of being part of an elite group.

Some followers of Christ behave as if God intended Christians to be an elite group. Visitors to church services may feel like outsiders who don't know the secret password. Christianese, an insider language, confuses those who haven't learned the vocabulary. New Christians may be asked to "jump through hoops" before they are accepted by the local church.

Jesus did not suffer on the cross to create an elite group of believers. He is the "Savior of the world" (John 4:42). His suffering and death on the cross enabled Him to "taste death for everyone" to bring "many sons to glory" (Heb. 2:9, 10).

Our goal is not to keep people out. Our goal is to do all we can to bring as many as will receive Him into a restored relationship with the Lord. God is looking for a large family!

*Lord, keep me from erecting obstacles that prevent*
*others from being restored to You.*

What unintentional obstacles might I be creating that make it harder for people in my life to come to Christ? How can I begin taking down those obstacles today?

*Immanuel*

# THE INVASION
## Matthew 1:18–23

"They will call him Immanuel"—which means, "God with us."

Matthew 1:23 NIV

One of the not-so-new ideas floating around today is that God is found in everything—rocks, trees, skies, seas. This is actually a New Age rehash of an old age concept called pantheism. Pantheism teaches that God is not separate from the natural world around us.

God *is* separate from His creation. The Great "I AM" existed before He formed the universe from nothing. The Bible tells us He is present everywhere, but He is not *part* of creation.

However, an invasion occurred two thousand years ago. God stepped into His creation in the form of a human being, Jesus of Nazareth. God became man. *Immanuel*, God with us, walked with and among the crown of His creation.

When sin separated man from a holy God, God bridged the gap. No longer would God be "up there." He would now be here, in the company of the humanity who so desperately needed to reach Him, but did not have the ability to reach Him. We will never again be alone, for now that God is Immanuel, He will never desert us or forsake us (Heb. 13:5).

> *Immanuel, thank You for the assurance of knowing*
> *You are always with me. Help me never to take Your*
> *presence for granted.*

How does knowing that God is with me change how I face my day?

*Immanuel*

# WALKING WITH GOD
### Genesis 5:21–24

Enoch walked with God for 300 years.
Genesis 5:22 GW

Have you ever watched a parent walk with a preschooler? Sometimes the child hurries to keep up, taking several petite steps for each adult one. Other times, the child runs ahead with an occasional glance over his shoulder to confirm mom or dad is close behind.

What does it take to walk *with* someone? First, walking together requires both parties to be moving in the same direction. Second, walking together requires that both parties are moving at the same pace, neither party running ahead or lagging behind.

The same things apply to our walk with God. We change our direction through repentance, no longer following sin, but instead following the Savior. Then we walk according to the pace the Holy Spirit sets as He directs us. Trouble occurs when we run ahead of His leading or delay in obeying His commands.

Immanuel means *God* is with us. How we walk with Him determines if *we* are with God.

> *Immanuel, I confess the times I have run ahead of Your leading or lagged behind Your instruction. Help me walk with You in repentance and obedience.*

How have I run ahead or lagged behind the Lord this week? What can I do to walk *with* God today?

*Immanuel*

# WITH US, NO MATTER WHAT
## Daniel 3:13–30

> Was it not three men we cast? . . . I see four
> men loosed and walking about.
>
> Daniel 3:24–25

A friend faced cancer surgery. "I'm okay," she reassured her family and friends. "God is with me." After an unsuccessful surgery and a terminal diagnosis, her perspective did not alter. "No matter what happens, God is still with me," she said with the same assurance.

Daniel's three friends experienced similar faith in the reality of God's presence. They lived each day with a confident faith in God, and they faced the executioner's fire without any doubts. Whether He protected them from the fire or not, He would always be with them.

It is easy to have a confident, public testimony that God is with us when our lives are pleasant and successful. However, it is when our lives fall apart that the world watches us most closely. Are our claims of an intimate relationship with God real or the stuff of fairy tales?

Hurting people want to know that God's abiding presence does not depend on circumstances. We can show by how we live that the reality of God's abiding presence depends on the birth, life, death, and resurrection of Immanuel.

> *Thank You, Immanuel, for the assurance that You
> are with me. Help me live the reality of Your pres-
> ence, no matter what happens.*

Do those around me see my confidence in Immanuel, regardless of my circumstances?

# BEAUTIFUL TO ME
## Isaiah 4:2–6

In that day the Branch of the LORD will be beautiful and glorious.

Isaiah 4:2

B eauty is in the eye of the beholder." Nowhere is this more mean-ingful than in the person of Jesus Christ.

The prophet Isaiah wrote two seemingly contradictory statements about Israel's coming Messiah. First, he said, "The Branch of the LORD will be beautiful" (Isa. 4:2). Later, he said, "He has no stately form or majesty that we should look upon Him, nor appearance that we should be attracted to Him" (Isa. 53:2). Which is correct?

For those who have no part in His salvation, Jesus Christ was, at best, an itinerant preacher made larger-than-life by fanatical follow-ers . . . if He existed at all. At worst, He was a lunatic who claimed to be God.

For those whom Jesus has saved from the power and penalty of sin, He is everything beautiful. His beautiful words speak eternal life into our lives. His beautiful blood atones for our sin. His beautiful Spirit resides in our hearts, reconciling us to our heavenly Father.

To every Christian saved by the grace of God, Jesus Christ *is* beautiful.

*Beautiful Lord, thank You for surrounding me with the beauty of Your salvation.*

How can I reflect on the beauty of my Savior as I go about my daily routine?

# DECEPTIVE BEAUTY
## Ezekiel 28:11–19

Your heart became proud
on account of your beauty.

Ezekiel 28:17 NIV

How can something beautiful also be ugly at the same time? God created Satan to be a beautiful angel with the honor of serving and abiding in His presence. Satan was not content with his position, though, and wanted the worship accorded to God. After he failed in his quest to be as God, he caused man to fall for the same lie—that we can "be like God" (Gen. 3:5 NIV).

Pride is ugly. It causes us to think only of ourselves and to think of ourselves more highly than we ought. Pride also focuses on external beauty. Today, millions of people spend countless dollars preserving and promoting physical beauty. Regardless of how much we spend, however, external beauty will always be fleeting.

Only when we give our broken and corrupted lives to the Lord, asking Him to remove all that is ugly, do we become truly and eternally beautiful.

*Beautiful Lord, forgive me for the times I focus on
external beauty while ignoring the eternal beauty
You are working in me.*

Where has pride crept into my life? What can I do today to cooperate with God's Holy Spirit as He works to develop an eternal beauty in me?

# BEAUTIFUL FEET
## Romans 10:13–17

How beautiful are the feet of those who bring good news!

Romans 10:15 NIV

When we think of feet, we do not usually think of them as beautiful. Smelly, sweaty, dirty, with bunions and calluses maybe, but not beautiful.

So why does Scripture specifically call the feet of those who share the gospel *beautiful*?

Imagine a prisoner trapped in a dark dungeon for decades. He is beaten and abused, hungry and sick. He lies dejected in a corner, consumed by depression, despairing of ever breaking free. Suddenly, his cell door flies open, and a voice proclaims his freedom. Too weak to stand or raise his head, all he can do is look at the sandals of the one who brings his release. The prisoner does not see dust or dirt on those feet. He takes no notice of bunions or calluses. To him, the feet in those sandals are beautiful!

How beautiful are our feet today? Have we been bringing the Good News of salvation to those most desperate to hear it? When we obey God's call to share the gospel, we have the most beautiful feet in the world.

*Heavenly Father, make my feet beautiful. Help me be sensitive to opportunities to share the gospel today.*

How can I better prepare for opportunities to share the gospel with those around me?

# HUNGER NOT
## John 6:26–35

I am the bread of life. No one who comes
to me will ever be hungry again.

John 6:35 NLT

The photographs haunt us: starving children with distended stomachs, protruding bones, and limbs like sticks. Most of us have no concept of what it means to be truly hungry. We toss off phrases such as "I'm famished" or "I'm starving" a mere hour or two after a meal. If we have distended stomachs, it is probably because we are carrying excess weight.

Physical hunger may be foreign to us, but we have all felt the pangs of spiritual hunger—a gnawing in our spirit that dreams of more to life than what we see. We struggle with right living because of temptation's relentless attacks, and we are anxious at the sin that ensnares us.

Jesus answers our need with a profound statement. "I am the bread of life; he who comes to Me will not hunger." He gives us complete spiritual nourishment and satisfaction—everything we need to live, grow, and flourish.

We need never experience spiritual hunger when we feed on Jesus, the Bread of Life.

*Lord God, thank You for nourishing me with the*
*Bread of Life. Give me a growing hunger for You.*

How hungry am I for the spiritual nourishment that comes only from a relationship with Jesus Christ? How can I "feed" on Him today?

# JUNK FOOD
## Psalm 119:97–104

How sweet are your words to my taste; they are sweeter than honey.

Psalm 119:103 NLT

We live in a junk-food world. All too regularly, we satisfy our physical hunger with convenient or tasty foods that provide little nutrition.

Just as we can fill our bodies with unhealthy foods, we can also fill our souls with spiritual junk food. Spending time and energy on activities that do not have eternal value dulls our spiritual appetite for God's Word.

The psalmist not only hungered for God's words, he found their taste sweeter than honey. Can we say the same? Some of us read the Bible out of obligation; we do it because we know it is good for us, but it doesn't "taste" good. From there, we might progress to reading the Bible because it is spiritually satisfying. Better still is when we spend time in the Word of God because it is a delight—the equivalent of eating the most delectable dessert.

The world works tirelessly to draw us away from feeding on the Bread of Life. Don't be distracted by spiritual junk food.

> *Bread of Life, forgive me for filling up on things that do not satisfy. Help me feed on the spiritual nourishment that comes through Your Word and Your Holy Spirit.*

What spiritual junk food has been diminishing my appetite for God and His Word?

# BE DISCERNING
## Matthew 16:5–12

Watch out for the yeast of the Pharisees and Sadducees!
                                    Matthew 16:6 GW

For years, researchers said coffee was bad for our health. Now some studies have shown that a moderate amount of coffee may help in protecting us from certain diseases. The key word is *moderate*!

Just as we need to be wise about what we eat and drink, Jesus warned us to be discerning about the spiritual teachings we ingest.

Today, we hear God's Word quoted in a variety of venues, from churches to television, from books to the Internet. The Bible, however, tells us to be discerning, comparing the teaching we hear to the written Word of God. Even the Bereans verified the apostle Paul's teachings against the Scriptures "to see if what Paul said was true" (Acts 17:11 GW).

The determining factor in believing a particular teacher should not be friendships or the reputations of celebrities. We need to beware the "yeast" of corrupt teaching.

> Holy Lord, thank You for the clear teaching of Your Word. Help me be discerning in the teaching I receive, always confirming it against Your written Word.

What teachers or preachers have I listened to without taking the time to check their teaching against the written Word of God?

# THE BETROTHAL
## Hosea 2:18–23

I will betroth you to me forever;
I will betroth you in righteousness.

Hosea 2:19 NIV

A biblical betrothal is often likened to a modern engagement period, but it included much more. It was a promise to marry that could only be broken by divorce.

In biblical times, the husband provided his wife with basic needs, including food, clothing, shelter, and medical care. He took care of her in life and provided for her burial in death. In return, the husband received ownership of any resources or property she might inherit from her family.

God promises to be a bridegroom to His people, to fulfill all the responsibilities of a husband to His bride. He feeds us the bread of life, clothes us in His righteousness, shelters us under His wings, and heals our spirits. When this life ends, He provides for our eternal life with Him. All that we have belongs to Him, and we offer our lives to Him in return.

Believers are more than engaged. We are betrothed to our bridegroom, Jesus Christ.

*Lord, You are my bridegroom. Thank You for the care You provide me in this life, and the assurance that I will be with You for eternity.*

How has the Lord shown me the care of a bridegroom? What can I do today to respond to His loving care?

# THE WEDDING
## Revelation 19:4–9

*The marriage of the Lamb has come and*
*His bride has made herself ready.*

Revelation 19:7

I enjoy watching engaged couples. They spend almost every minute preparing for the day when they will be husband and wife. When they are together, they have eyes only for each other. Engaged couples devote themselves to learning everything they can about their loved one. They go out of their way to make the one they love happy. Their thoughts are never far from their love, and they make detailed plans to spend the rest of their life with this person.

Each day we spend here on earth is an opportunity to prepare ourselves to meet our Bridegroom. Do we have eyes only for Him? Do we devote ourselves to learning everything we can about Him as revealed in His Word? Do we go out of our way to make His heart smile? Do we live our lives in light of the eternity we will spend with Him?

Are we behaving like those betrothed to a holy Bridegroom?

> *Heavenly Father, I am eager to please my Bride-*
> *groom. Teach me, by Your Holy Spirit, how I can*
> *walk more closely with You.*

How much time will I spend today learning to know my Bridegroom more intimately? What can I do to demonstrate my love for Him?

# BELIEVERS, UNBELIEVERS, MAKE-BELIEVERS
## Matthew 25:1–13

Please give us some of your oil because our lamps are going out.

Matthew 25:8 NLT

Children love to play "make-believe." Their vivid imaginations create fantasies, and they sometimes have trouble distinguishing from reality. Playing make-believe is a fine game for children, but it is dangerous when adults pretend they have a relationship with God.

If the oil in this parable symbolizes the Holy Spirit, then the five foolish virgins represent those who enjoy being called *Christian*, but who have not had a true change of heart. At first glance, the prudent virgins seem quite harsh and selfish. Their behavior contradicts everything we have been taught about sharing with others. However, no one can give the Holy Spirit to someone else. Everyone must surrender individually to God—we cannot do it for someone else.

Family or friends may call themselves Christians, but without a personal surrender to the Bridegroom, they will share the fate of the five foolish virgins. The most loving thing we can do is encourage them to stop playing make-believe and to choose the Bridegroom for themselves.

> *Dear Lord, help me not to contribute to others' false
> sense of security regarding their spiritual condition.
> Show me how to encourage them to a true relation-
> ship with the Bridegroom.*

Who in my life has been trying to "borrow" oil from my lamp? How can I lovingly encourage them to enter into their own personal relationship with Christ?

# HOLDING IT TOGETHER
## Acts 4:1–12

He is the stone that the builders rejected, the
stone that has become the cornerstone.

Acts 4:11 GW

What helps you keep it together each day? Is it that first—or fourth—cup of coffee? Is it a morning workout? Perhaps it's a daily quiet time spent in prayer and reading the Bible.

In ancient times, the cornerstone fulfilled a critical role in holding buildings together. It was placed in the space where two walls met, aligning them and anchoring the structure.

Christians have a number of beliefs, including belief in one triune God—Father, Son, and Holy Spirit. We believe the Bible is the Word of God. We believe we are lost in sin apart from the redeeming work of God's grace. We believe the church is the body of Christ.

The cornerstone of our beliefs is that Jesus Christ is the Son of God, completely God and completely man. His virgin birth, sinless life, substitutionary death, and physical resurrection provide the way for our salvation by the grace of God.

The world may reject Him, but Jesus Christ is our Cornerstone, the One who holds us together and keeps us each day until we go to be with Him for eternity.

*Lord God, thank You that everything I am and all
that I believe is held together in Christ.*

When did I last take inventory of what I believe? Is Jesus Christ the cornerstone of *all* my beliefs?

# NEVER DISAPPOINTED
## 1 Peter 2:4–8

A PRECIOUS CORNER stone, AND HE WHO
BELIEVES IN HIM WILL NOT BE DISAPPOINTED.

1 Peter 2:6

If it sounds too good to be true, it probably is." I remind myself of these words each time I see an ad in print, on television, or on the Internet. They have saved me much disappointment—and money!

We have all been let down by people, by purchases, even by places. The higher our expectations, the greater the chance for disappointment. However, one person who will never disappoint us is our Cornerstone, Jesus Christ.

Jesus delivers exactly what He promises, and more besides. He gives us the absolute assurance of being freed from slavery to sin and the knowledge that the penalty has been paid once and for all. He provides the blessing of approaching the God of the universe as Father rather than as Judge. He offers the delight of experiencing the truest, purest form of love and joy.

When Jesus is our Cornerstone, our highest expectations will never be disappointed.

> *Dear Father, thank You that I will never be disappointed when I rely on Christ alone. Help me share with others the blessing of salvation from the penalty, power, and presence of sin.*

Is there something I have been afraid to trust God for because I fear being disappointed? Will I give Him this issue today and trust Him for the results?

# NO LONGER OUTSIDERS
## Ephesians 2:11–22

You are built on the foundation of the apostles and
prophets. Christ Jesus himself is the cornerstone.

Ephesians 2:20 GW

Second-class citizens. That's what some Gentiles felt like in the
early church. After all, Jewish believers were already God's chosen people and worshiped Him in the temple in Jerusalem. They
considered Gentiles to be unworthy outsiders. They did not allow
these outsiders beyond the wall separating the outer Court of the
Gentiles from the rest of the temple.

The apostle Paul reminded Gentile believers that Jesus had broken down the wall between Jew and Gentile. No longer outsiders,
Gentiles had the same access to God as the Jews. Both came to the
Father through Jesus Christ. He was the Cornerstone who held them
together.

Today, Christians raised in the church sometimes look down on outsiders who come to Christ without any background in the Scriptures
or familiarity with Christian worship. Regardless of our backgrounds,
Jesus Christ is still the Cornerstone who unites us all in Him.

*Father, forgive me for not being more welcoming
to visitors of different backgrounds who come to
worship You in my church. Help me break down
walls that may separate us.*

How do I respond to strangers who visit my church? What can I
do to make a visitor feel more welcome this week?

# TO GOD, THROUGH GOD
## John 10:1–10

I am the gate. Those who come in through me will be saved.

John 10:9 NLT

In biblical times, shepherds kept their sheep in pens at night to protect them from predators and thieves. The location of the flock determined the shepherds' options. Caves provided natural pens. The shepherds often used rock formations as one "wall," and then built the three remaining walls using thorn branches or rocks. Regardless of their construction, all sheepfolds shared a common characteristic: a single opening served as the one entrance and exit.

The shepherd would lie across the opening, using his own body for the gate to the pen. Daily, he put his life on the line. A predator or thief could not get to the sheep without going through the shepherd.

Jesus Christ identified Himself as the gate or the door. There is no entrance into the presence of God except through Jesus. Completely God and completely man, He did what we could not do for ourselves. He opened the door to heaven that was closed to us because of sin.

He showed us that the only way *to* God is *through* God!

> *Holy Lord, thank You for opening the door to heaven through Jesus Christ. Thank You that because of Him, I will never find the door locked.*

How does knowing that Jesus is the door to heaven change the way I approach God?

# NO BRIDGE JUMPING
## Matthew 7:13–23

For the gate is small and the way is narrow that leads to life.

Matthew 7:14

The majority is not always right. Or as my mother phrased it, "If everyone jumped off a bridge, would you?"

Why don't more people believe in, and follow, Jesus Christ? Maybe it is because the crowd travels a different road. It is challenging to go against the majority, to march to the beat of a different drummer. Our culture likes to create its own ways to God. Believe in Jesus or not, they say, but do what feels good to you. God will accept you anyway.

While the world proclaims an "easy believism" that requires little from us, Jesus declares that the wide gate is the wrong gate. Sadly, few are willing to hear it.

Do we have the conviction to go against the majority and enter the narrow gate? Others may mock, activities distract, and trials weigh upon us. Still, our own choices determine our eternal future.

Not only is the majority not always right, sometimes they are dead wrong.

*Heavenly Father, forgive me for the times I have listened to the majority, rather than listen to You. Show me where I have been seeking the wide gate instead of Your gate.*

How might my choices today affect the path I follow through God's small gate of salvation?

# Blocking the Entrance
## Matthew 23:13–24

You lock people out of the kingdom of heaven.

Matthew 23:13 GW

Have you been blocking salvation's entrance to others? That's what Jesus accused the Pharisees of doing. Not only would they not enter heaven themselves, their behavior prevented others from entering. They did this by requiring legalistic behaviors as a condition of salvation—a list so intricate that few people had any hope of success.

If we impose requirements on others before they enter a saving relationship with Jesus Christ, we are guilty of imitating the Pharisees. In our eagerness to be good Christian witnesses, we may imply that others must clean up their act before becoming a Christian. However, no one can make themselves pure enough to meet God's standards. This is why we need Jesus! Of course, salvation does require a repentant heart. Cleaning up, however, is what the Holy Spirit does in and for us as we surrender to the lordship of Jesus Christ in every area of life.

We must be careful not to impose anything on others that God does not impose on them. Blocking the entrance to salvation is a serious offense.

*Lord, help me not impose restrictions on others as Your Spirit draws them to You.*

How am I causing others to think they must meet a set of requirements *before* they come into a relationship with Jesus Christ?

# A FIRM FOUNDATION
## 1 Corinthians 3:9–15

For no man can lay a foundation other than . . . Jesus Christ.

1 Corinthians 3:11

Before God laid the foundation of the world, He laid the foundation for our salvation. Before God created man, who would rebel and need restoration, God laid the foundation for that restoration. The foundation for our salvation and restoration is Jesus Christ alone.

Today, assorted religions proclaim a variety of ways to God. Each one claims to be unique, but whether they realize it or not, they all have the same foundation: an emphasis on self-effort. If their adherents work hard enough, if they follow the right rules, if they do enough good works, maybe they will make it to heaven, nirvana, or utopia.

By contrast, Paul and the other apostles founded churches built on the solid foundation of the person and work of Jesus Christ. When we build on anything else, our foundation is faulty and our religion crumbles under the weight of our own efforts.

Jesus Christ is the only sure foundation that will last for eternity.

*Holy Lord, thank You for laying a firm foundation
for my salvation in Your Son. Help me never to
rely on anything or anyone else for my restoration
to You.*

Have I been trying to add my own work to the foundation God has already laid? What is the place for my good works, since they do not contribute to my salvation?

# FOOLISH BUILDERS
## Matthew 7:24–29

> Therefore, everyone who hears what I say and obeys it
> will be like a wise person who built a house on rock.
>
> Matthew 7:24 GW

Residents of south Florida are familiar with the annual threat of hurricanes. Evacuations are mandatory for those who live in mobile homes, since they do not have a foundation to withstand hurricane winds. Sometimes, though, long-time residents foolishly ignore the warnings because they've heard them so often. Their safety depends not only on hearing the evacuation orders but also on a wise response.

Have you ever sat in church and thought, "I've heard this before"? That it is safe to tune out the message because it's for the visitors? Some people sit in church their whole lives, hearing the words of Jesus, but not acting on them. That's as foolish as building a house on shifting sand.

Jesus said that it is not enough to hear His words. We must also act on them by receiving His gift of salvation and then obeying His instructions on how to live. When we do, we rely on a solid foundation, one that will support us in all the storms life brings.

> *Heavenly Father, You have clearly communicated*
> *Your salvation in and through Your Son. Help me*
> *hear the message and respond with obedience in*
> *every area of my life.*

In what area have I heard God's Word but not acted on it? How will I take action today?

# REACHING THE UNREACHED
## Romans 15:14–29

I aspired to preach the gospel, not where Christ was already named,
so that I would not build on another man's foundation.

Romans 15:20

Several international Christian mission organizations are focusing on the "10/40 window," also known as the "resistance belt" of the world. Identified by latitude coordinates from 10 degrees north of the equator to 40 degrees north of the equator, this band around the world includes 3 billion people in 60 nations, and 95 percent of the unreached people groups.

The apostle Paul also had a burden for reaching the unreached. He declared that he did not want to "build on another man's foundation." Paul was not speaking of laying a foundation other than Jesus Christ. Rather, he referred to his work with people who had not yet heard of Jesus Christ, instead of ministering where the gospel had already been preached.

Today, we still have the privilege and the obligation to reach the unreached. Some can go to the mission field. Some can give so that others may go. All of us can pray. What are we doing to share Jesus Christ, the foundation of our salvation, with a needy world?

> Lord God, forgive me for my casual responses to
> the urgency of sharing the gospel with those who
> have not yet heard. Show me what You want me to
> do to reach the unreached.

What can I do today to help reach the unreached? Is God asking me to pray, give, or go?

# WHO CALLS YOU "FRIEND"?

### Exodus 33:7–11

The LORD used to speak to Moses face to face
. . . as a man speaks to his friend.

Exodus 33:11

Who names you as their friend? Are they the same people you consider friends?

Today, we refer to almost everyone as a friend, although many qualify more as acquaintances. We should not take friendship lightly, especially friendship with God.

Moses had such an intimate relationship with God that the Lord spoke to him face-to-face. God named Abraham His "friend" (Isa. 41:8), as well. What made these men friends of God? Was it their good works, their holiness, or their position in the community?

Moses was not holy. He was a killer whose short temper prevented him from entering the Promised Land. Abraham lied about his wife Sarai. God considered them friends, not because of what they did, but because they took Him at His word, acting in obedience and faith.

God chooses His friends, not for what they can do for Him, but for what He can do *through them*. When we enter into a relationship with God through His Son, Jesus Christ, He receives the glory and honor, and we receive the blessing of friendship.

*Lord, thank You for the privilege of a relationship
with You, that I may be Your friend.*

Have I based my friendship with God on what I can do for Him or what He can do through me?

# NOT THAT KIND OF FRIEND
## Matthew 26:45–56

Jesus replied, "Friend, do what you came for."

Matthew 26:50 NIV

Calling some people "friends" does not guarantee their friendship or that they will always behave as friends should behave.

In the Garden of Gethsemane, Jesus watched three types of friends behave in decidedly unfriendly ways. Judas betrayed Him with a kiss. Peter flouted Jesus's teachings by attacking His enemies. All the disciples abandoned Him to His foes.

Friendship presumes both parties will act in mutual interest and support. We know our friendship with God begins with His choosing us. We also know God always acts to our benefit. Still, what does God expect from us in return? Jesus gave us the answer when He said, "You are My friends if you do what I command you" (John 15:14). God expects His friends to believe Him and obey His commands.

Living by faith and in obedience—that is how God's friends behave.

> *Heavenly Father, forgive me for the times I have called myself Your friend, but not behaved as Your friend.*

If faith and obedience are tests of friendship with God, would Jesus say I pass the tests? If not, what must change for my life to reflect my friendship with God?

# RIGHT FRIENDS
### Proverbs 12:1–28

Do not be misled: "Bad company corrupts good character."

1 Corinthians 15:33 NIV

Should we continue socializing with unbelievers after we become Christians, or should we replace those friends with Christians? Unlike neighbors or acquaintances, true friends know us intimately. They tell us the truth when no one else has the courage to do so. True friends want what is best for us, regardless of whether it is best for them. They share our goals and values and encourage us in our spiritual growth.

Jesus said we are to live for Him and be a witness in a world that does not know Him. At the same time, we are to remain separate. We are to influence without being influenced, pointing people to Christ without compromising ourselves with an unrighteous world. James wrote, "Whoever wants to be a friend of this world is an enemy of God" (James 4:4 GW).

God calls us to be salt and light in our relationships with unbelievers. Our most intimate friends, though, should be those who will encourage us to grow in the light and love of the Lord our God, the One who names us *friend*.

> *Dear Lord, help me develop relationships and friendships without compromising Your Word.*

In what relationships have I compromised my spiritual life for the sake of a friendship?

# IT BELONGS TO HIM
## Hebrews 1:1–14

He has spoken to us by his Son, whom he
appointed heir of all things.

Hebrews 1:2 NIV

Statisticians have forecast that the baby boomer generation will receive the largest inheritance of any generation to date, a total of more than ten trillion dollars. As large as that is, there is one heir who will receive significantly more than the baby boomers' combined inheritance. This heir is God's Son.

God appointed His Son, Jesus Christ, to be heir of all things. All of creation—every created thing—belongs to Him. Not only did Jesus make it all, He upholds it all by His Word. It is fitting, then, that He has full authority as Lord over what He created.

For now, Satan is the prince of a world in which sin reigns. We eagerly wait for the day when creation will be set free from his hold and sin's corruption, for the day when the heir will restore all things.

We rest in the promise that Satan's time is limited and his end is sure. No matter what he does, he cannot change the reality that Jesus Christ is heir of His creation.

*Lord God, thank You for the assurance that despite
the turmoil in the world today, You are in control
and the day will come when Your heir will restore
all things.*

How does knowing that Jesus is God's heir change how I view current events today?

# Someday
## Ephesians 1:3–14

Because of Christ, we have received an inheritance from God.

Ephesians 1:11 NLT

*Someday.* Think of the potential packed into this word. Someday, I will . . . Someday, we will . . . Someday, God will . . .

Someday, all things will be summed up in Christ. Someday, He will return and will rule over all creation—heaven *and* earth. Someday, we will be in the presence of God forever.

However, when the apostle Paul wrote about our inheritance, he used the past tense. We *have received* an inheritance. It may be in the future, but Paul wrote as if it has already happened. His confidence in the finished work of Christ on the cross left him no doubt as to the certainty of our inheritance. In Paul's mind, it is already done. No need to doubt God's Word, because God has given His Holy Spirit to each of us as a pledge of the fulfillment of our inheritance.

We can look forward to a glorious future. Get ready, because someday *will* come!

> *Heavenly Father, thank You for the certainty of my inheritance. Help me to rest in the assurance that nothing and no one can take it away from me.*

What circumstances in my life are causing me to doubt the certainty of my inheritance in Christ? How does the apostle Paul's certainty help me face those situations today?

# INHERITANCES
## Acts 20:24–32

Now I commit you to God and to the word of his
grace, which can build you up and give you an
inheritance among all those who are sanctified.

Acts 20:32 NIV

Grieving the death of a close family member can be gut-wrenching. Worse yet, the grief process may be intensified by painful family squabbles over wills and inheritances. Thoughts turn from the loss of a loved one to whether they will inherit as much of the deceased's estate as they think they deserve.

The apostle Paul warned the Ephesian elders that false teachers would distract them and their flock from their eternal inheritance. The elders needed to be alert against such influences.

Paul's warning is still relevant. False teachers sway many to ignore the eternal inheritance God prepared for those in Jesus Christ. Not only are we to protect ourselves from these influences, we must also be careful how we influence others.

When we rely on God's grace and His Word, we—and those we influence—will be built up to receive the eternal inheritance God has prepared for us.

*Holy Lord, protect me from relationships, teachers,*
*and influences that do not lead me to rely on Your*
*grace and Your Word.*

Who are the people who influence me the most? Whom do I influence?

# PERMANENT PRIESTHOOD
## Hebrews 7:11–28

It was fitting for us to have such a high priest,
holy, innocent . . . and exalted.

Hebrews 7:26

Agents have long played a role in such fields as acting, sports, and publishing. These "middle men" represent their clients to seek the best possible arrangement with an employer.

God established a different kind of "middle man" in ancient Israel: the position of high priest. As the spiritual leader of the people, the high priest represented God to them, teaching them His Law. He also represented them to God, offering sacrifices for their sin.

Prior to preparing and offering sacrifices for the people, the high priest needed to be consecrated, cleansed, and anointed. Then he offered a sacrifice for his own sin. After this, he could enter the Holy of Holies in the tabernacle. There, he sprinkled the blood of the sacrifice on the cover of the Ark, atoning for the nation's sin. When he died, a new high priest replaced him.

Jesus Christ is our perfect high priest. Because He was sinless, He did not need a sacrifice for His sin. Instead, He offered Himself as the spotless sacrifice whose blood atones for our sin.

We do not just have *a* high priest, we have the *best* high priest. He is also our *permanent* high priest—One who will never be replaced.

*Lord God, thank You for providing the perfect high*
*priest to reconcile me to You.*

How does knowing Jesus is my permanent high priest reassure me when I approach God?

# THE MEDIATOR
## Hebrews 8:1–6

We do have such a high priest, who sat down at the
right hand of the throne of the Majesty in heaven.

Hebrews 8:1 NIV

Jesus sat down in heaven.

This doesn't seem like it should be a big deal, until we remember the furniture in the tabernacle. God gave Moses detailed instruction for the construction and furnishing of the tabernacle. While it contained several different articles of furniture, it did not contain any chairs. Since the priests never completed their work of administering sacrifices, they had no time to sit.

The continuous animal sacrifice, however, pointed to the permanent sacrifice to come. Once Christ completed His work as our high priest, He was free to sit.

Now, Jesus's role as mediator of the new covenant provides everything we need as He represents us before God. We can enter God's presence without fear because Jesus has gone before us.

Through Jesus Christ, we have free access to our holy God. We need no other mediator.

> *Heavenly Father, thank You for providing my one*
> *and only mediator, Jesus Christ. Help me never to*
> *take His role for granted.*

Have I used other mediators in approaching God? What does His Word say about them?

# ROYAL PRIESTHOOD
## 1 Peter 2:9–12

You are . . . a royal priesthood . . . people who belong to God.

1 Peter 2:9 GW

We typically consider kings and priests in a class by themselves, rarified positions for those who have special roles in life. If we ever found ourselves in the company of kings and priests, we would be on our best behavior—reverent and deferential.

The apostle Peter called Christians "a chosen race, a royal priesthood, a holy nation, a people for God's own possession." Most Gentile believers have difficulty identifying with these roles. A chosen race? Israel. A royal priesthood? Royalty in Israel descended from the tribe of Judah, and priests descended from the tribe of Levi. A holy nation and God's own possession? Again, we think of the Israelites, descended from Abraham and chosen by God to be His people.

Christians are, indeed, "a royal priesthood." We are united with our high priest, Jesus Christ. Someday, we will rule with Him. Yet our behavior toward each other does not always reflect these identities. We don't treat each other as deferentially as we would treat earthly kings and priests, as deferentially as the personal, prized possession of God Himself.

If we did, we would live up to the title He has given us: a royal priesthood.

*Lord Jesus, forgive me for the times I have treated*
*Your royal priesthood disparagingly.*

What can I do today to encourage fellow Christians in the "royal priesthood"?

# Meek Is Not Weak
## Matthew 11:25–30

I am humble and gentle, and you will find rest for your souls.

Matthew 11:29 NLT

The world does not hold humility in high esteem. Even among Christians, humility is frequently something we know we *should* have, but we rarely *want* it.

We are told to stand up for ourselves and develop our "personal authority." Humble people are weak—doormats to be stepped on in the quest to advance in life.

However, true humility, or meekness, is far from weak. Jesus Christ, humble in His earthly life, exhibited far greater power than any of us can fathom. After fasting for forty days in the wilderness, it took great strength under great control to reject Satan's temptations (Luke 4:1–13). It was certainly not a weak person who overturned the tables of the moneychangers in the temple (Matt. 21:12–13). It took great strength to remain on the cross while the people He was dying for hurled insults at Him.

In meekness, our Savior submitted to the will of His Father, even to an agonizing death on a cross. Jesus's humility provided our salvation. In Him, we find rest for our souls.

*Lord God, thank You for the humility of Jesus that led to my salvation. Help me learn and exhibit humility in my own life.*

What have I learned from Jesus about humility that I can apply today?

# LIKE A CHILD
## Matthew 18:1–6

Therefore, whoever humbles himself like this child
is the greatest in the kingdom of heaven.

Matthew 18:4 NIV

Who are the greatest people in heaven?

The disciples asked Jesus this question, but He did not give them a direct answer. Instead, He warned them that without true humility, they could not even *enter* the kingdom of heaven.

Jesus said we have to become like a child—child*like*, not child*ish*. He did not mean that children are perfect. With no resources of their own, children depend completely on their parents. Children do not ask where their next meal will come from, or if there will be a roof over their head tomorrow night. They simply trust.

We do not easily identify with the dependence of children. We would rather focus on our independence. However, Jesus makes it clear that salvation produces change. New birth gives us a new perspective. We move from being consumed with pride to complete dependence on God.

Those with true humility do not care who the greatest people are. They only want to please their heavenly Father.

*Father, help me trust You in total dependence for
my every need.*

In what area does my attitude need to change today to be more dependent on God?

# WHO GETS THE CREDIT?

## 1 Peter 5:1–7

Furthermore, all of you must serve each other with humility.

1 Peter 5:5 GW

Academy Awards ceremonies often last longer than scheduled due to lengthy acceptance speeches by the recipients. These speeches drag on as winners thank everyone from their agent to their kindergarten teacher. True humility is not always the motivation for these extensive speeches, but the point is still made that we do not succeed on our own.

Pride causes us to take sole credit for our achievements. Humility recognizes that God is the One who gives the ability for those accomplishments. He also places people in our lives—family members, neighbors, co-workers, teachers, friends—who have contributed to who we are today. Good or bad, God uses each one to develop our character and prepare us for His purposes.

Humility also prompts us to defer to the other people in our lives, placing their needs and interests above our own. The world says such behavior makes us pushovers. God tells us that when we do things His way, He will honor us at a time that is best for our good and His glory.

*Lord, I confess the times I have taken credit for what You and others have done. Help me give You the credit for the abilities You have given me to accomplish Your purposes.*

Who has helped me accomplish my goals? How can I communicate my gratitude to them through a telephone call, card, or email today?

# COVERED IN PRAYER
## John 17:13–26

He always lives to make intercession for them.

Hebrews 7:25

Did you know that Jesus prayed for us when He walked on earth two thousand years ago?

In what is known as His "High Priestly Prayer," Jesus prayed for His disciples. He also added, "I do not ask on behalf of these alone, but for those also who believe in Me through their word" (John 17:20). The people He referred to are you and me!

He prayed for us to be sanctified, unified, and that we would glorify God. He prayed we would be kept safe from the devil and that the love of the Father for the Son would be in each of us. He prayed these things then, and the writer of Hebrews tells us Jesus *still* intercedes for us.

What's more, when overwhelming troubles snuff out the slightest whisper of our prayers, we have the added assurance that the Holy Spirit also intercedes for us (Rom. 8:26–27).

When life becomes so difficult that we find ourselves wishing for an "in" with God, remember that the Son and the Spirit are interceding with the Father for His children.

> *Dear Lord, thank You that when I do not know what to pray, Your Son and Your Holy Spirit are interceding for me.*

How does knowing that Jesus is interceding for me with the Father change the way I will approach my problems today?

# SHOULD I PRAY?

## 1 Samuel 12:19–24

It would be unthinkable for me to sin against
the LORD by failing to pray for you.

1 Samuel 12:23 GW

Is intercessory prayer an option or an obligation?

For the prophet Samuel, praying for his fellow Israelites was more than an option or even an obligation. He considered it a sin against God Himself if he did not intercede for them.

Why is intercessory prayer so important? First, it is a measure of our prayer life in general. If we are not praying for others, we are probably not doing much praying at all. Second, when we pray for others, God not only changes them, He changes us. Intercessory prayer causes us to look beyond our own interests as we become aware of the needs and burdens of others. Finally, intercessory prayer is critical if we are having difficulty forgiving someone else. It is almost impossible to stay angry with a person when we ask God to help us see them through His perspective, and pray for Him to bless them abundantly!

Samuel considered intercessory prayer to be more than an option or an obligation. He considered it part of his life's work. We should, too.

*Father, forgive me for the times I have neglected the
privilege of praying for others.*

How much of my daily prayer time is devoted to interceding for others?

# WHAT SHOULD I PRAY?
## Colossians 1:3–12

We have not stopped praying for you.

Colossians 1:9 GW

Praying for unbelievers is usually a straightforward task. Our hearts yearn for them to be reconciled to their heavenly Father and to know their Savior. What about praying for Christians? Since they already have an intimate relationship with God, what should we be praying for them?

The apostle Paul gave us an excellent example of how to pray for other believers. He prayed for the Colossian Christians to be filled with the knowledge of God's will with wisdom and understanding. He prayed this would result in their walking in a manner worthy of the Lord, pleasing Him and bearing fruit in good works. He also prayed for them to *increase* in the knowledge of God, to be strengthened in His power, and to persevere with patience. Finally, he prayed for them to be filled with joy as they gave thanks for their inheritance in Christ. In all these things, Paul prayed with an earnest desire for others to know Christ as intimately as he did.

The next time we want to pray for another Christian but are not sure how to begin, Paul's prayer for the Colossians is a good place to start.

*Heavenly Father, help me pray for others as Your
Holy Spirit brings them to my mind. Show me what
You want me to pray for each person.*

Who is God prompting me to pray for today? How can I intercede for them?

# WHERE IS SIN JUDGED?
## Revelation 20:11–15

Doesn't the Judge of all the Earth judge with justice?

Genesis 18:25 Message

The Judge opens the books. In a loud voice, He reads from the lists, and the defendants hang their heads in shame. Finally, He opens the last book, peruses the names, and then bangs His gavel. Every sin and every person is judged . . . guilty.

The Bible describes a time of final judgment. Those who trust in Jesus Christ's salvation already know their deeds do not measure up to God's holy standards, and they have received the righteousness of Christ. Those who claim to be righteous apart from Jesus Christ will be judged and found guilty according to their deeds. Without Christ's perfect righteousness, their names will not be in the Book of Life and their destiny will be sealed.

God must judge all sin. However, our righteous Judge gives us a choice as to *where* He will judge it: at the foot of the cross of Christ, or at His great white throne of judgment.

God gives us the choice to make, and we live with the consequences.

> *Holy Lord, You are the righteous Judge. Thank You*
> *for showing me how to have my sin judged at the*
> *cross so I will not face Your judgment throne.*

Has my sin been judged at the cross of Christ? If not, why not? If it has, how can I thank God today for the assurance that I have Christ's righteousness?

# JUDGE NOT
## Matthew 7:1–6

Do not judge so that you will not be judged.

Matthew 7:1

"Judge not, lest you be judged" is probably the most frequently quoted Bible verse by non-Christians. Did Jesus mean for us to accept sinful behavior as okay—to *never* judge?

He could *not* have meant for us never to judge, because a few sentences later Jesus warned His followers, "Do not give what is holy to dogs" (Matt. 7:6). The very act of discerning who is or is not a "dog" requires making a judgment. Jesus is saying to use God's standards, not our own (v. 2), and that we must start by judging ourselves (vv. 3–5).

Jesus had already warned His followers not to be like the hypocritical and judgmental Pharisees. Instead, we are to be poor in spirit, mourning sin, meek, hungering and thirsting for God's righteousness, merciful, pure in heart, and peacemakers. Since only God sees the heart, we must never judge another person's motives, but always lovingly point them back to God.

A Christian's judgment is never for *condemnation*, it is always for *restoration*.

> *Heavenly Father, forgive me for the times I have judged the speck in my brother's eye before addressing the log in my own eye.*

By God's standards, am I judgmental? What areas in my own life does the Lord want me to examine and judge?

# NO MAN IS AN ISLAND
## Romans 14:1–13

> Therefore let us stop passing judgment on one
> another. Instead, make up your mind not to put any
> stumbling block or obstacle in your brother's way.
>
> Romans 14:13 NIV

I once ran an obstacle course for a teamwork exercise. Under, over, around, through—the race lasted ten minutes, and I was exhausted by the time I navigated the final obstacle. I took great comfort in knowing that this was a one-time experience, and I have no plans to repeat it!

The apostle Paul noted that Christians place obstacles in the paths of fellow believers every day. We do it whenever we judge other Christians as inferior because we consider them less mature, worldlier, or less knowledgeable than we are.

Some Christians abstain from drinking alcohol, while others enjoy wine in moderation. Some believe women should wear long hair, while others consider hair length a personal preference. Some mark Saturday as our Sabbath, while others honor Sunday as the Lord's Day.

Paul reminds us that we all belong to Christ, and we are answerable only to Him. Rather than judge fellow believers, let's encourage them by not placing obstacles in their path.

> *Dear Lord, help me encourage fellow believers instead of judging them.*

Which other Christians have I judged inferior because they have different preferences? How does the Lord want me to relate to them?

# WHO RULES?

## 1 Samuel 8:1–8

*They have rejected me as their king.*

1 Samuel 8:7 NIV

How many different forms of government can you name? Dictatorship, monarchy, republic, parliamentary, and totalitarian are several types that exist in our world today.

After God delivered the Israelites from Egypt, He gave Moses the law by which He required them to live. Moral laws reflected His holy nature and taught them right from wrong; ceremonial laws included the sacrificial worship that pointed to the coming Messiah; and civil laws established Israel as a theocracy. Other nations had their kings; Israel's ruler was God.

Israel was not content to remain a theocracy. Much like children who want what everyone else has, the people asked the prophet Samuel for a king "like all the nations" (1 Sam 8:5). God told Samuel that by asking for an earthly king, Israel had actually rejected His rule over them.

Although our government today is not a theocracy, Christians still answer to God as our King. He rules our spirits and He reigns in our lives as our supreme authority. May we never reject Yahweh from being King over us.

> *Lord, You are my King and I worship You. Help me submit to Your reign in my life.*

Are there areas of my life where I have been like the Israelites in rejecting God as my King? How can I bring those areas into obedience to my supreme ruler?

# ALLEGIANCE
## Matthew 4:17–23

Listen to my cry for help,
my King and my God.

Psalm 5:2 NIV

*I pledge allegiance to the flag . . ."* How often do we think about the meaning of these words as we say them? Allegiance. Fidelity. Loyalty. Words reminiscent of imperial majesties resplendent in royal regalia, and seemingly out of place in our modern world of chrome and computers.

Our country's flag is not the only thing to which Christians pledge allegiance. We also pledge allegiance to God, our King.

Jesus began His earthly ministry with a message of repentance, "for the kingdom of heaven is at hand" (Matt. 4:17). Then he appointed His disciples and proclaimed the message of the kingdom, a message of spiritual healing and restoration to the Father. He healed physical sickness to illustrate the spiritual healing enjoyed by citizens of His kingdom.

Every kingdom must have a king. Jesus is not just *a* king, He is *the* King. He is *my* King and *your* King, and He demands our allegiance.

*Lord God, You are worthy of all my allegiance.*
*Protect me from anything that would cause me to*
*be disloyal to You.*

Have I been disloyal to the Lord in my thoughts, words, or deeds this past week?

# KING OF NATIONS
## Revelation 15:1–8

King of the nations!
Who will not fear, O Lord, and glorify Your name?

Revelation 15:3–4

Empires rise and fall, eventually passing into oblivion. Ancient history saw Egypt, Assyria, Babylon, Persia, Greece, and Rome rise and fall as world leaders, their names evoking fear among their contemporaries. In the past century, the development of nuclear power and the rise of superpower nations such as the United States and Russia influenced world events.

Today, things like terrorism, epidemics, and natural disasters cause nations to fear.

Christians should not look to governments for solutions to humanity's problems. We must remember our earthly citizenship is temporary. The apostle Paul reminded us, "For our citizenship is in heaven, from which also we eagerly wait for a Savior, the Lord Jesus Christ" (Phil. 3:20). We need not fear economic meltdowns, news of the latest epidemic, or terrorist strikes. We need only look to our king.

Someday, the nations of the world will fear the King of nations—the Lord God. Jesus Christ will take His rightful place to rule over the earth, and all the nations will worship Him.

*Lord, You are my King. Help me be an example to others as I look to You for security.*

How have I expected the government to solve problems only my God and King can solve?

# THE LAMB

## Revelation 5:11–14

Worthy is the Lamb, who was slain.
Revelation 5:12 NIV

Why a lamb? Of all the animals on earth, why would the God of the universe choose to call His Son a lamb?

Israel's annual Passover sacrifice commemorated the substitute accepted by God during the final Egyptian plague. Death had "passed over" His people because they placed lamb's blood on their doorposts. The Passover lamb was more than an annual sacrifice, though. It pointed to another Lamb—God's perfect Lamb, killed so that we would also escape death.

Lambs are gentle, harmless, and defenseless. God's Son stood before His accusers and did not defend Himself. His silence fulfilled Isaiah's prophecy, "He was oppressed and afflicted, yet he did not open his mouth; he was led like a lamb to the slaughter, and as a sheep before her shearers is silent, so he did not open his mouth" (Isa. 53:7 NIV). The unblemished Passover lamb pointed to the sinless Savior who died for our sins instead of His own.

Jesus Christ is not *like* a lamb; He *is* "the Lamb of God who takes away the sin of the world!" (John 1:29).

*Lamb of God, I can never thank You enough for taking away my sin with Your sacrifice.*

How does knowing the Lamb of God affect how I approach my heavenly Father?

# MY LAMB

Exodus 12:3–11

On the tenth day of this month each man
is to take a lamb for his family.

Exodus 12:3 NIV

It doesn't take long to become attached to a pet. A few days and a name are often enough.

When the Israelites celebrated the Passover, each family selected a lamb. Then they kept the lamb for four days, from the day they chose it to the day they sacrificed it.

The family would feed and care for the lamb, knowing that in a few days it would give its life for them. The children might even play with it until the fateful day. Parents might have warned their children not to become too attached, knowing that this new playmate would soon be sacrificed on their behalf. A sacrifice that became personal.

Israelite families would look for *a* lamb among the flock and then select *the* lamb to care for until Passover. Finally, as they sacrificed the lamb, they would acknowledge that it was *their* lamb, killed in their place.

God didn't just provide *a* lamb for our salvation, He provided *the* Lamb—His Son. When we trust Christ's sacrifice for us, He becomes *my* Lamb and *your* Lamb. He becomes personal.

*Heavenly Father, how it must have wrenched Your heart to see Your Son sacrificed for my sin. I worship the Lamb—my Lamb—today.*

How personal is Jesus Christ's sacrifice to me? How personal *should* it be?

# LAMBS AMONG WOLVES
## Luke 10:1–16

Go! I'm sending you out like lambs among wolves.

Luke 10:3 GW

Military experts agree that the most lopsided battle in history is the Battle of Thermopylae in 480 BC, where the Persians outnumbered the Greeks twenty to one. Other lopsided battles include the Battle of the Alamo in 1836, where the Texans were outnumbered ten to one, and the invasion of Poland in 1939, where Germans outnumbered Polish forces ten to one.

Sometimes, as Christians, we may feel outnumbered as we try to live our relationship with Christ in our daily routines. At work, at school, in the community, or in our own families, we may feel like the only Christian, outnumbered by the unbelievers around us.

When Jesus sent seventy of His followers out, He warned them they would be "lambs in the midst of wolves"—outnumbered and vulnerable. If they were rejected, He told them not to argue, debate, or battle, but simply proclaim the truth, wipe the city's dust from their sandals, and leave.

We can learn from their example. Arguing may win us the battle but lose us the person. Outnumbered or not, God calls us to respond to others according to who we are: His lambs.

*Lord God, help me follow the example of Your
Lamb as I go out into a hostile world.*

How is Jesus's response to His enemies an example to me today?

# A NEW HEART
## John 3:1–13

I am the way, the truth, and the life.

John 14:6 GW

Irreversible heart failure was once an automatic death sentence. Today, heart bypasses, valve replacements, and heart transplants provide patients new life.

Heart transplants may be relatively recent medical procedures, but the Lord has been in the business of transplanting new hearts for thousands of years. Speaking through the prophet Ezekiel, God described how He would replace the old covenant with the new covenant. "I will give you a new heart and put a new spirit within you; and I will remove the heart of stone from your flesh and give you a heart of flesh" (Ezek. 36:26).

Jesus fulfilled Ezekiel's prophecy and instituted the new covenant. He told Nicodemus that without a new heart, there is no hope of salvation. "Unless one is born again he cannot see the kingdom of God" (John 3:3). Entrance into the kingdom of heaven is only by new life.

A new heart means new life, and both are found only in Jesus Christ.

*Lord God, You have given me eternal life where death once reigned. Help me live this new life according to the Holy Spirit You have placed in me.*

How is the new heart God has given me different from my old heart? How can I live out these differences today?

# NOW
## John 5:18–24

He who hears My word, and believes Him
who sent Me, has eternal life.

John 5:24

When does eternal life begin?
Some Christians believe eternal life begins at the moment of physical death, when our spirit goes to be with the Lord for eternity. That is not what the Bible tells us.

Jesus said that if we believe in Him, taking God at His Word that our salvation is found in Christ alone, we have eternal life *now*. Yes, we will be with the Lord when we die, but we do not have to wait until then to experience the joy and the power of eternal life.

Salvation is more than a formula prayer spoken in anticipation of the day we face death. Salvation provides a restored relationship with God *now*. It gives us the indwelling of God's Holy Spirit *now*. It brings power to say no to sin *now*.

We who trust Christ as our personal Savior have already "passed out of death into life" (John 5:24). For us, the gift of eternal life has already begun.

*Heavenly Father, thank You for the gift of eternal life. Help me rely on Your Holy Spirit to partake of all the blessings eternal life brings me in this life.*

What aspects of my eternal relationship with God have I been neglecting to apply? How can I begin to apply them today?

# CULTIVATE LIFE
## Proverbs 18:19–24

The tongue has the power of life and death.

Proverbs 18:21 GW

I killed another potted plant today. First I forgot to water it; then I drowned it to make up for my neglect. It finally gave up the fight for life as its last leaf dropped off the shriveled stem.

I made several mistakes with this plant. I did not read the instructions for its care that accompanied it. Of course, that meant I did not know how much water and sunlight it required. I also did not consider the cultivation of this plant a priority in my daily list of things to do.

People are more important than plants, yet we often treat them with even less care. Think about the people God has placed closest to us. What are their hopes, dreams, and aspirations? What are their hurts and insecurities? How do they express and receive love? Do they know the Lord? If they do, are they growing in Him? If we do not know the answers to these questions, we will not be able to speak blessing into their lives. Instead, we may speak irreparable harm.

Rather than alternating between neglect and killing others with kindness, let's use our tongues to cultivate life.

*Dear Lord, help me to be sensitive to the heart's desires of those around me. Thank you for the opportunity to cultivate life by speaking blessing into their lives.*

In what specific way can I use my tongue to cultivate life in those around me today?

# DISPELLING THE DARKNESS
## John 9:1–12

*While I am in the world, I am the light of the world.*

John 9:5 NIV

One match. One candle. One light bulb. One source of light is all we need to send darkness scurrying. This is what God did when He invaded our sin-sick world.

Spiritually dark forces work overtime to keep us from being restored to our Creator. Because of our sin nature, we are spiritually blind. If our heavenly Father had not taken the initiative, we would be helpless to find our way to Him.

God did not leave us to stumble around, helpless and alone, searching for Him in the dark. The light of His presence invaded our darkness when He sent His Son. Jesus called Himself the Light of the world. The Source of light sent His Light to show us the way back to the Father.

Jesus illustrated the spiritual sight He brings when He healed the man who had been born blind. When the disciples asked why the man was blind, Jesus explained that the purpose for the blindness was to display the work of God.

Today, God is still dispelling the darkness to light our way to Him, using our lives as a canvas to display His glory.

> *Light of the World, thank You for sending Your light into my darkness.*

How is God using my life to display the light of His works?

# WALK IN THE LIGHT
## Ephesians 5:7–14

Do not participate in the unfruitful deeds
of darkness, but . . . expose them.

Ephesians 5:11

Headlines broadcasting details of public figures caught in sin occur with disturbing regularity. Public apologies follow close behind. The apologies, however, usually label the behavior as a lapse in judgment, a mistake, or an inappropriate action—anything but sin.

Before we point fingers at others, what is the first thing *we* do after we sin? If we are like many, we might explain it, excuse it, or blame someone else—anything but identify it as sin.

God tells us the first thing we must do when we sin is to expose it. We are to bring the sin into the light by confessing it to Him. Confession means agreeing with God, calling sin what God calls it. No more justifying, denying, or rationalizing. When we confess sin, He exposes it for what it is and shines the light of His forgiveness and cleansing.

Sin's darkness keeps us from the light of God's presence. Confession keeps us walking in His light.

*Heavenly Father, forgive me for the times I have delayed running to You when I sin. Help me to quickly confess sin, so that nothing blocks the light of Your presence in my life.*

What sin in my life have I been excusing, justifying, or denying? What will I do today to bring that dark area into the light of God's forgiveness and cleansing?

# ILLUMINATION
## Isaiah 58:1–12

Then your light will rise in darkness
And your gloom will become like midday.

Isaiah 58:10

Look at me, God! Look at all the good, religious things I'm doing! Aren't You impressed with my self-denial and my fasts and my spirituality?"

Like a child showing off for a parent, the people of ancient Israel tried to impress God with their religious behavior. But God was not impressed because of the huge inconsistency between their religious behavior and every other part of their lives. They mistreated employees, oppressed the less fortunate, and turned their backs on the hungry and the homeless.

What about us? Would the people we worship with on Sunday recognize us Monday through Friday? Are our lives so consumed with our own interests that we neglect the less fortunate around us? Have we made any effort to defend those who cannot defend themselves?

Shining the light of the gospel of Jesus Christ involves more than walking around with a Bible and preaching to people. Jesus met the physical needs of others to show how much their heavenly Father cared for them. He calls us to shine His light and make it our own by doing the same. When we do, our light illuminates our dark world and God is glorified.

*Dear Lord, help me shine Your light by meeting the needs of others in Jesus's name.*

What can I do today to shine the light of Christ in my world?

# HE RULES
## Genesis 49:1–2, 8–12

The Lion from the tribe of Judah . . . has won the victory.

Revelation 5:5 GW

In the pecking order of the animal kingdom, few animals are a threat to the lion. No wonder, then, that the king of the jungle symbolizes the power and status of the tribe of Judah.

Jacob summoned his sons for a final word of blessing and prophecy prior to his death. The three oldest brothers—Reuben, Simeon, and Levi—had disqualified themselves from positions of blessing by their past behavior. Jacob elevated Judah to a position of honor, and illustrated his tribe's prosperity by describing an abundance of the fruit of the vine.

Judah's tribe was also to be the kingly line, and it was from him that King David descended. The Messiah, Israel's long-awaited king and the One from whom "the scepter shall not depart" (Gen. 49:10), would also be a descendant of Judah.

Jesus Christ *is* the Lion of Judah. To Him is "the obedience of the peoples" (Gen. 49:10). Those who do not bow before Him now will bow before Him when He returns.

> *Lion of Judah, I worship You as the One who rules*
> *and reigns forever. Take Your rightful place as ruler*
> *of my life.*

Is there an area of my life I have not brought under the rule of Jesus, the Lion of Judah? How can I honor Jesus's kingship in my life today?

# RIGHTEOUS BOLDNESS
## Proverbs 28:1–12

Righteous people are as bold as lions.

Proverbs 28:1 GW

There is something to be said for a clear conscience.

A guilty conscience causes us to lose sleep as we worry about the consequences of discovery. It triggers us to check and double-check our "story" to ensure that we have not contradicted one falsehood with another. A guilty conscience forces us to look over our shoulder, constantly expecting to be discovered and found guilty.

The righteous are spared from suffering these consequences. They sleep peacefully, their conscience clear. The righteous need not worry if their words are contradictory, since they only speak the truth. The righteous also do not fear discovery, since they have nothing to hide.

As a result, righteous people are confident and secure. They can face people and circumstances with a holy boldness that comes from belonging to a righteous God.

When we belong to the Lion of Judah, we have His righteousness. When we have His righteousness, we can be "bold as lions."

*Lion of Judah, thank You for Your righteousness.*
*Strengthen me to stand boldly and confidently in Your*
*righteousness no matter what my circumstances.*

In what situation do I need the boldness of a lion? What might be sapping my boldness?

# A BALANCED VIEW
## Revelation 19:11–16

A sharp sword comes out of his mouth to defeat the
nations. He will rule them with an iron scepter.

Revelation 19:15 GW

The first time Jesus came, He did not look like a lion. He did not act like a lion. He did not roar like a lion. Meek and mild, Jesus seemed to be more of an annoyance to His enemies than a threat. Yet they feared Him enough to have Him executed.

If they feared Him then, how much more will His enemies fear Him when He returns?

Today, non-Christians dismiss a coming judgment as an absurd notion. To them, Jesus was nothing more than a philosopher known for the Golden Rule. Perhaps that is because Christians often speak of Him as the tender Shepherd, the wise Teacher, and the loving Forgiver.

However, someday Jesus will return in a different role. The next time He appears on earth, it will be to wage war and bring judgment. He will strike His enemies and rule creation.

We have a responsibility to provide a balanced view of Jesus Christ to non-Christians. Yes, He is the tender Shepherd who cares for His lambs, but He is also the Lion of Judah who will subdue His enemies.

*Lord, help me share a balanced view of who You
are with those who do not know You.*

Do I speak more of the Lord's love or His judgment? How can I accurately share both?

# SORROW UPON SORROW
## Isaiah 53:1–5

He was a man of sorrows, familiar with suffering.

Isaiah 53:3 GW

Despised and forsaken. Grieved and stricken. Pierced, crushed, and scourged. The prophet Isaiah's graphic description of the Messiah validates the title *Man of Sorrows*.

God became man—a man whose life overflowed with the joy of doing His Father's will, but a man whose life also brimmed with sorrow.

At the beginning of Jesus's life, a king wanted Him dead. Thirty years later, His cousin was executed for speaking truth, foreshadowing Jesus's own death. Despite His miraculous displays of authority and power, the religious leaders rejected Him. A fickle populace first hailed, then turned on Him. One follower betrayed Him, and the remaining eleven abandoned Him. After a sham trial, He was brutally beaten and cruelly executed. Worst of all, in His final agonizing moments, His Father turned His face from Him.

Jesus did it all for you and me, so we would never have to know the sorrow of the Father turning His face away from us.

*Jesus, thank You for suffering for my sin and taking my penalty so I will never have to.*

How much do I appreciate the unbroken fellowship I have with the Father because of Jesus's death on the cross? How can I show my appreciation to Him today?

# SORROWFUL REPENTANCE
## 2 Corinthians 7:1–11

For behold what earnestness this very thing,
this godly sorrow, has produced in you.

2 Corinthians 7:11

Little Missy was caught shoving her sister. "What do you say?" her mother asked. "I'm sorry," Missy said. "Sorry for what?" Mom asked. Missy scrunched her nose and thought for a moment. "I'm sorry I got caught!"

True sorrow for sin is critical. In the course of the apostle Paul's ongoing correspondence with the Corinthian church, he had found it necessary to rebuke them in a previous letter. In this letter, however, he rejoiced in their response. Rather than reacting with a shallow or hypocritical response, they eagerly repented in godly sorrow.

What about us, today? Are we more like little Missy or more like the Corinthian Christians? When we are caught in sin, are we sorrowful for the embarrassment and consequences of being caught, or are we sorrowfully repentant for our offense against our holy God?

*Man of Sorrows, give me a heart that is sorrowfully repentant for my sin.*

What causes me greater sorrow: the embarrassment of being caught in sin or the knowledge that I have offended God? How can I develop a godly sorrow in repentance today?

# WEEPING WITH OTHERS
## Romans 12:14–21

Rejoice with those who rejoice, and weep with those who weep.

Romans 12:15

"Jesus wept." The shortest verse in the Bible (John 11:35) is also one of the most emotional verses in the Bible. *God* wept. God *wept.*

Humans have a wonderful capacity for empathy. Unfortunately, we also have an immense capacity for self-centeredness. Self-centeredness comes naturally; empathy is nurtured. Because of this, the apostle Paul exhorted us to cultivate an outward focus. We are to "rejoice with those who rejoice, and weep with those who weep."

It should be easy to feel sorrow for someone else's bad news. Unless, of course, we don't like the person or they have hurt us. Then it is not so easy. However, Paul wrote that we are not to look down on others. We are not to return evil for evil or take revenge. Rather, we are to bless our persecutors and be kind to our enemies. If they weep, we are to sorrow with them.

Empathy with others flows out of our relationship with the Man of Sorrows. He is the One who gives us the capacity to "weep with those who weep."

> *Man of Sorrows, thank You for Your compassionate love. Help me to sorrow with those who weep, regardless of how they have treated me.*

Who needs me to weep with them today? How can I share this person's sorrow?

# WITH THE NAKED EYE
## 2 Peter 1:16–21

I am the bright morning star.

Revelation 22:16 GW

Venus is regularly visible as a radiant light in the dark, early morning sky. The brightest of the planets—only the sun and moon are brighter—it can be seen with the naked eye. In ancient times, people named it the "morning star" because it appeared right before the rising of the sun.

Jesus Christ referred to Himself as the "bright morning star" (Rev. 22:16 GW). The mystery of the coming of the Messiah was finally revealed in Him. His appearance enabled people to see God with the naked eye. Unlike when the Lord told Moses "no man can see Me and live" (Exod. 33:20), God walked among and with men and women in the person of Christ, and they were "eyewitnesses of His majesty" (2 Pet. 1:16).

The light of prophets, priests, and kings shined brightly throughout Israel's history, but Jesus shined the brightest in each of these roles. As prophet, He proclaimed the words of His heavenly Father. As priest, He offered up the only sacrifice that could restore us to God. As king, He rules and reigns forever.

Someday, our Bright Morning Star will return, brighter than the sun, moon, or Venus, and every eye will see Him.

*Lord, I praise You, for the brightness of my Bright Morning Star has drawn me to You.*

Do I begin each day by spending time with the Bright Morning Star? If not, why not?

# WANDERING STARS
## Jude 10–16

> They are wandering stars, heading for
> everlasting gloom and darkness.
>
> Jude 13 NLT

The tabloid headlines shout to me as I stand in line at the supermarket checkout. I shake my head at the shocking lifestyles and wonder what has become of former stars as new celebrities grab the headlines and compete for my attention.

The Bible speaks of such people as stars who wander from their courses, following their own designs. Their "end is destruction, whose god is their appetite, and whose glory is in their shame" (Phil. 3:19). They will pass into darkness.

Yet others labor for God without recognition: missionaries toiling in foreign fields; parents who adopt special-needs older children; pastors who minister in anonymity to the sick, hungry, and homeless. These are true bright lights.

To whom are we drawn? Do we know as much about the life of missionary Hudson Taylor as we do about the latest politician who had an affair? Are we as interested in the life of hymn writer Fanny Crosby as we are in the famous rock star who divorced the diva?

Wandering stars will be forever forgotten. True bright lights will shine for eternity.

*Father, help me remember that the light of a life*
*lived for Your glory will last for eternity.*

Am I drawn more to lights who will fade or lights who will shine for eternity?

# CELESTIAL NAVIGATION
## Philippians 2:12–18

You shine like stars in the universe.

Philippians 2:15 NIV

Prior to the advent of satellite navigation systems such as the Global Positioning System (GPS), travelers relied on celestial navigation. Using bright celestial bodies such as the moon, planets, or stars, seafaring navigators determined position and direction. Even lost campers have found their way home by relying on the dependable North Star.

The apostle Paul said we are to live out our salvation in daily life by clinging to God's Word and holding it out to others. When we do, we shine like stars in a dark world. Our consistency and integrity provide the light and direction needed by those around us.

Non-Christians watch us to see if what we have is real. If we respond to difficulties and trials with complaints and arguments, we are no different from unbelievers. When our behavior is consistent with what we claim to believe, others see the reality of a relationship with Christ.

People are desperate for dependable direction. Live in a way that lights their world.

*Dear Lord, I want my life to shine for You. Help me live in a way that demonstrates to others the reality and power of a relationship with Jesus Christ.*

Has my behavior this week been a light to others? How can I hold out the light of God's Word to those around me today?

# TOTALLY PURE
## 1 John 3:1–10

Everyone who has this hope fixed on Him
purifies himself, just as He is pure.

1 John 3:3

What is the longest you have lasted without sinning before you became a Christian? A minute? An hour? How about after you became a Christian? Are you frustrated by your failure to grow in purity?

The only One who is truly pure is God. John wrote, "In Him there is no sin" (1 John 3:5). Not the smallest hint of the slightest contaminant. Not a wrong thought or a wrong motive. Not a wrong plan or a wrong action. No sin *at all*.

It is almost impossible for us to wrap our minds around the concept of such purity. The innocence of a newborn is not as pure as God. The brightest, most intense light does not achieve His purity. The fragile, crystalline structure of the whitest snowflake is not as pure as He is.

Yet God tells us we can be made pure, just as He is pure. Christ's sacrifice enables us to exchange our sin for His righteousness. Someday we will be like Him, and we will see God just as He is. Until then, we fix our hope on the purity He provides, and thank God for Jesus Christ.

> *Holy Lord, I worship You because You are pure beyond my understanding. Although I do not deserve it, I thank You for giving me Your purity.*

How can I "fix my hope" on Christ today to gain the purity God gives?

# CLEAN ROOMS
## 2 Timothy 2:14–26

> Pursue righteousness . . . with those who
> call on the Lord from a pure heart.
>
> 2 Timothy 2:22

Fragile or sensitive products, such as microchips or pharmaceuticals, are often manufactured in environments called *clean rooms*. Air filter systems minimize contamination from pollutants. Workers wear protective clothing. Even the type of furniture and equipment that may be brought into the room is restricted.

In his classic booklet, *My Heart—Christ's Home*, Robert Boyd Munger imagines his heart to be a home, with Jesus walking through the rooms. Munger views the contents of each room—including closets—through the eyes of Jesus, and he realizes his home is not as free from sin as he had thought.

When we come to Christ, He forgives our sin. Still, temptation hounds us as we face hundreds of choices each day. We can become vessels of dishonor by giving in to wickedness and lust, or we can pursue righteousness with those "who call on the Lord from a pure heart."

Although we are bombarded with pollutants from the world around us, Christ makes us cleaner than any clean room.

*Heavenly Father, I give You every room of my heart*
*to clean to Your standard of purity.*

What closets in my life have I been holding back from God's cleansing touch?

# ABOVE REPROACH
## Titus 1:5–16

To those who are corrupted and do not believe, nothing is pure.

Titus 1:15 NIV

C hristians are a bunch of self-righteous killjoys." "I don't go to church because of all the hypocrites." "Christians quote the Bible to justify their own agendas."

These are a few of the negative stereotypes the world has of Christians. It is true that *some* Christians are self-righteous, *some* Christians are hypocritical, and *some* Christians quote the Bible for self-serving reasons, but not *all* Christians do these things.

Stereotypes are not new. The apostle Paul left Titus in Crete to establish leadership for the local church. He also gave Titus standards for selecting leadership to dispel stereotypes about Cretans. Still, Paul understood that despite impeccable leadership, non-Christians would still not recognize true purity because their minds are defiled. They preferred stereotypes, because the alternative leads to truth, which leads to Christ. They would rather deny Him than bow to Him.

We may not be able to eradicate the world's stereotypical perspective of Christians. We can, however, live in a way that is above reproach and point them to the One who will give them the purity they lack and the restored relationship they need.

> Lord God, help me depend on You to live a pure
> life, above reproach.

How have I contributed to negative Christian stereotypes held by unbelievers around me?

# NO LONGER ENEMIES
## Romans 5:6–11

*While we were enemies we were reconciled to God.*

Romans 5:10

Do you know someone who is sitting on a fence? When it comes to God, many people today consider themselves fence-sitters, the religious version of a neutral Switzerland. They have nothing against God, but neither are they ready to align themselves with Him.

Yet the Bible tells us that we were enemies of God before we knew Christ. *Enemies* is a strong word. It means we were hostile to God. Jesus said, "He who is not with Me is against Me; and he who does not gather with Me, scatters" (Luke 11:23). There is no such thing as neutral ground in a relationship with God. Those who are not in Christ are, in effect, at war with Him.

Even so, God initiates a restored relationship with Him. He reaches into the trench of sin we have dug for ourselves, and He reconciles us to Him through His Son. Our choice is to stay in the trench at war with God, or receive the salvation and restoration He offers.

When it comes to God, people cannot sit on a fence . . . because there *is* no fence.

> *Lord God, thank You for reconciling me to You while I was still Your enemy. Thank You, even more, for doing it through the precious offering of Your Son.*

How does knowing that I was once God's enemy help me view the salvation I now have in Christ? How does it help me view the nonbelievers around me?

# BE THE FIRST
## Matthew 5:21–26

First go and be reconciled to your brother;
then come and offer your gift.

Matthew 5:24 NIV

Relationships can shift from friendship to enmity in an instant, the consequence of a word spoken in anger or an action viewed as a betrayal. It is much more difficult to restore such a relationship back to intimate friendship. At best, we may permit ourselves a grudging tolerance of the other person.

Christians can be particularly skilled at veiling grudges. We know anger toward others is wrong, so we hide it, allowing it to smolder into seething resentment. We play word games: "I'm not bitter, I'm *hurt*." We wait for the other person to make the first move.

However, in order to continue in our reconciled relationship with God, Jesus said we should seek reconciliation with others, rather than settle for a grudging tolerance. Regardless of whether we are responsible for the offense, we must initiate reconciliation, as God did with us.

We cannot force others to reconcile with us, but we *can* make the first move.

*Father, it is difficult to seek reconciliation with one who has hurt me. Help me remember that I have hurt You more, yet You initiated reconciliation with me.*

Is there someone in my life who has something against me? How can I take a first step toward reconciliation today?

# ONE MINISTRY FOR ALL
## 2 Corinthians 5:10–21

God, who reconciled us . . . gave us the ministry of reconciliation.

2 Corinthians 5:18 NIV

What is your ministry? Every Christian has one. You might be an usher, a greeter, or a groundskeeper. You could be a member of a prayer team, the hospitality team, or the nursery staff. You might serve in the bookstore, work in the church office, or volunteer as a youth leader. In addition to these and other options, every Christian also has a ministry of reconciliation.

While some people wonder at the future of humanity and the world, we already know what will happen. God will judge humanity for sin and rejection of His Son. Therefore, the apostle Paul said, "knowing the fear of the Lord, we persuade men" (2 Cor. 5:11).

We do not persuade them to our way of thinking, nor try to convert them to a particular church denomination. We do not persuade them to be better people, nor to live a moral life. Paul said our ministry is to make a single appeal: "on behalf of Christ, be reconciled to God" (2 Cor. 5:20).

We may serve in many different ministries, but we *all* have the ministry of reconciliation.

*Holy Lord, help me speak the message of reconciliation through Jesus Christ to a world separated from You and destined for judgment.*

When I speak to others of my faith, do I focus more on persuading people to my way of thinking or to a relationship with the person of Christ?

# REDEMPTION
### Job 19:23–29

I know that my Redeemer lives.

Job 19:25 NIV

We don't speak much of *redemption* today. The word may pop up in an old movie or two, but apart from the Bible, the only experience many people have with redemption is when they redeem coupons at the supermarket.

The theme of redemption runs through the entire Bible. Redemption describes the process by which a ransom was paid to obtain a slave's freedom. God redeemed—bought back—His people from Egyptian slavery. Then He used this event to illustrate how He would one day redeem His people from slavery to sin and the clutches of death.

When Job spoke the precious words, "I know that my Redeemer lives," he did not know when, where, or how God would redeem His people. We have the advantage of looking back to the cross and knowing the purchase price of our redemption was the life of God's own Son.

Jesus Christ, our Redeemer, does indeed live.

> *Redeemer, You are the only One who could pay the price to purchase me out of the slave market of sin and death. Help me remember the price You paid for me.*

What was my life like before God redeemed me? How can I thank Him for my redemption?

# TRAPPED
## Romans 7:14–25

Who will set me free from the body of this death?

Romans 7:24

Trapped, with no way out. This is how it feels to be a slave to sin. Even if we want to change, we can't. Waves of despair engulf us. We may feel like we are stuck in a pool of quicksand: the more we struggle and fight to get out, the faster and deeper we sink.

The apostle Paul understood the frustration of this slavery. He wrote, "For the good that I want, I do not do, but I practice the very evil that I do not want" (Rom. 7:19). His cry echoes across history to pierce our hearts. "Wretched man that I am! Who will set me free from the body of this death?" (Rom. 7:24).

There is only one answer to his question. Only one Redeemer. Only one way out. "Thanks be to God through Jesus Christ our Lord!" (Rom. 7:25). Freedom comes from receiving His redemption and surrendering to His authority in our lives, moment by moment and day by day.

We can try harder and sink faster. Or we can cling to our Redeemer, Jesus Christ, and rely on the freedom He has purchased for us.

*Heavenly Father, help me remember that it is Your redemption, not my efforts, that frees me from slavery to sin.*

What habit has me trapped? How can I rely on Christ's redemption for freedom in this area today?

# FUTILITY
## 1 Peter 1:17–25

> You were not redeemed with perishable things
> . . . from your futile way of life.
>
> 1 Peter 1:18

Have you ever watched a hamster on a wheel? Round and round he goes, but he goes . . . nowhere.

When the apostle Peter wrote to the early Christians, he reminded them that they had been redeemed from a futile way of life. Peter spoke of the futility of trying to keep God's laws while struggling against the power of sin's slavery. Jesus redeems us from this discouraging way of life. He entered sin's slave market, paid our purchase price, and released our shackles.

However, it is not enough to live in the freedom of our redemption without a thought for those who are still trapped in slavery. Others told us about the Redeemer. It might have been through a conversation, a book, a church service, or a television program. Now it is our turn to communicate the gift of redemption to free others from the slave market of sin.

If we love the people around us, we will not leave them trapped in a life of futility. Whose shackles will we help release today?

*Dearest Lord, help me share the gift of redemption
today with other slaves to sin.*

---

Who do I know who is struggling with the futility of life? How can I begin to share the gift of Christ's redemption with this person today?

# OUR RECEIPT
### John 20:1–18

I am the resurrection . . . he who
believes in Me will live even if he dies.

John 11:25

I am a stickler for keeping receipts. After a frustrating experience in which I failed to retain proof that I had paid for an expensive service, I now keep receipts for all my purchases. A receipt proves that my purchase is paid in full.

When Jesus Christ was dying on the cross, one of the last things He said was, "It is finished" (John 19:30). This same phrase was also used in New Testament times to describe the full payment of a commercial debt. His death paid our sin-debt and fully satisfied God's justice.

Jesus Christ declared Himself the resurrection and the life as He looked beyond His approaching death to what He knew would follow. His resurrection would prove His claim to be the Great "I Am." It would also prove God's acceptance of His substitutionary sacrifice. We need never worry that God will demand an extra payment. Nothing more is required for our salvation other than the price Christ already paid.

Our sin-debt really is paid in full, and the empty tomb is our receipt.

*Holy Lord, I rejoice in the resurrection of Jesus*
*Christ, my Savior, and in the knowledge that my*
*sin-debt to You has been paid in full.*

What does it mean to me today that God requires nothing more for payment of my sin?

# FIRST FRUITS
## 1 Corinthians 15:12–28

And if Christ has not been raised, our preaching is useless.

1 Corinthians 15:14 NIV

I spent most of my life living with cold, dreary winters. Each February I dreamt of spring as I shoveled snow from the sidewalk and scraped ice from my windshield. Just when it seemed winter would never leave, a tiny crocus would poke through the snow, reminding me new life was on its way.

Jesus's resurrection is our promise of new life. The apostle Paul referred to the resurrection as "the first fruits" (1 Cor. 15:20)—a reference to what each person who trusts in Christ will experience. When we die, our spirit will go to be with the Lord. A day will come, however, when He will also raise our bodies to resurrected life.

Everything we believe hinges on the resurrection. This earthly existence is only the beginning of life. As Paul said, "If we have hoped in Christ in this life only, we are of all men most to be pitied" (1 Cor. 15:19).

When we find life cold and dreary, when it seems that death surrounds us, look to the resurrection. New life is on its way.

*Father, thank You for the assurance of life You give*
*me through Christ's resurrection.*

What situation causes me discouragement today? How can the promise of resurrection change my perspective?

# UNLESS I SEE
## John 20:19–29

I refuse to believe this unless I see the nail marks in his hands.

John 20:25 GW

Poor "Doubting" Thomas! He has gotten a bad rap ever since he asked for positive proof of Jesus's resurrection. Then again, the rest of us are not so very different. How many times have *we* asked God for a "sign" before we obey His promptings?

It should be no surprise, then, that non-Christians are skeptical of Jesus Christ's resurrection. They question biblical accounts and object to anything that requires what they call "blind faith." Too often, Christians respond fearfully and defensively to these perceived attacks.

God does not ask us to argue with unbelievers. Neither should we be afraid of their questions. The resurrection of Christ—and everything else about Him—stands up to any and all scrutiny. There is actually nothing "blind" about our faith. We have the written testimony of the Bible, two thousand years of history to look back on since the cross, and the personal experience of the indwelling of the Holy Spirit to validate every claim of Christ, including His resurrection.

People will always have questions. Jesus Christ always has the answers.

*Lord, help me share Jesus and His resurrection with*
*a world searching for answers.*

How do I respond when non-Christians ask me about my faith? What can I do this week to better prepare to answer those questions?

# SOLID GROUND
## Psalm 62:1–12

He only is my rock and my salvation,
My stronghold; I shall not be shaken.

Psalm 62:6

Humans can feel only about 20 percent of the 500,000 detectable earthquakes that shake our world each year. Of those, only one-tenth of one percent are strong enough to cause damage. However, these numbers offer little comfort to someone whose world has just been rocked by a severe earthquake.

Some earthquake survivors lose confidence in the very ground they walk on. One moment the earth beneath their feet is stable, the next moment it is shifting. What does one hold on to when the very foundations are shaken?

The Bible reminds us that God is the one reliable reality in an unstable world. In 1 Corinthians 10:4, the apostle Paul described Jesus Christ as the "rock." Not only is God *the* rock, the psalmist called Him "*my* rock." God is a personal anchor who will never fail.

When our very foundations are shaken, we hold on to our Rock.

> Lord God, I praise You, for You are the solid ground
> in my changing world. Help me cling to You alone
> for the security and stability I need.

Who or what do I hold on to when my world is shaken? What do those around me see me holding on to?

# FIRM FOOTSTEPS
## Psalm 40:1–10

He set my feet on a rock and made my steps secure.

Psalm 40:2 GW

How long were you trapped in sin before the Lord rescued you? Was it early or late in life that God set you on the solid rock of Jesus Christ? Some of us had been caught in sin for so long that we may not have realized its effects until Christ rescued us.

Thankfully, we know that Christ *did* rescue us. The psalmist described how He did it. First, God brought us up out of the pit of destruction, a pit that did not easily release us. Then He set us on the strong rock of Jesus Christ. We are no longer caught in the miry clay of sin that impeded our walk with the Lord. Our steps are now secure. Finally, He gave us a new song, so that we might praise our Redeemer and our Rock.

Once He has set us safely on the Rock, we can live one of two ways. We can hide in a corner, fearful of slipping back into the pit, or we can walk boldly in the confidence that He will keep our footsteps secure.

Stretch your legs and walk confidently upon your Rock.

*Heavenly Father, help me stand boldly on the solid rock of Jesus Christ.*

How have I been hesitant or fearful in living out my salvation? In what area is God beckoning me to step out with confidence in Him?

# THE SHAKING
## Hebrews 12:18–28

Therefore, we must be thankful that we have
a kingdom that cannot be shaken.

Hebrews 12:28 GW

A shaking is coming, worse than the most powerful earthquake or the strongest hurricane. Our world as we know it will be shaken from its foundations. Those who belong to Christ, however, belong to an unshakable kingdom that will remain when all else passes away.

The writer of the book of Hebrews noted that those who belong to the unshakable kingdom should have one response. "Because we are thankful, we must serve God with fear and awe in a way that pleases him" (Heb. 12:28 GW). A life of reverential service to God will always touch the lives of others. Worship and service proclaim who we are and to whom we belong. Our service, along with our words, offers others the opportunity to discover what they are missing before their world is shaken with finality.

As we serve God with hearts full of gratitude, we become living testimonies of what it means to belong to an unshakable kingdom and an unshakable God.

*Holy Lord, help me worship and serve You with*
*gratitude, as I point others to Jesus.*

Do I worship and serve the Lord reluctantly or with gratitude?
What opportunities for service do I have today?

# BEAUTY FROM BARRENNESS
## Song of Solomon 2:1–7

I am the rose of Sharon,
The lily of the valleys.

Song of Solomon 2:1

Scientists have recently proven what women have known for centuries: flowers have the ability to influence human emotions. What is it about flowers that attracts us so? Is it their vivid colors, their fragile petals, or their intoxicating scents?

Jesus Christ is known as the Rose of Sharon, a name taken from the Song of Solomon. The Song is a stirring love poem describing the relationship of Solomon and his bride. It is also seen as a portrayal of God's relationship with Israel and Christ's relationship with the church.

In the Song, Solomon likened himself to the rose of Sharon, and the name later became associated with Christ. The rose of Sharon is a plant known for growing almost anywhere. Regardless of whether the landscape is harsh, has heavy vegetation, or is shaded by trees—the rose of Sharon still flourishes.

When we come to Christ, our lives can provide some of the harshest growing conditions for any plant. Yet Jesus Christ comes in and brings the beauty of the rose of Sharon where once only barrenness reigned.

*Rose of Sharon, thank You for planting Your beauty
in the barren landscape of my heart.*

How can I cultivate the soil of my heart for the Rose of Sharon to blossom?

# Bloom Where You're Planted
## Jeremiah 17:5–8

For he will be like a tree planted by the
water . . . its leaves will be green.

Jeremiah 17:8

Beautiful gardens look effortless, but they do not just happen. They require countless hours of planting, weeding, fertilizing, watering, and pest control.

When God makes us His garden, it doesn't just happen. He sent his Son as the purchase price for our lives. He planted the new life of the Rose of Sharon in our hearts. He gave us His Spirit to water, fertilize, and weed out spiritual enemies. Our job is to trust Him as the Gardener.

So dig into His nourishing Word and dine on its sustenance. Drink from the revitalizing stream of living water. Enjoy the refreshing rain of forgiveness as it washes the sin from each day. Allow the storms of life to fortify your roots and strengthen your resolve to trust Him even more. Open the tender leaves of your life to bask in the healing warmth of the Son.

God has planted the Rose of Sharon in our lives. Trust the Gardener and delight in the blossoms of His planting.

*Heavenly Father, forgive me for the times I have not trusted You as my Gardener. Help me respond to Your touch so the Rose of Sharon will blossom in my life for all the world to see.*

Have I been trusting the Gardener of my soul to enable my life to blossom? How can I cooperate with the Holy Spirit's "gardening" today?

# FRAGRANT FRAGRANCES
## 2 Corinthians 2:14–17

*For we are a fragrance of Christ to God
among those who are being saved
and among those who are perishing.*

2 Corinthians 2:15

O f our five senses, the sense of smell is the strongest in helping trigger memory recall. Certain scents can remind us of events from childhood, decades after they occurred.

No wonder then, the apostle Paul spoke of Christians as being "the sweet aroma of the knowledge of Him in every place" (2 Cor. 2:14). As flowers are fragrant and crushed flowers even more so, Christians are also a fragrance of Jesus Christ, regardless of what life brings.

The aroma is not the same for everyone we encounter. To some, we are an aroma of life, an encouraging reminder of what Christ has done and is doing in the lives of His people. To others, we are an aroma of death because they will reject Christ.

We do not know how people will respond to our "fragrance." Those who respond with hostility today may later recall the aroma, and be led to Christ at another time. Our job is to be a fragrant aroma and let God bring the recall in His time.

*Lord God, in all my life experiences, whether times
of rejoicing or times of suffering, help me to be a
fragrant aroma of Christ to others.*

What kind of fragrance have I radiated in my circumstances this week?

# NO MORE RIVERS OF BLOOD
## Hebrews 10:1–10

He has appeared once to remove sin by his sacrifice.

Hebrews 9:26 GW

Few things offend our modern sensibilities more than the bloodshed of innocent victims. When we read the Old Testament, we wonder how a loving God could require rivers of blood from thousands of sacrificed animals in the name of worship.

God used substitutionary sacrifice to teach His people the seriousness of sin and the need for atonement. He began with the death of an innocent animal for Adam and Eve. Later, the sacrificial system included a Passover lamb for each family and a scapegoat killed annually to cover the sins of the nation. With each level of sacrifice, God expanded His people's view of the atoning work of a single sacrifice. However, He never meant these sacrifices to last forever.

Jesus made the old covenant sacrifices obsolete by ratifying the new covenant with His own death. His perfect, eternal sacrifice stopped the rivers of blood once and for all.

God has woven the theme of substitutionary sacrifice through all of His Word. It begins with one sacrifice for each person, expands to one sacrifice for each family, then one sacrifice for the nation, and finally culminates in one perfect sacrifice for the entire world.

*Holy Lord, thank You for sending the perfect sacrifice to pay for my sin once and for all.*

Which offends me more: the shedding of innocent blood or my sin against God? Why?

# LIVING SACRIFICE
## Romans 12:1–8

I encourage you to offer your bodies as living sacrifices.

Romans 12:1 GW

*L*iving sacrifice. Isn't that a contradiction? Doesn't a sacrifice imply death?

The apostle Paul urges us to become living sacrifices in response to all Jesus has done for us. Living sacrifices have died to their own interests and agendas. Their focus is on what God wants to do through them. To be a living sacrifice is to be set apart by God for His service.

Paul explained that becoming a living sacrifice begins with presenting our bodies. Since Jesus offered His body on the cross as our substitute, how could we then hold back from offering our bodies to God? The world tells us to fight for our rights, live for the moment, and gratify our desires without regard for the consequences. A living sacrifice does not conform to the pattern of this world. Still, we may not realize we are conforming to the world's pattern until it is too late.

The presentation of our bodies and the transformation of our minds require a continuous process of yielding to the Holy Spirit through obedience to His Word. It is a daily lifestyle of surrender in thanksgiving for the sacrifice of Jesus Christ on our behalf.

> *Heavenly Father, I belong to You because of Jesus Christ's sacrifice for me. Help me to present myself to You as a living sacrifice, set apart for Your service.*

Is there a part of my body or mind that I have withheld from complete dedication to God?

# COSTLY PRAISE
## Hebrews 13:15–21

Through Him then, let us continually offer
up a sacrifice of praise to God.

Hebrews 13:15

When is a sacrifice not a sacrifice? The answer is simple: when it costs us nothing.

Throughout the Old Testament, God's people came to Him on the basis of costly sacrifices—the best of their flocks and the first fruits of their harvests. After the death and resurrection of Jesus Christ, we no longer need those sacrifices. Now we are to present *ourselves* as living sacrifices.

God also expects another kind of sacrifice: a continual expression of praise for the One who sacrificed Himself for us. Praise for God when things are going well is only the beginning. Praise becomes a costly sacrifice when we offer it to Him when life does not meet our expectations. The apostle Paul noted that the sacrifice of praise also extends to "doing good and sharing" (Heb. 13:16).

Those around us will see a consistency between our sacrifice of praise and our actions, regardless of the events in our lives. Such sacrifice is pleasing to God and a blessing to others.

*Lord God, I want to do more than speak Your praise when things go well in my life. Help me praise You every day and in every circumstance as You use me to serve others.*

How has my failure to praise God because of unmet expectations affected my witness?

# THE GREATEST SERVANT
## John 13:1–17

No servant is greater than his master, nor is a
messenger greater than the one who sent him.

John 13:16 NIV

We rarely apply the adage, "Do as I say, not as I do," with pride. It generally means our words and behavior are inconsistent.

In New Testament times, dusty roads created the need for foot washing, a job usually done by the lowest of the servants. When Jesus shared a last meal with His disciples, no one in the room had performed this service. Instead, the disciples argued over who was the greatest.

If anyone had a right to claim the position of "greatest," it was Jesus. Instead of demanding they serve Him, however, He served them. The God of the universe stooped to perform a task everyone else thought too beneath them. He had taught them about servanthood; now, once again, He demonstrated servanthood by His own behavior.

Jesus had every right to spurn the role of a servant, but He didn't. His actions proclaimed, "Do as I say *and* as I do."

> *Lord God, forgive me for the times I have avoided*
> *service I viewed as too menial for me. Teach me*
> *how to serve You in whatever task You have for*
> *me today.*

How is God asking me to serve Him by serving those around me today?

# SUFFERING SERVANTS
## Matthew 20:20–28

Whoever wishes to become great among you shall be your servant.

Matthew 20:26

The mother of disciples James and John seems like a typical stage mother. *Her* boys were brighter and more deserving than the other disciples were, or so she thought. *Her* boys should have positions of honor in the kingdom of heaven. Of course, *her* boys agreed with her.

The remaining disciples were indignant at the audacious appeal, probably because they wished they had thought of it first! None of them had a clue as to the true cost of the request.

For Christ, suffering preceded glory. He came as a suffering servant to achieve for us the salvation we could not achieve for ourselves. That meant drinking the full cup of God's wrath against sin. The two brothers would soon learn what this meant. James, the first to die for Christ, was executed by the sword. John endured exile on the island of Patmos.

Suffering still comes before glory. Jesus suffered for us, and we are not exempt from suffering. Jesus came to serve, rather than be served, and our lives should not be any different.

In the kingdom of heaven, honor is not requested; it is bestowed on those who live for Christ alone, and that includes suffering.

*Dear Father, strengthen me to serve You in times of success and in times of suffering.*

How can I serve the Lord today through my suffering so that He gets the glory?

# SERVANT LEADERSHIP
## Matthew 23:1–12

The person who is greatest among you will be your servant.

Matthew 23:11 GW

We often measure successful leadership by the leader's celebrity, his following, and his financial success. Jesus taught us a different way.

The Pharisees in Jesus's day loved the attention their position brought. They enjoyed places of honor at the best dinners, front-row seats in the synagogues, and respectful greetings in their community. They also worked to attract even more attention. They wore extra-large phylacteries—small cases that held Bible passages worn on their arms and across their foreheads. They adorned their robes with extra-long tassels as a mark of holiness.

Jesus cautioned against seeking celebrity status and lifting ourselves so high that we enjoy titles and respect reserved for God alone. Instead, our leadership should be a direct function of our servanthood. The greater the servant, the greater the leader.

How do we know if we are practicing true servant-leadership? The proof is in whether we behave like a servant when we are treated like one.

*Heavenly Father, keep me from seeking the attention*
*and recognition that comes from exalting myself.*
*Help me to lead through serving and to follow You*
*as I lead.*

How can I be a better servant-leader of the people God has placed in my life?

# THE BEST TEACHER
## Psalm 32:8–11

I will instruct you and teach you in the way you should go.

Psalm 32:8 NIV

Good teachers are passionate about their students and their message. They are knowledgeable, dedicated, and patient. Perhaps you have the privilege of knowing a teacher like this. He may be the elementary school teacher who taught you to read. She might be the high school teacher who encouraged you to follow your passion into a career. Perhaps he is the Sunday school teacher who led you to Jesus Christ.

God Himself is our teacher. He promises to teach us, giving us the direction we need for life. He promises to watch us and counsel us with His wisdom and His presence. Most of all, He proved His passionate love for us by sacrificing His own Son.

For any teacher to be successful, the student must have a desire to learn. God warns us against stubbornly going our own way. If we trust the Lord and come to Him with a heart willing to learn, He will surround us with His lovingkindness and teach us everything we need.

Of all the many good teachers who have blessed our lives, the best teacher of all is the One who gave His life so that we might hear what He has to say.

*Lord, thank You for teaching me everything I need.*
*Help me live a life that pleases You.*

What lesson has God been teaching me this week? Have I been a willing student?

# TEACHABLE SPIRIT
## Acts 18:23–28

They took him aside and explained to him
the way of God more accurately.

Acts 18:26

D o you have a teachable spirit? Giving and receiving constructive criticism is not easy, especially when the one being corrected is acting out of a sincere love for the Lord. The alternative, however, encourages persistent misinformation or wrong behavior.

As the gospel spread in the early church, a man named Apollos knew of John the Baptist's ministry to prepare for the Messiah. Apollos also knew Jesus was the Messiah. He eloquently shared the Old Testament Scriptures with the Ephesians, but he did not have the complete picture. Priscilla and Aquila, discipled by the apostle Paul, explained the full gospel to Apollos, including Jesus's substitutionary death on the cross and His victorious resurrection.

Apollos had a teachable spirit. He received the correction with grace, and later God used him as a significant influence in the early church in Corinth.

May we each be as teachable as Apollos.

> *Heavenly Father, give me a teachable spirit. I ask*
> *You for the grace to receive Your correction through*
> *the people You have placed in my life.*

How do I usually respond to criticism? Are my responses dependent on the person delivering the criticism?

# KNOW-IT-ALLS
## 1 Timothy 1:1–7

> The goal of our instruction is love from a
> pure heart . . . and a sincere faith.
>
> 1 Timothy 1:5

Nobody likes a know-it-all. We've all met them. They give the answers before we ask the questions, eager to impress us with the wealth of their knowledge.

When the apostle Paul wrote to his young protégé, he urged Timothy to pay special attention to his own teaching and the teaching of others in his church. It appears that strange doctrines had spread, fueling endless speculation and hindering the growth and maturity of the local Christians.

Paul reminded Timothy the goal of our teaching is not to impress others or amass large collections of trivia. Nor should our teaching be caught up in useless speculation. Rather, the goal of our teaching is transformed lives among those we teach. Whether a parent with a child, a youth leader with a teenager, or one adult discipling another, our goal is to see hearts filled with love for the Lord and others, lives lived in purity with clear consciences and sincere faith.

When we feel the urge to teach, let's be sure to check our motives and our goals.

*Lord God, use me to teach others so that lives are*
*transformed and You are glorified.*

Whom has God placed in my life to influence or teach? What has my goal been in teaching this person?

# WHO IS TRUTH?
## John 18:28–38

"What is truth?" Pilate asked.

John 18:38 NLT

W hat is truth?" Pontius Pilate's question echoes through the centuries. The search for the answer has led people to a variety of philosophies and an abundance of answers.

Their conclusions, however, are woefully inadequate: "There are no absolutes; truth is relative; what's true for you is not true for me." Those who say such things do not realize their own statements are absolutes that contradict themselves!

God not only *told* us about truth, He sent His Son, Jesus Christ, to *show* us truth. His name *is* Truth. He said of Himself, "I am . . . the truth" (John 14:6); He told us knowing the truth sets us free (8:32); and He told Pilate, "I have come . . . to testify to the truth" (18:37).

When we know Jesus Christ, He reveals the truth of who God is, who we are, how God sees our sin, and what God's answer is to restore our broken relationship with Him.

Pilate asked the wrong question two thousand years ago. The question is not, "*What* is truth?" The question is, "*Who* is truth?" The answer is, "Jesus Christ."

> *Lord God, You revealed absolute truth when You revealed Your Son. Help me look only to You as the source of all truth.*

How has knowing the Truth set me free from the world's lies? With whom can I share this?

# DISCERNING THE LIES
## John 8:31–47

The devil . . . is a liar and the father of lies.

John 8:44

The easiest lie to believe is a half-truth. Mix a bit of truth with a lie, and people have a difficult time identifying right from wrong. The devil knows this and uses it against us. Jesus identified him as the "father of lies" (John 8:44), and deceit is one of Satan's most potent weapons.

We fall for lies about God—that He deprives us by withholding something good from us. We fall for lies about ourselves—that we will not be judged because we are not as bad as the next guy. We fall for lies about God's forgiveness—that He will withhold forgiveness because we have failed Him for the umpteenth time. We fall for lies laced with a tiny amount of truth.

God may indeed be withholding something good from us . . . in favor of giving us something better. We may not be as bad as the next guy . . . but we all fall short of God's holiness. We may have failed God for the umpteenth time . . . but He lavishly pours out His grace on us the moment we turn to Him.

When we surrender to the Lord, He speaks truth into our lives and gives us the ability to discern the slightest error.

*Father, help me to reject the adversary's lies. Fill me*
*with Your absolute truth.*

What compromised areas in my life do I need to line up with the truth of God's Word?

# SPEAKING TRUTH
### Ephesians 4:1–16

Speaking the truth in love, we will in all things grow up into him.

Ephesians 4:15 NIV

I had always thought the focus of the verse "Speaking the truth in love" was to help *others* grow in their relationship with the Lord. When we speak the truth of God's Word in love, others experience new birth and grow as they yield to the Holy Spirit's work in their life.

Yet the remainder of the verse clearly refers to the speaker's own growth and maturity as well. Speaking truth without love leads us to legalism. Showing love without truth opens us to compromise. Truth spoken *in* love manifests the love of Christ without sacrificing His holiness. It changes the lives of the listener *and* the speaker.

This balance produces a church working together, growing under the headship of Christ. God's truthful Word becomes our defense against every crafty doctrine and deceitful scheme that might inhibit our growth.

Speaking the truth in love is not optional. It is required for every Christian's maturity.

> *Dear Lord, help me speak the truth in love, so that I and others in my life may grow in both Your holiness and Your compassion.*

Do I share the gospel using truthful words delivered with a loving spirit? How can I develop a greater balance of truth and love in my relationships?

304

# THE CONQUERING HERO
## Colossians 2:8–15

God disarmed the evil rulers and authorities. He shamed them
publicly by his victory over them on the cross of Christ.

Colossians 2:15 NLT

Hail the conquering hero!" In the ancient Roman Empire, victorious military leaders would return to the city of Rome in triumphant parades. Cheering crowds lined the streets as generals led their captives in public displays of conquest.

Also in Roman times, when a criminal was crucified, his crimes were written and nailed to his cross to explain his death sentence.

The apostle Paul used both of these images to describe Christ's victory on our behalf. Although Jesus had committed no crime, our sin-debt against God was placed on Him—nailed to His cross when He was crucified. He then proclaimed His victory to the devil and the demonic host. Satan's power over us was broken, and Christ's triumph is public knowledge for all to see.

Today, some Christians mistakenly behave as if Jesus is still battling Satan and the outcome is uncertain. The war has been fought, and Jesus Christ won the victory over sin, death, and the devil when He died for us. He truly is our conquering hero.

*Victorious Lord, I gratefully rejoice in Your victory
over the enemy of my soul.*

How can I celebrate Christ's victory over sin on my behalf
today?

# NO LONGER PRISONERS
## Colossians 1:13–17

He rescued us from the domain of darkness.

Colossians 1:13

Psychologists have identified a condition known as Stockholm syndrome to explain the emotional bond that sometimes develops between a hostage and their captor. Over time, the hostage can become sympathetic to their captor and distrust law enforcement's rescue efforts.

God created us to be in fellowship with Him. However, when sin entered the world, we became prisoners of Satan. Humanity settled into a life of captivity, and the memory of what it was like to be truly free faded. Many people have developed the equivalent of Stockholm syndrome, viewing the devil as harmless and responding to God with distrust.

Jesus Christ's death and resurrection provided the victory necessary for our freedom. When we trust Him for salvation, He rescues us from the enemy's dark territory and transports us to His kingdom of light. Yet even after our rescue, the emotional pull of the world we left behind may cause us to distrust the One who freed us.

To enjoy our freedom in Christ, we must destroy any shred of Stockholm syndrome.

*Victorious Lord, forgive me for the times I have*
*distrusted You and Your plans for me.*

How have I become comfortable or sympathetic with the ways of the world that conflict with God's kingdom of light? What will I do today to show my trust in the One who freed me?

# MORE THAN CONQUERORS
## Romans 8:31–39

In all these things we overwhelmingly
conquer through Him who loved us.

Romans 8:37

D o you have a critical person in your life, perhaps a boss, neighbor, or family member? He behaves as if his purpose in life is to evaluate and correct your every action. She may reject you unless you conform to her standards for your life.

People may be entitled to their opinions, but that does not mean we have to listen to or believe them. Our standard for living is the Bible, and God's Word tells us that if we are in Christ, no one can condemn or bring a charge against us. Nothing can separate us from His love. Not suffering or persecution. Not famine or danger. Not angels or demons. Since God is on our side, it does not matter who or what is against us. To be conquerors, we must focus on the One who has conquered on our behalf.

Criticism and persecution will come—sometimes from those closest to us. We can choose to believe their words, or we can choose to believe the Word of God. When we take God at His Word, we become overwhelming conquerors.

*Victorious Lord, help me to keep the eyes and ears
of my heart focused on You alone.*

How have I allowed the opinions of others to interfere with my relationship with the Lord?

# ABIDING BRANCHES
## John 15:1–6

Then Jesus said, "I am the true vine."

John 15:1 GW

There are vines, and then there are *vines*. Jesus spoke of Himself as the true vine, but today people may misinterpret His words.

We might think of a vine as an ivy that clings to bricks or concrete. We may picture a twining vine, such as wisteria, that climbs by encircling a pole in a spiral pattern. We may think of sprawling vines, such as bougainvillea, whose long runners may need to be supported across a brace to thrive.

Jesus's disciples would not have considered any of these vines. Their thoughts would have immediately centered on the most familiar vine to them: a grapevine. Grapevines have sturdy trunks. Their branches extend outward, lifted along supports to encourage fruitfulness.

When Jesus said He is the vine, He referred to the trunk. As long as the branches remain attached to the trunk, they draw life and nourishment to produce abundant crops of grapes.

Jesus is the vine; we are the branches. When we abide in Him, rightly related to Him, we enjoy the blessing of life, health, and fruit.

*Lord God, help me remain rightly related to my*
*Vine, continually abiding so I might be fruitful for*
*Your kingdom.*

Why do I struggle at times to abide in Christ? How can I better abide to bear more fruit?

# GRAFTED IN
## Romans 11:1–24

Some of the branches were broken off, and you, being a wild olive,
were grafted in . . . do not be arrogant toward the branches.

Romans 11:17–18

Some plants, such as the navel orange tree, do not produce fruit
with seeds. These plants are cultivated by grafting a branch of
one plant onto the trunk of another to give it a strong root system. The new plant is completely dependent on the "old" trunk for
survival.

Today, although individual Jewish people have come to know Jesus
Christ, Israel as a nation has yet to acknowledge her Messiah. Some
Christians can be condescending—even arrogant—to those of the
Jewish faith, belittling them for missing the One they waited for.

We have no right to be arrogant. The apostle Paul reminded us
that Israel is still God's chosen people, the nation who gave the Savior to the world. Gentiles are "grafted" onto Israel's stock, enjoying
the opportunity for salvation because of Israel's unbelief. Someday,
though, Israel will be saved, her broken branches grafted back where
they belong.

In the meantime, we should be eternally grateful for the stock that
brought us salvation.

*Heavenly Father, give me a heart of gratitude for*
*Your chosen people. Help me remember that it*
*is from Israel that You sent Your Son to offer me*
*salvation.*

What can I do to share Messiah's love with someone of the Jewish faith this week?

309

# DEPENDENT FOR GROWTH
## John 15:7–17

> This is My commandment, that you love one
> another, just as I have loved you.
>
> John 15:12

John Donne said, "No man is an island." We all rely on the intricacies of interdependent relationships.

Jesus spoke to His disciples about the importance of abiding in Him, as a branch must remain attached to the vine's trunk to stay healthy and fruitful. Then He went on to describe the relationships that accompany the act of abiding.

First, He spoke of the intimate relationship between God the Father and God the Son: "Just as the Father has loved Me" (John 15:9). Our relationship with Christ begins with their intimate relationship. Jesus spoke of a second relationship in verse 9: "I have also loved you; abide in My love." When we abide in Him, we reap obedience and joy.

Third, in verse 16, Jesus said that when we abide in Him and bear fruit that glorifies the Father, our requests will be in accordance with His will and He will grant them. Finally, Jesus again commands us to "love one another" (v. 17), as He explained in verse 12, "just as I have loved you." His nourishing love flows through us just as nutrients flow from the grapevine's trunk to its branches.

*Lord, help me remember the interdependencies of*
*all my relationships, beginning with You.*

How does Christ's love flowing in me make it easier for me to love even the unlovable people in my life?

# ONLY WAY
## Matthew 26:36–44

My Father, if this cannot pass away
unless I drink it, Your will be done.

Matthew 26:42

The world belittles Christians as narrow-minded and intolerant. With billions of people on earth and hundreds of belief systems, how could Christians say there is only one way to God?

Jesus said, "I am the way . . . no one comes to the Father but through Me" (John 14:6). Not *a* way among several ways, but *the* way. The only way. Or are we misinterpreting His words?

Beyond Jesus's words about Himself, we have additional proof that He is the only way to God. The night He was betrayed, Jesus went to the Garden of Gethsemane with His disciples to pray. He asked His Father to allow the "cup" to pass (Matt. 26:39)—a reference to God's wrath against sin that would be atoned by Jesus's death for us. Three times He asked His Father, and three times the answer was no. If there was another way to God, Jesus would not have had to die in our place. There was no other way for Jesus Christ because there is no other way for us.

People wonder how there could be only one way to God. The more we learn of God's holiness, righteousness, and justice, and the more we understand our own sinfulness, the more we realize the extent of God's mercy in providing a way *at all*!

*Holy Lord, thank You for providing the way for me
to be intimately restored to You.*

How can I share the truth that Jesus is the only way to God with someone today?

311

# WRONG WAY
## 2 Peter 2:1–16

False teachers will be among you.

2 Peter 2:1 GW

Many bestselling books quote the Bible, yet deny that Christ is the only way of salvation. Leaders in several major church denominations have claimed the name *Christian*, yet denied the virgin birth of Christ. Have you ever wondered why people who do not believe Jesus Christ is the only way to God still identify themselves as *Christians*?

To guard against false teachers, we need to know how to identify them. The apostle Peter said they infiltrate the church, secretly introducing destructive teachings. These heresies include denying Jesus Christ is the Savior and the only way to God. False teachers gratify their own desires, motivated by their greed. They forsake the right way—the only way—and instead follow the foolishness of their own supposed wisdom.

Peter warned that God will not spare false teachers from judgment. It does not matter how large a following these leaders have or the extent of their celebrity status. If we are not following *the* way, we are following the *wrong* way.

*Lord, help me discern those who do not follow the
way of Your Son, despite their claims.*

How alert am I to false teachers who claim to be Christian? How can I better guard against false ways?

# FIND THE WAY
## John 14:1–6

Thomas said to him, "Lord . . . how can we know the way?"

John 14:5 GW

What if you discovered the only way to cure cancer? Would it be narrow-minded to share that cure with others? Would it be intolerant to let them know the other supposed cures are wasting valuable time and money and will only result in death? Of course not. You would not worry about offending others if it meant saving lives.

During Jesus's final evening with His disciples, He assured them that He was leaving to prepare a place for them and that they "know the way" to where He was going (John 14:4). Thomas spoke for the twelve when he asked, "How do we know the way?"

Yet these confused men became the same ones who turned Jerusalem, and the Roman Empire, upside down. Jesus's resurrection confirmed *who* He is—the Christ, and *what* He is—the only way to the Father. Their relationship with Him compelled them to share what they knew.

In the face of countless philosophies of salvation and satisfaction competing for our attention, how compelled are we to share the One we know who provides the *only* way to the Father?

*Father, forgive me for the times I hesitate to speak*
*of Jesus as the only way to You.*

What causes me to hesitate in speaking of Jesus Christ as the only way to God? How can I overcome my hesitation?

# GOD SPOKE
## John 1:14–18

In the beginning was the Word . . . and the Word was God.

John 1:1

How would a human being communicate with ants in a way they could understand? We would have to learn their language or become an ant ourselves.

How could a holy, righteous God communicate with sinful man in a way we could understand? He did it by speaking our language, using words through men such as Abraham and Moses. Later, He spoke through the prophets. Finally, God spoke through the Word, His own Son, who was with Him from before time began, and who became one of us.

The Word *was* God and the Word *is* God. Through Jesus Christ, God spoke to our hearts. The Word spoke grace and peace to us. He communicated love and compassion for us. He spoke healing and hope into our lives.

The Word—Jesus Christ—expressed God's holiness and is the only One who met that standard of holiness. He expressed God's justice and then satisfied that justice with His life. He was cruelly executed and then spoke forgiveness to His executioners.

God sent His Word. Are we listening?

*Holy Lord, thank You for speaking to my heart through Your living Word, Jesus Christ.*

How is God speaking to my heart through His Son this week? How well am I listening?

# THE BIBLE SPEAKS
## 2 Timothy 3:16–4:4

Every part of Scripture is God-breathed and useful.

2 Timothy 3:16 Message

I s every word of the Bible truly necessary? Consider all the genealogies, all the measurements, all the repetition. Is every word of
the Bible really true? Think of the Garden of Eden, Jonah and the
whale, Daniel in the lions' den. Allegories and fables, or the Word
of God?

Hebrews 4:12 tells us "the word of God is living and active and
sharper than any two-edged sword, and piercing as far as the division
of soul and spirit, of both joints and marrow, and able to judge the
thoughts and intentions of the heart."

God's Word expresses His love, teaches us His standards, convicts
us when we fail to meet them, corrects us, and trains us to move forward according to His direction. Every word of the Word is necessary
and useful. Even the genealogies show us the importance of speaking
God's Word to succeeding generations. Every word is true, including the miraculous events that remind us our sovereign God created
natural laws and can suspend them anytime He chooses.

Most important of all, Jesus is The Word, and all the words of
Scripture point to Him.

*Heavenly Father, speak to me through Your whole
Word. Cause me to see applications I have missed
in the past, and show me how to apply them to
my life.*

How is God using His Word to pierce my soul and spirit today?

315

# WE SPEAK
## Matthew 12:33–37

For out of the overflow of the heart the mouth speaks.

Matthew 12:34 NIV

"Sticks and stones may break my bones, but words can never hurt me." Remember this rhyme from childhood? Unfortunately, it is not true. Words are powerful and they do hurt, causing deep wounds that can last a lifetime.

Words also expose the condition of the heart. No matter how much we try to hide our feelings, our words give us away. Angry words reveal a short temper. Sarcasm exposes resentment. Flattery discloses insincerity. Careless words damage relationships and create obstacles that prevent people from coming to the Savior. Godly words come from a heart that has been changed by Christ. They uplift and draw people to Him.

What does our speech say about us? What message are we sending to those around us? Is it a message of life-change and love, or hypocrisy and harm? People around us need to hear the gospel, and they need to hear it from us.

Our most powerful testimony occurs when our words and actions are consistent with *the* Word of God.

*Lord, help me speak from a heart changed by Your Son. Use my words to uplift others today.*

How can I share the Word today with someone who has not yet heard God's message?

# WITH AND IN
## Psalm 139:7–12

Where can I go to get away from your Spirit?

Psalm 139:7 GW

Jesus spent three years teaching and training His disciples. On His last night with them, He said it was time for Him to leave, but He was not abandoning them. Instead, Jesus told them He would send the Holy Spirit—the third person of the Trinity.

The Holy Spirit has many names in Scripture, including Advocate, Comforter, Counselor, Helper, Intercessor, Strengthener, and Spirit of Truth. He is the same Spirit of God who was active in the creation of the universe, and who overshadowed Mary to conceive Jesus.

During the Old Testament period, the Holy Spirit temporarily rested on individuals, anointing them for their God-ordained tasks. Aware that his sin could cause the Holy Spirit to leave, King David sorrowfully pled, "Do not take Your Holy Spirit from me" (Ps. 51:11).

Now, because of Christ's victory over sin and death, the Holy Spirit dwells permanently in all believers. The apostle Paul told believers they are "sealed in Him with the Holy Spirit of promise" (Eph. 1:13).

God is always *with* us in the most intimate way possible because He is always *in* us.

*Holy Spirit, help me never to take Your precious, indwelling presence for granted.*

How will I live differently today because God is both with me *and* in me?

# BODIES AND TEMPLES
## 1 Corinthians 6:12–20

Do you not know that your body is a temple of the Holy Spirit?

1 Corinthians 6:19

Fitness centers are popping up everywhere. Members get access to state-of-the-art equipment, exercise programs, and personal trainers. Lose weight, tone up, get in shape—the goal is to have the body we always wanted, or at least the body we used to have! We should take care of our bodies, though, for a more important reason.

Before the time of Christ, God's Spirit dwelt among the Israelites, first in the tabernacle, and later in the temple in Jerusalem. The people responded to the privilege with awe and reverence. The God of the universe had chosen to dwell in their midst.

Christians have an even greater privilege today. The Holy Spirit dwells in every believer. That makes our bodies the temple of God. The Bible doesn't exhort us to pursue sculpted bodies, but it does have much to say about how we *use* our bodies. We are to pursue righteousness and flee immorality. We are not to allow anything to master our body, including gluttony and lust. We never want to grieve God's Holy Spirit by anything we think, say, or do (Eph. 4:30).

Treat your body like the very temple of the living God—because it is.

*Heavenly Father, help me properly care for my body—Your dwelling place.*

Which of my habits grieve the Holy Spirit? How can I begin changing this habit today?

# WHOM DO YOU RELY ON?

## 1 Corinthians 2:1–5

> My message and my preaching were . . .
> in demonstration of the Spirit.
>
> 1 Corinthians 2:4

During an evangelism class several years ago, I role-played with a woman who struggled to apply the training. In my arrogance, I privately concluded that she would confuse her listeners if she shared the gospel without more practice. A week later, she told us she had led two people to Christ during hospital visits, while I had failed to share Christ with anyone that week.

The apostle Paul had every reason to be confident of his own background and abilities. A descendant of the tribe of Benjamin, he had been trained to be a teacher of the Law by one of the premier Pharisees in Israel. Few Israelites knew the Hebrew Scriptures better than Paul.

Yet when Paul preached the gospel, he did not rely on his persuasiveness, training, or wisdom. Rather, he focused on Christ, speaking with "weakness and in fear and in much trembling" (1 Cor. 2:3). The message of salvation required total dependence on the Holy Spirit.

Speaking of Christ to others does not require a head full of knowledge; it requires a heart that relies on the Holy Spirit. We need only obey His promptings and trust Him for the outcome.

*Lord God, forgive me for the times I have relied on*
*my natural skills and abilities to share the gospel*
*instead of relying on Your Holy Spirit.*

How can I rely more on the Holy Spirit, and less on myself, when I share Christ?

# OUR DEFENSE ATTORNEY
### 1 John 1:5–2:2

> We have an Advocate with the Father, Jesus Christ the righteous.
>
> 1 John 2:1

It has been said that a man who is his own lawyer has a fool for a client. Nowhere is that more true than when sinful man stands in the presence of the holy God of the universe. If ever we would need a good defense attorney, it will be then.

The Bible tells us Satan is the adversary of believers, accusing us "before our God day and night" (Rev. 12:10). Think of Satan as a prosecuting attorney. He has all the evidence he needs to use against us, and we hand him more evidence with each passing day. Sins in our thought life, in our conversations, and in our behavior. Sins of omission and sins of commission. Intentional sins and unintentional sins.

Christ is our Advocate—our defense attorney. He is the One who stands with us before God, the righteous Judge, to plead our case. Jesus proclaims to the court that He has already died to atone for our sin. He has served our guilty sentence, and we can never be accused again.

Our Advocate not only defends us, He already paid the sentence for our guilty verdict.

> *Holy Lord, thank You for being my Advocate. I place myself in Your hands and throw myself on the mercy of Your court.*

What do I communicate when I plead for my Advocate's defense but continue to sin?

# TOO DEEP FOR WORDS
## Romans 8:18–27

The Spirit Himself intercedes for us with
groanings too deep for words.

Romans 8:26

Have you ever been tongue-tied? Perhaps a situation is too wonderful—or too horrific—for description. You run to your heavenly Father, heart pounding with emotion, but the words do not come. Maybe you have a need so deep you are afraid to speak, afraid to ask for answers because you are not even sure of the questions.

Jesus Christ is our Advocate, and so is the Holy Spirit. When we are too weak to pray, He intercedes for us according to the Father's will. When we are not sure what is in our own hearts, the Holy Spirit searches our hearts and speaks to God on our behalf. When we do not know what words to use, He communicates with the Father in a language deeper than words.

It is difficult, though, for us to stop talking and rely on His intercession. To stop rambling when we are not really saying anything, or to keep silent when we are speaking foolishly.

When we are at a loss for words, we can trust God's Holy Spirit to know just what to say.

*Heavenly Father, thank You that when I do not have*
*the words, Your Holy Spirit speaks on my behalf.*
*Help my heart to rest in His advocacy.*

How does knowing that the Holy Spirit intercedes for me with my heavenly Father affect how I pray? In what situation do I need to rely on His intercession today?

321

# PUBLIC DEFENDERS
## Micah 6:1–8

What does the LORD require of you?

Micah 6:8 NIV

Is it enough "to act justly and to love mercy" (Mic. 6:8 NIV) in our own little corner of the world if people elsewhere receive neither? Like Cain, we may ask, "Am I my brother's keeper?" (Gen. 4:9). After all, we can't fix *all* the injustice in the world. What difference can one person make?

In a sense, we *are* our brothers' keepers. Edmund Burke once said, "All that is necessary for the triumph of evil is that good men do nothing." Throughout history, injustice has flourished because people pretend not to see what is happening. They do not want to get involved.

In the legal system, the Public Defender is an advocate for those who cannot afford legal counsel. Advocacy, though, is not limited to attorneys. Each one of us can speak up for those who cannot speak for themselves. We can volunteer at a crisis pregnancy center to help mothers and babies, or as a guardian *ad litem*, advocating for children whose family members are unable to act in their best interests. We can speak up for people being trafficked for slave labor around the world. We can pray, write letters, make visits, or pick up the phone. We can do *something*.

We may not eradicate all injustice, but we can make a difference, one person at a time.

*Dear Lord, give me Your eyes to see those who are hurting. Help me advocate for them.*

Has God placed someone in my life who needs an advocate? How can I respond today?

# COMFORT IN DISCOMFORT
## John 14:16–20

I will pray the Father, and he shall give you another Comforter.

John 14:16 KJV

Comfort has become the standard by which many people live. We want comfortable cars, comfortable clothes, and comfortable shoes. We even reach for comfort foods to give us an emotional boost. Far be it from us to be uncomfortable!

With His crucifixion imminent, Jesus promised the disciples He would not abandon them; He would send "another"—different, yet equal to Himself. The King James Version translates this name as *Comforter*, one who would be with them, and us, forever.

Within hours of Jesus's promise, the disciples would enter the most trying period of their lives. Their Master would be executed, and they were about to enter an intense period of persecution. Jesus promised that the Comforter would dwell in them, bringing the strength, hope, and intimate presence of God. He would ease their fears and answer their questions.

The Comforter does not promise a trouble-free life. Rather, He encourages our hearts in whatever life brings. His presence reminds and reassures us that God is always with us. When life becomes uncomfortable, He does not eliminate our suffering; He carries us through it.

*My Comforter, thank You for the assurance that I*
*am not alone in my trials and suffering.*

How has God comforted me with His presence in the midst of my trials this week?

# MOURNING FOR SIN
## James 4:6–10

Blessed are those who mourn. They will be comforted.

Matthew 5:4 GW

If we had the option, most of us would choose joy and laughter over mourning and weeping. Yet the apostle James urges us to seek mourning instead of laughter and heaviness rather than joy. Does this mean God wants us to be miserable?

God resists the proud but gives grace to the humble. One of the ways we exhibit our humility is when we mourn over sin—our own and the sin of others. The presence of sin should break our hearts. Deep sorrow should wash over us as we realize that our sin—yours and mine—nailed Christ to the cross.

When we mourn over sin, the Comforter enfolds us in His love and pours His grace on us. He enables us to view our sin from His perspective, and He gives us a desire for His holiness. Throughout this process, He wraps us in His comfort.

We do not mourn over sin to be miserable; we mourn over sin to touch the heart of God.

*Heavenly Father, help me see my sin as You see it.*
*Help me mourn over my sin and give me a desire*
*for Your holiness.*

Do I mourn more for the consequences of my sin or for the sin itself?

# THE COMFORT OF THE COMFORTED
## 2 Corinthians 1:3–7

> We can comfort those in any trouble with the
> comfort we ourselves have received from God.
>
> 2 Corinthians 1:4 NIV

The question of suffering has disturbed people for centuries. As far back as the book of Job in the Old Testament, Job and his friends debated why the righteous suffer misfortune.

The Bible describes various reasons for our trials. God permits us to suffer to test our faith, mature our character, or manifest the reality of our heavenly Father's care. We may suffer to share in Christ's suffering, learn to trust God more, or be pruned for greater fruitfulness.

The apostle Paul explained yet another reason for our trials. When our heavenly Father comforts us, we are able to comfort others with the same comfort we have received from Him. To do this, though, we must be willing to be open with others about our struggles.

The more transparent we are regarding our own trials and the comfort we have received, the more God can use us to touch the lives of our brothers and sisters in Christ.

*Comforter, help me be open with others about my trials, so that I might help someone else suffering with the same struggles.*

Is someone in my life struggling with a trial similar to one in which I have experienced God's comfort? How can I extend comfort to this person today?

# WORLD MINISTRY
## John 16:7–15

He will come to convict the world of sin.

John 16:8 GW

When we think of the Holy Spirit, we usually think of Him in relation to His ministry in the lives of Christians. He comforts, counsels, and encourages. He guides, helps, and transforms. He convicts us of sin and manifests His fruit in our lives.

Jesus said the Holy Spirit has a three-fold ministry in the world. God's Holy Spirit convicts unbelievers of sin, righteousness, and judgment. He is the One who opens the eyes of the spiritually blind that they might know that Jesus Christ is both God and Savior. The Holy Spirit is also the One who causes people to see the insufficiency of their own righteousness and their need for the righteousness of Christ. Finally, God's Holy Spirit brings the realization that the god of this world—Satan—has already been defeated. Whether the devil admits it or not, the war has already been won and his guilty verdict has been pronounced.

It is only through the convicting work of the Holy Spirit that God draws us to a restored relationship with Him.

> *Holy Lord, thank You for convicting me of sin and opening my eyes to Your salvation. Help me live in the light of Your righteousness as I respond to the conviction of the Holy Spirit.*

How can I thank God today for the role of His Holy Spirit in my salvation?

# UNQUENCHED
## Ephesians 4:17–32

Do not quench the Spirit.

1 Thessalonians 5:19

Christians have the ability to quench the work of the Holy Spirit in our lives. We do it every time we sin.

The Holy Spirit convicts the world of sin. After we are in a restored relationship with God, though, He still convicts us of areas in our lives that do not honor Him. We are no longer to behave like unbelievers. Rather, the way we live should reflect the work God is doing in us. Inconsistency between our words and actions will cause God's Spirit to bring conviction.

We quench the work of the Holy Spirit when we allow sin to interfere with the work He is doing through us. Instead of using us to advance the kingdom of Christ, the Holy Spirit's ministry in our lives turns to convicting and correcting us. He may prompt us with a quiet thought or through the written Word of God. He might speak truth to us through another believer or even through an unbeliever.

Whichever method He chooses, the Holy Spirit will get our attention to convict us of sin.

*Father, help me remain sensitive to the Holy Spirit's*
*conviction and promptings.*

How sensitive am I to the conviction of God's Holy Spirit? What has He challenged me to apply from the Bible today?

# NO LONGER FRUSTRATING
## Acts 16:22–34

Sirs, what do I have to do to be saved?

Acts 16:30 GW

Sharing the gospel can be satisfying or it can be frustrating. One person comes to Christ, while another refuses. The gospel is clear to us, but may not be clear to family members, friends, or co-workers. Regardless of how creative we are in sharing God's Word, they either reject it outright or shrug it off with indifference.

God knows what every person needs to receive His salvation. That point will be different for each individual. A stirring restlessness in their soul may drive some to Him. Others will suffer the loss of everything dear to them before they turn to God. For some, a quiet word is enough. Still others may never come to Him. We must be sensitive to the Holy Spirit's leading for each person we approach.

Sharing the gospel will not be frustrating if we remember that our job is to live out and communicate the new birth Christ offers. The Holy Spirit's job is to convict and create new life.

*Lord God, Your Spirit is the One who convicts man of sin, of righteousness, and of judgment. Help me do my part in sharing the gospel and leave the job of heart-change to You.*

Whom can I pray for today, that the Holy Spirit will convict them and soften their heart? How can I be prepared to share the gospel with those He calls me to influence for Him?

# ASSURED COUNSEL
## Psalm 16:1–11

I will praise the LORD, who counsels me;
even at night my heart instructs me.

Psalm 16:7 NIV

Where do you first turn in your search for answers to life's problems?

Difficult situations and unanswered questions often cause us sleepless nights. We toss and turn in bed, our minds racing as we search for elusive solutions to our troubles.

King David had the responsibility of ruling a nation. Despite all the advisors in his royal court, he made a conscious choice to turn first to God for the answers he needed. God was always before him and at his right hand. This gave David an unshakable confidence, regardless of his circumstances. David received the Lord's counsel because he placed God first. Others might lie awake, staring at the ceiling in desperation, but God instructed David's thoughts in the night hours.

God is still our Counselor. Like David, we too have the assurance of the Lord's instruction. Running to God as a last resort when all else fails is good, but looking to Him *first* for the answers we need is better.

*Holy Lord, thank You for being my Counselor. Help*
*me to place You first in every situation, so that Your*
*counsel is the first thing I seek, and You are the first*
*one I turn to.*

For what problem do I need answers? How is God counseling me in this situation?

# BAD COUNSEL FROM GOOD PEOPLE
## Matthew 16:21–28

Heaven forbid, Lord! This must never happen to you!

Matthew 16:22 GW

When we seek godly counsel, how do we know God is the one who is speaking?

Jesus told His disciples He would suffer and die, but Peter disagreed—"This shall never happen to You." Although Peter wanted to believe this, he was wrong.

Today, difficult situations such as an unreasonable boss at work or a strained marriage at home may spur us to seek advice. Well-meaning family members and other Christians, motivated by love for us, may tell us what we want to hear. "Get out," they may say. "God doesn't want His children to hurt. Move on to a better situation."

Yet God may want us to remain in that circumstance, not because He delights in causing us pain, but because He has a greater goal. Perseverance develops deeper character or a stronger trust in the Lord. Authentic testimony under trial may lead to the salvation of someone watching from a distance. Heartache now may enable us to comfort someone later in a similar situation.

Good people can give bad counsel. Discernment comes from knowing God's Word.

*Heavenly Father, help me discern godly counsel according to the truth of Your Word.*

Do I know the Bible well enough to recognize bad counsel, even when it comes from other Christians? If not, what can I do to begin an in-depth study of God's Word today?

# AN APT ANSWER
## Proverbs 15:21–28

A man has joy in an apt answer,
And how delightful is a timely word!

Proverbs 15:23

Being asked for advice can be an ego boost. Someone else values our opinion enough to consider applying it. However, giving good counsel is not as easy as we might think, especially if we desire to give *godly* counsel.

So, how should we respond? Before we say a word, we should pray that our Counselor would give us wisdom and discernment to speak *His* counsel. Second, resist the urge to offer opinions. Good counsel is never about personal opinions; it is always rooted in the wisdom of God's Word. We also need to understand all the facts of the situation. People often neglect to tell us certain details so they'll receive advice they *want* instead of the counsel they *need*.

Once we understand the complete situation and we know what the Bible says, the next step is to point the other person to the Word of God. Rather than telling him the answer, help him see what the Bible says as he opens God's Word for himself.

When we provide counsel in accordance with the Word of God, it truly is an "apt answer" and a "timely word."

*Lord, forgive me for when I have been quick with*
*my opinion and slow with Your Word.*

How can I guard against giving opinions instead of God's Word when asked for advice?

# MORE THAN SURVIVAL
## 2 Corinthians 4:7–18

God, who gives . . . encouragement.

Romans 15:5 NLT

The devil rarely plays fair. Problems come when we least expect them and often when we have exhausted our resources to respond to them.

The apostle Paul knew what it was like to live with trouble. He had been beaten, whipped, and shipwrecked. He had suffered hunger, thirst, and persecution.

However, Paul did more than merely survive these troubles. Regardless of what he suffered for the sake of the gospel, Paul could declare that he did not lose heart. God encouraged him as he worked to advance the kingdom of Jesus Christ.

God still provides encouragement, many times from unexpected sources and in unexpected ways. He infuses us with courage through Bible verses that speak to our spirits during our quiet times with Him. He cheers our hearts with music or messages that seem to be written just for us. He lifts our souls with the joy of leading others to a relationship with Christ.

We can go through life in survival mode, reeling from problem to problem, or we can enjoy the encouragement of God, trusting Him for our future. Which way do *you* want to live?

*Lord God, thank You for the encouragement You bring in the midst of my circumstances.*

In what area of life am I in "survival mode"? How might God be encouraging me today?

# NAYSAYERS OR YAY-SAYERS?
## Acts 9:10–28

Barnabas . . . (which translated means Son of Encouragement).

Acts 4:36

Are you a naysayer or a yay-sayer? Naysayers are motivated by fear. They object to most everything, using phrases such as *we can't, we've always done it this way*, and *it will never work*. Yay-sayers pepper their conversations with phrases such as *we can*, and *let's give it a try*.

Naysayers and yay-sayers are nothing new. In the early church, God had used the disciples who had been with Jesus to spread the good news of salvation in Christ. However, the Lord was about to shake things up even more. He grabbed hold of Saul, changed his name to Paul, and made him God's missionary to the Gentiles as well as to Israel.

Most of the disciples allowed fear to govern their initial response to Paul. Ananias and Barnabas, however, moved beyond their fears to be an encouragement. Ananias referred to him as "brother" and healed him. Barnabas, the Son of Encouragement, put his life and his reputation on the line. He took hold of Paul and brought him to the other apostles.

True encouragers are not motivated by fear. They use positive words, and then follow them with positive action, always depending on their heavenly Encourager.

*Heavenly Father, give me a heart like Barnabas and help me be an encouragement today.*

Do I have a reputation as an encourager or a discourager? Whom can I encourage today?

# MINISTRY OF ENCOURAGEMENT
## Romans 1:8–12

> I'm eager to encourage you in your faith, but I
> also want to be encouraged by yours. In this way,
> each of us will be a blessing to the other.
>
> Romans 1:12 NLT

A friend of mine has a ministry of encouragement. In person and by email, all who speak with him leave their encounter infused with renewed encouragement to live for the Lord in their present circumstances. What makes him unusual is that for thirty-three years he has had Lou Gehrig's disease, a neurodegenerative condition producing muscle weakness and atrophy. Even in his wheelchair, he is still at his post as a greeter in church every Sunday morning.

The apostle Paul was a great encourager. He filled his epistles with words of appreciation and intercessory prayer. He urged believers to be all God intended for them to be. Paul also understood that encouragement is a two-way street. Not only did he desire to encourage the Christians in Rome, he also longed to be encouraged *by* them.

Faithful obedience to the Lord not only brings blessing to us, our lives become a testimony of encouragement to others in the body of Christ, and they encourage us, too!

> *Lord God, use me to be an encouragement as I am*
> *encouraged by my brothers and sisters in Christ.*
> *Help us work together to advance Your kingdom.*

How is God using the body of Christ as a source of mutual encouragement in my life?

# HE HOLDS OUR HANDS
## Psalm 37:23–27

The steps of the godly are directed by the LORD.

Psalm 37:23 NLT

Whenever I vacation in a new city, the first thing I do is take a short bus tour. In a matter of hours, I am able to enjoy an overview of the city while listening to a tour guide describe the sites. Then, armed with maps and written guides, I determine which locations I want to revisit, and which less touristy sites I want to explore. The tour guides—both written and human—are indispensable in helping me find my way around.

Life can be like a new city. Unfamiliar roads lead to unexpected destinations. Goals we worked hard to achieve fail to bring us happiness. Instead, the less-traveled path provides the greatest satisfaction. However, we would be hopelessly lost without our Guide.

God promises in His Word to guide us. He directs our steps and holds our hands as we travel through each day. He accompanies us and provides for us throughout our journey. He catches us when we fall. Most of all, He never leaves us alone.

Our Guide knows the way. Why follow anyone else?

*Holy Lord, thank You for being my Guide. You have shown me the way of salvation, and You keep me in Your salvation each day of my life.*

What situation is causing me uncertainty? How is God guiding me today?

# STRAIGHTEN CROOKED PLACES
## Proverbs 3:1–6

In all your ways acknowledge him,
and he will make your paths straight.

Proverbs 3:6 NIV

A growing attitude in our culture encourages us to compartmentalize our lives. A box for religion, another for work. One for family and another for school. Each section separate and distinct from the others.

When we live this way, our lives become crooked. We fall for the world's lie that different values apply to different areas. We are kind and gracious on Sunday mornings but cutthroat and competitive Monday through Friday, because "that's how you get ahead" in the corporate world. We teach children about our great Creator-God, but tell college biology professors what they want to hear about evolution, because "that's how you pass the class."

God's Word reminds us that success does *not* depend on having a different set of values and standards for the various parts of our lives. If we are His children, we will live by His standards and His guidance in every area of life, regardless of the day or the location.

When we acknowledge Him, He will straighten all the crooked places in our lives.

*Father, forgive me for the times I failed to acknowledge You and follow Your guidance.*

What area of life have I compartmentalized and failed to acknowledge God in? How can I apply His guidance in that area today?

# SAME GUIDE, DIFFERENT GUIDANCE
### Romans 8:14–17

All who are guided by God's Spirit are God's children.

Romans 8:14 GW

Growing up in the same family does not mean family members will be the same. Sisters may look alike, but have vividly different talents. Brothers may have similar builds, but wildly differing aspirations. Even identical twins will have different personalities.

In the family of God, Christians have the same heavenly Father, but also have unique combinations of personalities, experiences, talents, and abilities. As we work together to further Christ's kingdom, God directs us according to our distinct temperaments and gifts.

We need to avoid comparing ourselves to each other. Consider two men who come to Christ the same day in the same church. God may lead one to the foreign mission field to labor among aboriginal tribes, while He appoints the other to share the gospel with his country-club neighbors. Other Christians may judge the one who goes overseas as spiritual and the one who stays as carnal or selfish. Yet each one is being obedient to God's leading.

God guides all His children, but He does not guide us all the same way.

*Lord, help me obey Your leading without judging*
*how other Christians are obeying You.*

Have I been comparing the tasks God has for me to the work others are doing for Him? How can I encourage another Christian in his or her calling today?

# NOT SECOND-CLASS
## John 14:21–26

> But the Helper, the Holy Spirit, whom the Father will
> send in My name, He will teach you all things, and
> bring to your remembrance all that I said to you.
>
> John 14:26

The term *helper* often carries second-class connotations. We have been conditioned to believe that those who can, *do*, while those who can't, *help*. Classroom "helpers" assist "real" teachers. Job listings for skilled trades such as carpenters, electricians, and plumbers often include "helper" entries—positions so low, they rank below apprentices. Even some wives associate the label *helper* with second-class status.

The Bible frequently refers to God as our Helper. Helper also describes the Holy Spirit's broad role in equipping us to be all God intended as His children. The Holy Spirit is the One who regenerates, sanctifies, and comforts us. The Holy Spirit within each believer empowers us to say no to sin. He guides, teaches, and seals us.

The Holy Spirit was essential in creation (Gen. 1:2) and in the incarnation of Christ (Matt. 1:18). Our salvation depends on Him as much as it does on the Father and the Son. There is nothing second-class about the Helper.

*Helper, thank You for the assurance that I have Your
help every hour of every day.*

How do I react to being called a helper? How can the Holy Spirit help me to help others?

# Practical, Prayerful Help
## 2 Corinthians 1:8–11

He will rescue us because you are helping by praying for us.

2 Corinthians 1:11 NLT

I wish I could do more to help, but I'll pray for you." An air of helplessness often accompanies these words as we come alongside someone facing daunting circumstances. We may not be able to do anything *practical*, but at least we can pray as a last resort.

The early church had a very different view of prayer. Prayer was the *first* thing they did, not the last. Both practical and powerful, prayer enlisted the intervention of God Himself. Prayer unlocked jail cells and set prisoners free. Prayer brought direction and healing.

In his second letter to the Corinthian church, the apostle Paul described the suffering he experienced in Asia. The perils were so severe that death seemed to be their only future. Paul's gratitude to God accompanied his gratitude to the Christians in Corinth for the help they provided through their prayers.

If we want to be helpful, prayer is always the best place to start.

*Heavenly Father, forgive me for the times I have viewed prayer as a last resort rather than as a first priority. Help me to help others by praying for them.*

In what situation have I felt helpless? How can I pray for God's help in that situation today?

339

# GIVING AND RECEIVING
## Romans 16:1–16

Help her in whatever matter she may have need of you; for she herself has also been a helper of many, and of myself as well.

Romans 16:2

Some of us are born helpers. If anyone needs help, we are right there. Need a meal or someone to watch the kids? No problem. Need a lift to the airport or help moving? Sure thing.

Just don't expect *us* to ask for help. No matter how difficult the situation, we do not want to admit that we are not in complete control. Things may be difficult, but we'll muddle along quite well, thank you very much.

When the apostle Paul closed his letter to the church in Rome, he included a list of greetings, and acknowledged several fellow workers in the cause of Christ. One of those mentioned was Phoebe, the person who carried Paul's letter to Rome. He described her as "a helper of many," including himself. He also requested that the Christians in Rome provide her with whatever help she needed to enable her to continue serving the Lord.

Paul and Phoebe understood that even helpers need help. Following their example is much better than muddling along.

*Lord God, help me to give and receive help as I serve
You in the cause of Christ.*

In what area have I been reluctant to ask others for help? What help can I ask for today?

# WATER OF LIFE
## John 7:14–39

Rivers of living water will brim and spill out of the depths of
anyone who believes in me this way, just as the Scripture says.

John 7:38 Message

More than 50 percent of the human body is composed of water.
For infants, it can be as high as 75 percent. Water, then, is
critical to sustaining physical life. We may be able to last
four to six weeks without food, but we could not survive more than
ten days without water.

The ancient Israelites associated water with the Feast of Taber-
nacles. On the last day of the feast, the high priest would draw water
from the Pool of Siloam and lead a procession back to the temple,
where he poured out the water as a sacrifice to God. The water represented the water from the rock during their wilderness wanderings,
as well as the rain needed for the next harvest.

On the last day of this Feast, Jesus chose to proclaim Himself the
source of living water. He invited all listeners—then and now—to
come to Him to satisfy the thirst in their souls.

Just as there is no physical life without water, there is no spiritual
life apart from Jesus Christ, the source of living water. His Holy Spirit
quenches every thirst.

*Holy Lord, You alone provide eternal life. Thank
You for quenching my spiritual thirst with living
water.*

What part of my life has been feeling dry? How am I looking for
God to rain in this area?

# HOT OR COLD
## Revelation 3:14–21

Because you are lukewarm, and
neither hot nor cold, I will spit you out.

Revelation 3:16

Nothing beats a glass of ice-cold water on a hot day. And on cold, winter mornings, a hot shower is the perfect thing to get us going.

When Jesus rebuked the Laodicean church, He referred to hot and cold. His words might not make sense to us at first glance. "I wish you were cold or hot." Why would Jesus *want* people to be cold if "hot" people are enthusiastic and on fire for a cause, and "cold" people lack passion?

Laodicea's location gives us a clue to the meaning. It was near two cities, Hierapolis and Colossae. People traveled to Hierapolis for its soothing, therapeutic hot springs. Colossae was situated near refreshing, cold springs. Laodicea's water supply, however, came through an underground conduit system. By the time the water reached the city, it was lukewarm and foul.

Jesus Christ gives us living water, but what do we do with it? When our goal is to be as inoffensive as possible by keeping quiet about our Savior, then He is the One we will offend!

We are to live in a way that refreshes and soothes; we cannot do that by being lukewarm.

*Heavenly Father, help me be a conduit of Your re-
freshment and healing as I reflect Jesus.*

How can I reflect Christ today in a way that will be either refreshing or soothing to others?

# VULNERABLE FOR CHRIST
## John 4:7–42

The woman left her waterpot, and went
into the city . . . "Come, see."

John 4:28–29

A friend once confided in me, "I could never tell my family about Christ—you don't know the things I've done. They would throw my past in my face."

It's a good thing the Samaritan woman at the well did not feel that way. Jesus told her about the living water that quenches spiritual thirst and brings eternal life. In the course of their conversation, He also exposed her life of sin and revealed Himself as the long-awaited Messiah.

The woman could have quietly returned to the city without telling anyone of her encounter. Why would the respectable residents of her city listen to her? Still, she chose to make herself vulnerable. "Come, see," she said, and they not only listened, they came to see for themselves. Because she spoke up, "many of the Samaritans believed in Him" (John 4:39).

Our enemy celebrates when we keep quiet, ashamed of our pasts and fearful of how others will respond. However, Jesus redeemed our pasts—they are no longer counted against us. He calls us to be vulnerable with others, to show them what He can do with a surrendered life.

*Lord, give me a willing heart to share Christ with*
*others. Help me look beyond my own vulnerability*
*to see their need for You.*

How has fear or shame kept me from speaking about Jesus? How can I share Him today?

# FAMILY RESEMBLANCE
## 2 Corinthians 3:12–18

> But we all . . . are being transformed into the
> same image from glory to glory.
>
> 2 Corinthians 3:18

Do people say things like, "You've got your father's nose" or "You've got your mother's eyes"? The older I become, the more people tell me how much I resemble my mother. More than eye color or the shape of my nose, my mannerisms—the half-smile I sometimes have, the way I raise my eyebrows, and the inflections in my voice—remind people of my mother.

We cannot control which family members we look like, but there *is* someone we should always want to resemble. When we yield to the transforming power of God's Holy Spirit as He works in our lives, God conforms us to the image of His Son, Jesus Christ. He gives us the fruit of His presence: love, joy, peace, patience, kindness, goodness, faithfulness, gentleness, and self-control (Gal. 5:22–23) as we surrender to Him each minute of every day.

It doesn't matter whether we look like our mothers or our fathers, Aunt Ellen or Uncle Bob. The One we really want to resemble is Jesus.

*Holy Lord, thank You for Your transforming work*
*in me. Continue working in me until I become Your*
*masterpiece and look just like You.*

Do others see more of Jesus in me with each passing day? If not, why not?

# SINNER OR SAINT?

## James 1:19–27

But prove yourselves doers of the word, and not merely hearers.

James 1:22

Many of us have wondered at the transformation of a caterpillar into a butterfly, or marveled at the development of a tadpole into a frog. Yet every Christian has experienced an even more amazing transformation.

As Christians, we frequently refer to ourselves as "sinners, saved by grace." We remember how God rescued us from the muck and mire of a life controlled by sin and separated from Him. However, we are *no longer* sinners, we are "a new creature" (2 Cor. 5:17).

Butterflies do not crawl like caterpillars, frogs do not swim the same way as tadpoles, and Christians should no longer behave like sinners. The apostle James noted the various ways we have changed. We are no longer to be quick-tempered. We should be putting aside all immorality and wickedness, while increasing in humility. Our lives should consistently manifest God's Word in action as we progressively sin less and less.

Butterflies have transformed from caterpillars, frogs have changed from tadpoles, and Christians are no longer "sinners, saved by grace." Now, we are "saints who occasionally sin."

*Heavenly Father, help me see myself as You see me:*
*a child of God set apart for You.*

How can viewing myself as a saint instead of a sinner change the way I behave?

345

# TEAM MEMBERS
## 1 Corinthians 15:50–58

Not all of us will die, but we will all be changed.

1 Corinthians 15:51 GW

Aday is coming when, "in the twinkling of an eye" (1 Cor. 15:52), every Christian will be changed beyond anything our imaginations can conceive. Jesus Christ will give the signal, the dead will be raised, and we will be given immortal bodies.

We do not know when that day of final change will come. Until then, Christians are in the unique position of having been transformed into new life, yet still needing the Holy Spirit to apply His righteousness to our daily behavior. The process of this transformation will continue until we go to be with Him forever.

The apostle Paul compared our journey through life to running a marathon (Heb. 12:1). Since we are all running the same race, we need to cheer each other on as members of the same team. There is no room for jealousy or competition.

We have the opportunity to help or to hinder other Christians every day as they travel toward the finish line. Which will we choose?

*Dear Lord, help me to be a cheerleader for other Christians as we run this race together until we stand in Your presence forever.*

Have I been jealous of other Christians? How can I cheer on another Christian today?

# IT WASN'T THE NAILS
## 1 John 4:7–10

God is love.

1 John 4:8 Message

Why does God forgive our sins? Many Christians would say He forgives our sins because He loves us, but that is not what the Bible says.

God does not forgive us because He loves us. If God forgives us simply because He loves us, He would compromise His own character. His love cannot accept what His holiness judges. God's holiness cannot tolerate sin, no matter how small the sin might be or how great His love is.

God forgives us because Christ paid the price of our redemption through His death on the cross. The apostle John said, "This is love: not that we have loved God, but that he loved us and sent his Son to be the payment for our sins" (1 John 4:10 GW). God showed us His love by satisfying His holiness and justice through the sacrifice of His Son. The *reason* He sent His Son, however, is because He loves us.

God's holiness sent Jesus to the cross. The soldiers used nails, but it was His love for us that held Him there.

*Holy Lord, thank You for loving me so much that
Jesus satisfied Your justice for me.*

Do I focus on God's holiness apart from His love? How is my relationship with the Lord affected by the way I view His holiness *and* His love?

# HEART, SOUL, AND MIND
## Matthew 22:34–40

Jesus answered him, "Love the Lord your God with all your
heart, with all your soul, and with all your mind."

Matthew 22:37 GW

How complete is your love for God? Some measure their love
for God by how often they attend church or by the size of
their donations. Others evaluate their love for God by how
much time they spend in prayer or how often they share the gospel
with others.

Jesus said that if we really love Him, we will do so with every fiber
of our being. We will love Him with our whole heart—the center
of all our desires. We will also love Him with our whole soul—the
essence of our personality. Finally, we will love Him with our whole
mind—our thoughts, reasoning, and intelligence.

When we love the Lord with all our heart, soul, and mind, it will
be evident in our lives. The ultimate test, however, is whether intimacy
with Him produces obedience to His Word. "If you love me, you will
obey my commandments" (John 14:15 GW).

How complete is our love for God? The answer will be found in
the completeness of our obedience to Him.

*Lord, forgive me for when my obedience has not
matched my profession of love for You.*

Would Jesus Christ say I love Him with all my heart, soul, and
mind? If not, why not?

# AGAPE

## 1 John 4:11–21

Beloved, if God so loved us, we also ought to love one another.

1 John 4:11

The world tells us that love is all that is needed to solve our problems and deepen our relationships. But what kind of love?

*Eros* is a physical love that is selfish and conditional. It communicates, "I love you as long as you continue to please me." Brotherly love communicates, "I love you because we have something in common." Brotherly love includes mutual interest, but it is also a conditional love.

God's unconditional love is different. *Agape* says, "I love you, not because of who you are, but because of who I am." God loves us because of who *He* is, not because we have done anything to be worthy of His love. When we agape others, we are saying, "I love you, not because of what you can do for me, but because God's love flows through me to you."

The apostle Paul described agape in 1 Corinthians 13:4–8. He said agape is patient and kind. It is not jealous, bragging, or arrogant. Agape is not easily provoked and does not keep a record of wrongs. It rejoices with the truth and endures all things.

We need love in all our relationships, but the only type of love that will last is agape.

*Loving Lord, help me to be a vessel through which*
*You agape those around me.*

Who does God want to agape through me today? In what specific way can I show this person His love?

# JOYFUL TOMORROWS
## Zephaniah 3:12–20

He will rejoice over you with shouts of joy.

Zephaniah 3:17

*T*omorrow. It overflows with potential and uncertainty. Depending on our perspective, *tomorrow* can prompt shivers of fear or squeals of anticipation.

The prophet Zephaniah spoke of Israel's tomorrows. First, Zephaniah warned the people of coming judgment. Because of their idolatry and rebellion, God had previously judged the northern kingdom of Israel through Assyria's conquest. The southern kingdom of Judah would soon fall to the Babylonian empire.

Zephaniah also prophesied a more distant future. Someday, Messiah would return and dwell in their midst. God Himself would judge Israel's enemies and restore His people to their land. The Lord will rejoice over them when He gathers them back to shower them with blessing.

Your immediate future may appear as bleak as Israel's did. Uncertainty may be driving you to fear tomorrow. Remember that God has already won our eternal victory. Trust the One who rejoices over us today and holds our tomorrows in the palms of His nail-scarred hands.

*Heavenly Father, thank You for making me the object of Your joy. Help me rest and rejoice in the eternal victory You have won for me.*

How can I prevent fear of tomorrow from stealing my joy today?

# SOURCE OF JOY
## Luke 10:17–21

Rejoice that your names are written in heaven.

Luke 10:20 NIV

Many things can make us happy. A promotion at work, a marriage proposal, or a new baby can bring smiles to our faces. But is that the same as being truly joyful?

Jesus had sent seventy of His followers on a "mission trip" to spread the gospel message. When they returned, they were filled with joy at the results. They had been successful in sharing the Good News, and the demons had responded to their authority as Christ's representatives.

While Jesus was pleased with the outcome of their travels, He also gave them a gentle rebuke. They rejoiced in the wrong thing. Rather than rejoicing in their success over the spiritual world, they should have been rejoicing in their salvation.

Christians rejoice in knowing who God is—our loving heavenly Father, the Redeemer who sacrificed Himself for us, and the Holy Spirit who is always with us.

The true source of our joy is not things, experiences, or even service to God. The true source of our joy is that we—and others—are in a right relationship with God Himself.

*Holy Lord, help me look to my relationship with*
*You as the source of my joy.*

How have I been depending on my circumstances for happiness instead of looking to Jesus for my joy?

# GROW, SERVE, REJOICE
## 3 John 1:1–4

I have no greater joy than this, to hear of my
children walking in the truth.

3 John 1:4

Church ministries are always looking for volunteers to help in
advancing the kingdom of Jesus Christ. Some Christians assume only those in full-time ministry are qualified for certain
tasks, but pastors can do just so much. They are already responsible
for the spiritual growth of the flock through preaching, teaching,
and counseling. Pastors frequently have financial and administrative
duties as well.

As the apostle John shepherded the early Christians, he knew the
joy that came from seeing others grow in their relationship with Christ.
John wrote this particular letter to a beloved fellow Christian whose
obedience to the truth of the gospel gave him great delight.

Pastors need our support today. We can increase their joy as we
grow in Christ and obey the truth of God's Word. We can also share
in the work of ministry through giving and serving.

As we grow in our relationship with Jesus and serve Him through
the local church, we will also know the joy that comes from seeing
people come to Christ and grow in Him.

*Lord, give me a heart that desires to serve You and
rejoices when others find You.*

Does the spiritual growth of others cause me joy? How can I
encourage someone in his or her spiritual growth today?

# COMPASSIONATE PATIENCE
## 2 Peter 3:1–9

The Lord is not slow in keeping his
promise. . . . He is patient with you.

2 Peter 3:9 NIV

Patience may be a virtue, but we do not always appreciate this trait. We may dismiss patient people as timid, cowardly, or non-confrontational. Some people have even misinterpreted God's patience as a negative quality.

The apostle Peter described a time when unbelievers will mock God's patience. Peter noted that Christians will be rejected when they speak of sin and judgment. False teachers who relish their own sin will conveniently forget two significant events: creation and the worldwide flood. The act of creation established God's ownership of the universe. The flood proves that God holds us accountable to Him.

God is not slow in fulfilling His promise of coming judgment; His judgment will come in His time. God's patience, however, is motivated by compassion for people as He gives humanity persistent opportunities to be restored to their Creator and to acknowledge Him as Lord.

As we consider our relationship with God, how grateful we should be that He did not run out of patience before He restored us to Him!

*Holy Lord, thank You for Your patience in drawing
me to You despite my stubbornness.*

How has God revealed His patience in my salvation and in my daily walk with Him?

# WAITING

## Hebrews 11:32–40

None of them received all that God had promised.

Hebrews 11:39 NLT

In a culture that promotes instant gratification, "wait" is a four-letter word. Grocery aisles are filled with instant coffee, instant tea, and "homemade" ready-to-eat cookies. Internet access provides a world of information in seconds, but it is still not quick enough as we seek faster and faster downloads. Email is now too slow and has been replaced by texting, which will be replaced by something else even faster. When we want something, we want it *now*.

Contrast this mindset with God's people throughout history. Hebrews 11 lists many who followed the Lord and waited on His promises. Although these Old Testament believers waited on the Lord, many of them endured adversity and suffering without ever seeing the fulfillment of those promises and prophecies.

How willing are we to wait on the Lord? Some of us have been praying for good things, such as the salvation of loved ones. Will we trust God for His timing, even if it means we may never see the answer ourselves?

*Heavenly Father, help me patiently trust You as I*
*wait on Your answers and Your timing.*

How willing am I to wait on God's timing for my requests? How can I use my waiting time to honor Him?

# COMPLAINING OR PATIENT?
## James 5:7–11

> You too be patient. . . . Do not
> complain, brethren, against one another.
>
> James 5:8–9

It is a bit ironic that the Christian life would be so much easier if it were not for all the people we have to deal with. We all have difficult people in our lives, and you're probably thinking of a particular person right now!

After Jesus Christ's resurrection, the early Christians eagerly awaited His return. Many expected Jesus to return in their lifetime. While they waited, they had little patience for the unfair practices of the rich and powerful, even among believers. They looked for Christ to come quickly to make all things right.

Injustice also angers the Holy Spirit, and He used the apostle James to rebuke those who abused their wealth and power. James also urged believers to be patient as they waited for Christ's return. Today, we are still to be patient in adversity, trusting the Lord to convict those who misuse their privileges. They will respond to His conviction or face His judgment.

In the meantime, an attitude of complaining only reinforces our discontent. God calls us to be as patient with others as He is with us.

*Lord, help me reflect Your patience in my relation-*
*ships with the difficult people in my life.*

---

Who in my life consistently causes me to lose patience? Why does this person get to me?

# OUR TENDERHEARTED GOD
## Titus 3:3–11

I am the LORD, who exercises kindness.

Jeremiah 9:24 NIV

What qualities combine to make a person *kind*? We may think of characteristics such as warmth, gentleness, and sensitivity. However, kindness is more than an attitude of warm fuzzies. Kindness is attitude in action. Kind people are tenderhearted toward the needs of others. This tenderness moves them to meet the needs they see.

The Bible reminds us that kindness is also a characteristic of God. In His mercy, He tenderly cares for His children, meeting our needs. He began with our greatest need, the need to restore our broken fellowship with Him. The apostle Paul spoke of the "kindness of God" appearing in the person of Jesus Christ, our Savior (Titus 3:4).

God is kindness personified. His tender mercy did not abandon us. Rather, His kindness reached into the ugly world of our sin and met our need at the ultimate cost of His Son's life. Kindness in action!

*Holy Lord, thank You for Your tenderhearted response to my sinfulness. Help me always respond with gratitude to Your everlasting kindness.*

God demonstrated His kindness to me in salvation. How does He continue to express His kindness to me as I walk with Him each day?

# GROWING IN KINDNESS
## 1 Peter 2:1–3

> Grow in respect to salvation, if you have
> tasted the kindness of the Lord.
>
> 1 Peter 2:2–3

New mothers watch their children's development closely. They celebrate their babies' growth from infancy to toddlerhood, and on to childhood, adolescence, and youth. Physical, mental, and emotional milestones indicate normal development. Missing a milestone may indicate a problem.

New Christians should also develop and progress in their faith. The apostle Peter reminded us that if we are the recipients of God's kindness, our lives will reflect the changes His kindness brings. We should be putting aside our former way of life, no longer behaving as unbelievers. Holding on to anger, hypocrisy, or wrong conversation will stunt our growth.

Do those around us see a difference in our lives since we tasted God's kindness? If we want people to respond to Jesus Christ, we ought to live in a way that manifests the reality of spiritual birth *and* spiritual growth.

> *Heavenly Father, forgive me for not responding to*
> *Your kindness when I fail to put aside old habits*
> *and ways. Help me love Your Word and yield to*
> *Your direction.*

Is there a difference in my life since I "tasted the kindness of the Lord"? How have I grown compared to last week, last month, or last year?

# KINDNESS TO THE LEAST
## Matthew 25:31–46

Whatever you did for one of the least . . . you did for me.

Matthew 25:40 NIV

When I worked in New York City, I became accustomed to seeing an occasional homeless person begging on the sidewalks. Family and friends cautioned me to resist the urge to give money. They assumed that poor choices had led to the beggars' circumstances and the money would be used for substances other than food.

Jesus told His followers to meet the needs of those around them. Feed the hungry, show hospitality, clothe the needy, and visit the sick and those in prison. He did not say anything about *deserving* help. After all, if merit is the determining factor, then He should not have saved *us*!

So, how did I respond to the beggars on the city streets? When I had the opportunity, I offered to buy them a meal at the closest diner or fast-food store. The truly hungry accepted with gratitude. The others declined.

Kindness does not see a need, pat the person on the head, and send them off with a "Praise the Lord, God will provide." Kindness meets needs in practical ways with the same tender heart God demonstrates to us.

*Lord God, help me reflect Your tender kindness as
I respond to the needs around me.*

How can I respond with kindness to the needs of someone else today?

# GOD ALONE
## Luke 18:18–27

> Why do you call me good? No one is good except God.
>
> Luke 18:19 GW

How good is God? Good enough not to leave us in the mess we make of our lives. Good enough to summon us to something higher and purer than we would pursue on our own. Good enough to challenge us to settle for nothing less than an intimate relationship with Him.

The young man who approached Jesus had the right destination in mind but he followed the wrong track. He was interested in salvation, but made some critical errors. First, he called Jesus "good" without realizing that true goodness belongs to God alone. Jesus *is* God, but the man did not realize this when he spoke to Him. Next, he thought of eternal life as something to be earned, rather than a gift offered by God. Finally, he had an inflated opinion of himself. He believed he had kept the whole Law, but no one had ever been able to do that other than Jesus Christ. Jesus cut through the man's self-deception with one challenge: "Sell all that you possess" (Luke 18:22).

God will always say the hard thing to us—hard things we do not want to hear, but things we *need* to hear. He does it because He is truly good. No one else comes close.

> *Lord, I praise You because You are good. Thank You for offering Your goodness to me.*

What hard thing has God spoken to me this past week? How does He want me to respond?

# CLINGING TO HIS GOODNESS
## Psalm 27:1–14

We know that God causes all things to work
together for good to those who love God, to those
who are called according to His purpose.

Romans 8:28

If God is good, why doesn't He accomplish His purposes without allowing bad things to happen to His children? Christians have struggled with this question through the ages.

The psalmist trusted he would see the goodness of God in this life as well as in the life to come. This does not mean unpleasant things will never occur. Regardless of events, we can cling to God's goodness, knowing He will work all things for our ultimate good and His glory.

A few years ago, a follower of Christ stopped to help a stranded motorist. His teenage son was with him, but stood several feet away. A drunk driver crossed the highway, killing the man and the motorist. A year later, when his widow was asked how she was coping, she said, "All I know is God is good. When I can't seem to do one thing in a day, when I don't understand why God would take my husband, a man with so much to give, I remind myself that God is good."

God's goodness is not contingent on our understanding. God's goodness is part of His nature. When we do not understand God or His goodness, we can still trust . . . and cling.

*Father, thank You for surrounding me with Your*
*goodness regardless of my situation.*

How has God revealed His goodness to me in my most difficult experiences?

# DO GOOD, REAP BETTER
## Galatians 6:6–10

Let us not lose heart in doing good, for . . .
we will reap if we do not grow weary.

Galatians 6:9

The Pareto Principle, also known as the 80/20 Rule, states that 80 percent of what we measure is caused by 20 percent of the initiating factors. Many churches experience a simple application of this rule every week: 80 percent of the work is done by 20 percent of the people.

After a while, the 20 percent may become discouraged and weary, especially if there is a lack of appreciation in addition to the lack of assistance. The apostle Paul must have understood what it felt like to be part of this group. He experienced life-threatening travels, hardships, and persecution—all for the good of the early church and advancing the kingdom of Jesus Christ.

There is another rule we should consider. The Bible often speaks of the rule of sowing and reaping. Paul reminded us that when we sow to the desires of our flesh, we reap corrupt fruit. When we obey the Spirit in our sowing, we enjoy the blessings of eternal life.

Do not be weary in doing good, even if you are one of the 20 percent. Our good God sees what you are doing for Him, and He will reward.

*Lord, help me look to You for my motivation and encouragement to continue doing good.*

In what area of service am I experiencing a lack of appreciation and help? How do Paul's words encourage me to continue doing good?

# DICTUM MEUM PACTUM
## Lamentations 3:19–25

Great is your faithfulness.

Lamentations 3:23 NIV

For thousands of years, a handshake was enough to seal a deal. People could be trusted on their word alone, as reflected in the original motto of the London Stock Exchange: *dictum meum pactum*, literally "my word is my bond." While we still engage in oral contracts today, the weight of a handshake has dissipated. Written contracts for legally binding agreements have become standard practice.

After Babylon conquered Judah and destroyed Jerusalem, the prophet Jeremiah still proclaimed Yahweh's faithfulness. The God of Israel had not abandoned His people; He had simply fulfilled His promise to discipline the nation for its sins. Because the Lord is faithful, Jeremiah knew that God would deliver His people at the right time.

People may not always be faithful to their word, but God is always faithful to His. We can always rely on our Heavenly Father. He has proven Himself dependable through His Word and faithful in the lives of those who belong to Him.

> Holy Lord, thank You for revealing Your faithfulness in Your Word and in me.

When has God acted in a way that *seemed* unfaithful to me? What did He teach me about His faithfulness through that experience?

# PROMISES, PROMISES
## Revelation 1:1–7

> Jesus Christ, who is the faithful witness.
>
> Revelation 1:5 NIV

Broken promises hurt. They cut us where we are most vulnerable. We depended on that person to keep his word and he failed us. We may vow never to trust again.

Disappointments with other people cause some to view God with similar cynicism. Will God's promises be as empty as the promises of the father who abandoned you? Will He fail to keep His Word like the husband who broke his marriage vows?

God always keeps His Word. When sin first entered the world in the Garden of Eden, the Lord promised victory over Satan (Gen. 3:15). Hundreds of prophecies throughout the Old Testament speak in great detail of the coming Messiah. He said He would come, and He sent His Son. He said He would save us, and He sacrificed His Son in our place. He said He would never leave us, and He gave us His Spirit. He said He will come again, and He will!

God is not like other people. If God said it, we can believe it, because He is faithful.

*Heavenly Father, thank You for Your faithfulness
to me, even when I have been faithless.*

---

How has God shown Himself faithful to me? How does His past faithfulness give me assurance in what I am facing today?

# RELAY RACES
## 2 Timothy 2:1–13

The things which you have heard from me
. . . entrust these to faithful men.

2 Timothy 2:2

Relay races incorporate added suspense over standard races. The outcome is dependent on individual skill *and* the runners' ability to work as a team in passing the baton.

Christians are also engaged in a relay race. The apostle Paul had trained and discipled young Timothy to pastor a local church. In a previous letter, he had encouraged Timothy not to give anyone an excuse to disdain his youthfulness. Now Paul urged Timothy to take the training and teaching he had received and "pass the baton" to others to advance the kingdom of Christ. Paul exhorted Timothy to select faithful men for this important task.

We are still responsible to pass on what we have learned about our relationship with God. Mature Christians who have been walking with the Lord for many years should be discipling, training, and teaching others the precious truths God's Holy Spirit has taught them. Those new in their faith should seek others who will disciple them to grow in the grace and knowledge of Jesus Christ.

Are you on the sidelines or in training? Grab a baton and get in the race!

*Lord, help me participate in passing the baton to
others as Your kingdom advances.*

How can I disciple others or participate in being discipled within the body of Christ?

# THE GENTLE LAMB
## Matthew 21:1–11

Your king comes to you,
gentle and riding on a donkey.

Matthew 21:5 NIV

Throughout history, kings have carefully chosen the animals they rode. One famous story is told of the wild stallion sold to twelve-year-old Alexander the Great. No one could tame the superb horse but him, and Alexander went on to ride Bucephalus his entire military career.

When Jesus made His triumphal entry into Jerusalem, He could have chosen to ride a magnificent horse. Although it would have befitted His position as King of the universe, He didn't, because horses were associated with war. He chose a donkey, the preference of kings during peacetime.

Jesus's choice reflected His purpose in coming to Jerusalem. Before the week ended, He would be sacrificed as the gentle, sinless Lamb of God.

Make no mistake about our gentle Jesus, however. The first time He came to earth, He came in gentleness. When He comes again, Revelation 19:11 tells us, He will return on a white horse to execute judgment and wage war against His enemies.

*Gentle Jesus, thank You for tenderly drawing my heart to You.*

How has the Lord used gentleness to draw me to Him? How can I develop a greater sensitivity to His gentle promptings of my heart?

# HOT BUTTONS
## Proverbs 15:1–18

A gentle answer turns away wrath,
but a harsh word stirs up anger.

Proverbs 15:1 NIV

Do you know what your "hot buttons" are? Even worse, do other people know what your hot buttons are?

Many of us have people in our lives who seem to have a talent for getting under our skin. Our normally calm demeanor shifts in their presence. We may become tense, watching for the slightest offense. We may even prepare snappy comebacks, anticipating their negative remarks.

God's children are to respond differently to the difficult people in our lives. He calls us to bathe our responses in gentleness. Rather than escalate tensions, a gentle answer "turns away wrath." Although gentleness may be dismissed as a sign of weakness, it is just the opposite. It is actually a sign of a strong person who is in control of his emotions and behavior.

As we learn to respond with gentleness, our hot buttons will soon cool off, and our gentle responses will yield the fruit of peace.

*Father, forgive me for the times I have responded defensively or with anger. Help me have gentle answers for those who push my hot buttons, until my hot buttons are no more.*

What are my hot buttons? How can I surrender these areas to the Holy Spirit so that I respond with gentleness, regardless of the person or the subject?

# GENTLE DISCIPLESHIP
## 1 Thessalonians 2:1–12

> But we proved to be gentle among you, as a
> nursing mother tenderly cares for her own children.
>
> 1 Thessalonians 2:7

No mother expects her baby to run before he learns to crawl, or eat solid food before he learns to drink milk. Yet as Christians we may become impatient with others in their spiritual walk, forgetting that spiritual development also requires crawling before running and milk before solid food.

The apostle Paul reminded the believers in Thessalonica that he had been as gentle as a "nursing mother" when he was among them. They were spiritual children, and he was their spiritual parent. Paul had poured his life into their lives, tenderly teaching and training them, asking nothing in return.

Just as children do not all develop at the same pace, we should not expect other Christians to grow in their relationship with the Lord as quickly as we may have. It is especially easy to fall into this trap with those closest to us—a husband or wife, children or close friends.

Paul was as gentle as a nursing mother around new believers. Are we?

*Lord, help me reflect Your gentleness as I disciple
new believers in their walk with You.*

How have unrealistic expectations of others' spiritual growth affected my relationships?

# DIVINE RESTRAINT
## Isaiah 42:1–17

I have kept silent for a long time,
I have kept still and restrained Myself.

Isaiah 42:14

We do not often think of self-control as an attribute of God. *We* cultivate self-control because we are prone to sin. But why should *God* practice self-control?

Speaking through the prophet Isaiah, the Lord said, "I have kept still and restrained Myself." Like many of the other Old Testament prophets, Isaiah proclaimed the need for God's people to turn their hearts back to Him. Isaiah devoted much of his writing to God's judgment for the nation's sin and their need for a deliverer.

God dealt with Israel's sin by sending controlled judgment. Everything that happened to His people—including their captivities at the hands of neighboring pagan nations—occurred as God carefully meted out judgment, but never completely destroyed the nation.

Israel deserved to be destroyed for their disobedience to God. So do we. However, God restrained His righteous judgment and combined it with mercy. Not only was Israel not destroyed, we are not either. Instead, He tempered judgment with mercy and restored us to Him.

*Holy Lord, thank You for tempering Your judgment and pouring Your grace on me through Your Son. Help me never to take Your mercy and grace for granted.*

How have I experienced the mercy of God's restrained judgment in my life this week?

# BROKEN WALLS
## Proverbs 16:25–32

Like a city . . . without walls
is a man who has no control over his spirit.

Proverbs 25:28

E ver lose your temper, or say something you wish you hadn't?
Ever wish you could control the thoughts, words, or deeds of
others?

All of us have something in our past that we regret. We may wonder
why we could not restrain our tongue, control our impulses, or break
a habit. It all comes down to self-control, the final "fruit" in the list
of the fruit of the Spirit in Galatians 5:22–23.

The writer of Proverbs compared an individual's lack of self-control
to a city whose walls are missing. In biblical times, a city's walls provided its main protection. The taller and thicker the walls, the more
difficult it was for the enemy to break through.

Self-control is not merely a nice character quality to possess; it
is a gift of protection from the Holy Spirit as we yield to Him. Self-
control safeguards us from the self-destructive results of shortsighted
behavior. It protects us from the damaging consequences of thoughts,
words, and actions that do not honor God.

Greater than the power of controlling others is the power of controlling ourselves.

*Heavenly Father, help me yield to the Holy Spirit
as He develops self-control in me.*

In what area do I need to submit to the Holy Spirit to patch up
the "holes" in my "walls"?

# JUST SAY NO
## Galatians 1:6–10

> If I were still trying to please men, I would
> not be a bond-servant of Christ.
>
> Galatians 1:10

No. It is a tiny word, yet when I am approached to volunteer, it is difficult for me to say. *Can you help at church?* Nnn . . . yes. *Will you chair this committee?* Nnn . . . yes. *Will you host this event?* Nnn . . . yes. The title of a song from *Oklahoma!* describes me perfectly: "I Can't Say No."

The desire to please others is generally a good thing. It is true that the Bible speaks of putting others' interests ahead of our own. Still, if we do not manifest self-control in our lives, we will find ourselves saying yes to some things God never intended for us to do.

When the apostle Paul rebuked the Galatian Christians for accepting false teaching, he reminded them that his priority was not to please men. Rather, he—and all Christians—should be concerned with pleasing Christ first. That means we need to discern false teaching.

We are also to discern false demands on our time. Being asked to do something does not mean we must be the ones to do it. Saying yes to a good work *someone else* wants us to do may prevent us from saying yes to the good work *God* has prepared for us to do (Eph. 2:10).

Sometimes the most loving and self-controlled thing we can do is to just say no.

> *Lord, forgive me for when I have failed to say no*
> *to things that take me away from You and your*
> *purposes for me.*

How can examining my motives help me determine what tasks to say yes to today?

# A CONFIDENT ANTICIPATION
## Colossians 1:18–29

God wanted his people throughout the world to know
the glorious riches of this mystery—which is Christ
living in you, giving you the hope of glory.

Colossians 1:27 GW

Hopelessness abounds in our world. Suicide rates have climbed, fueled by depression, drug use, and general anxiety over life's stresses. Reading the morning newspaper or watching the evening news certainly does not help.

Even when we speak of *hope*, the modern meaning differs from how the Bible speaks of it. Today, we often use this word to express desire in the face of uncertainty. We say things like, "I hope I get the job," or "I hope my husband remembered my birthday." We do not know *if* these things will happen, regardless of how much we may *want* them to happen.

However, biblical hope is not an *if*, it is a *when* . . . and it is a *person*. Biblical hope is a confident anticipation in Jesus Christ. He *is* the hope of glory. Our future in Him is certain. We may not know when He will return, but we know He *will* return. We also know that we will be with Him for all eternity.

Christ is our glorious hope. There is absolutely nothing *iffy* about Him.

*Lord, You are my hope. Help me confidently rely
on You in the midst of uncertain times.*

How does confident hope in Christ change the way I will face my fears today?

# A DIFFERENT GRIEF
## 1 Thessalonians 4:13–18

*We do not want you to be uninformed, brethren,
about those who are asleep, so that you will not
grieve as do the rest who have no hope.*

1 Thessalonians 4:13

Losing a loved one can make us feel as if we have lost a part of ourselves. Death prompts grief that may seem overwhelming. Yet some Christians teach that it is inappropriate to express grief—as if this indicates a lack of trust in God.

In the Thessalonian church, some taught that believers who had died would miss the return of Christ. In his letter, the apostle Paul corrected this misinformation by explaining the order of events when all Christians, living *and* dead, will go to be with the Lord.

Paul did *not* say we don't grieve; he said we do not grieve *like unbelievers*. Of course, we grieve the loss of those from whom death has separated us. Yet hopelessness must not corrupt our grief. For Christians, death is not the end. When God summons His children home, it is the beginning of life unfettered by sin, disease, and pain. It is ultimate and permanent healing.

Jesus Christ is the hope of glory, infusing us with His hope in our grief.

*Heavenly Father, thank You for the comfort that
comes from the hope You impart.*

Have I been grieving as the world grieves? In what ways does the hope of Christ comfort me as I grieve the loss of a loved one?

372

# A HOPEFUL EXPLANATION
## 1 Peter 3:8–16

Always being ready to make a defense to everyone
who asks you to give an account for the hope that
is in you, yet with gentleness and reverence.

1 Peter 3:15

I want what he has." These words often reflect envy and dissatisfaction with our own circumstances. We fall prey to desiring possessions, experiences, or relationships we don't have.

Yet when it comes to our relationship with the Lord, we should *want* others to desire what we have. We want them to be dissatisfied with an empty life of continuous striving and failing. We want to live in a way that creates a hunger and a thirst for an intimate relationship with the living God.

When we love our enemies in a world governed by vengeance, others will be curious. When we live with integrity in a culture of moral relativism, they will notice. When we exude hope in a hopeless world, people will yearn for what we have. When they ask, we must be ready to explain both the reason for our hope and how they can have it too.

We cannot share the answer until we live in a way that causes others to ask the question.

*Lord God, help me live in a way that causes people
to ask the reason for the hope I have.*

In what practical ways can I live out my hope today? Am I prepared to explain the reason for my hope if I am asked?

# LOOKING FOR MEANING
## Isaiah 44:1–8

I am the Alpha and the Omega—the Beginning and the End.

Revelation 21:6 NLT

Every good story has a curious beginning that piques our interest, a solid middle to hold us in the story line, and a strong, satisfying finish that makes us glad we stayed with it to the end.

Life is like a good story. We start with an exciting beginning, filled with potential. Twists and turns accompany decisions made throughout our lives. Though we don't know when our end will come, we know it certainly will arrive. Still, many throughout history have wondered if our beginnings and endings really mean anything in the grand scheme of life.

We cannot find meaning in our beginnings and endings apart from the Alpha and the Omega. He is not *a* beginning or *an* end; He is *the* Beginning and *the* End—the only one. Prior to creation, before the first word was spoken, God was. Long after all we know that is real ceases to exist, God will still be. Nothing has life, substance, or meaning apart from Him.

Alpha and omega are the first and last letters of the Greek alphabet. Letters have to be in the right combination to form words. Similarly, when we are in a right relationship with the one and only Alpha and Omega, He infuses our lives with meaning.

*Alpha and Omega, thank You for filling my life with meaning and purpose.*

How does knowing God is the Alpha and Omega give my life meaning today?

# COMPLETION
## Philippians 1:3–11

*I'm convinced that God, who began this good work in you, will carry it through to completion on the day of Christ Jesus.*

Philippians 1:6 GW

Do you have an unfinished project in your closet or garage? You began it with the best of intentions but never got around to completing it. Maybe you ran out of time, became bored, or the endeavor was more difficult than you anticipated.

When we enter into a restored relationship with our heavenly Father through Jesus Christ, we come to Him unfinished. Like a diamond in the rough, we need cutting and polishing to sparkle. God does not leave us unfinished because of the amount of effort we need. He is never surprised at our degree of sinfulness or our lack of cooperation.

The moment we surrender our lives to Him, God begins His work in us. His Holy Spirit chips, cuts, and sands us, day by day. He brings just the right pressure to bear until we think we will break. We expect damage or scarring, but we discover He knows exactly what He is doing.

When we go to be with Christ for eternity, we will find His work in us complete. He will have transformed us from unfinished projects to shimmering jewels.

*Father, thank You for the assurance that Your Spirit is working to make me complete.*

Where is the Alpha and Omega exerting pressure in my life as He works in me today?

# INTERVENTION
## Isaiah 46:5–13

I am God, and there is no one like Me,
Declaring the end from the beginning.

Isaiah 46:9–10

Deism is a philosophy that came to prominence in the eighteenth century. Deists believe God created the universe and left it to function according to natural law. They do not believe God miraculously intervenes in our world, and they reject the divinity of Jesus Christ.

Yet the Bible is filled with descriptions of God's intervention in His creation. He covered Adam and Eve's sin and delivered Israel from Egyptian slavery. He warned His people of His disciplining them through prophesied captivity, and then planned their restoration to their land through the Persian king, Cyrus, His "bird of prey from the east" (Isa. 46:11). He sent His Son, fully human and fully divine, to pay the penalty of man's sin, and He will return to judge the world.

As we share our faith, we will meet people with differing ideas as to who God is. Their belief—or lack of belief—does not change the truth that there is no one like our God, "declaring the end from the beginning." He is the Alpha and the Omega, the Beginning and the End, always accomplishing His pleasure, and always at work for our ultimate good and His perfect glory.

> *Holy Lord, thank You that You are everything and anything I will ever need, from the beginning of my relationship with You until the final day when You bring me home.*

What can I do today to show a watching world that the Alpha and Omega is my God?

# Alphabetical Listing

# Scripture Index

**Ava Pennington** is a contributing author to many books, including a number of Chicken Soup and A Cup of Comfort books, and has written for several magazines. This is her first solo project. She lives in Florida.